CITY OF A THOUSAND WORLDS

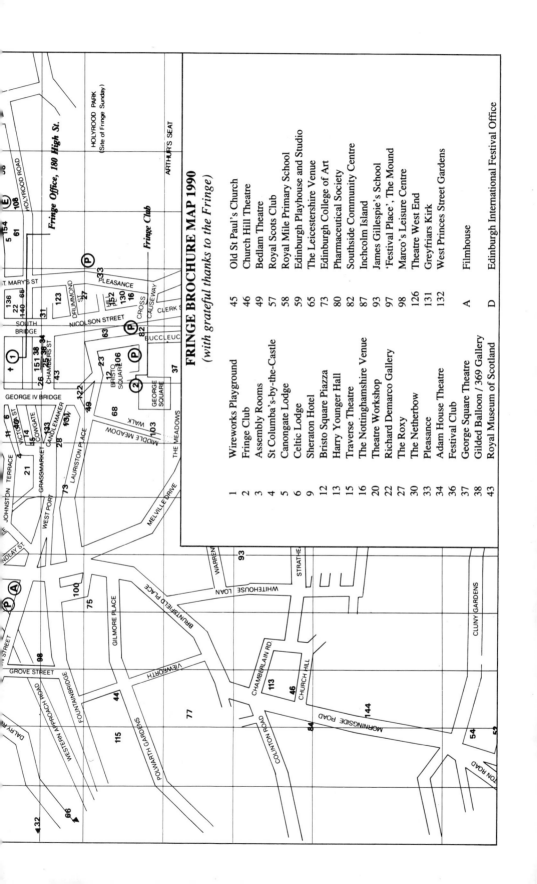

FRINGE BROCHURE MAP 1990
(with grateful thanks to the Fringe)

1	Wireworks Playground
2	Fringe Club
3	Assembly Rooms
4	St Columba's-by-the-Castle
5	Canongate Lodge
6	Celtic Lodge
9	Sheraton Hotel
12	Bristo Square Piazza
13	Harry Younger Hall
15	Traverse Theatre
16	The Nottinghamshire Venue
20	Theatre Workshop
22	Richard Demarco Gallery
27	The Roxy
30	The Netherbow
33	Pleasance
34	Adam House Theatre
36	Festival Club
37	George Square Theatre
38	Gilded Balloon / 369 Gallery
43	Royal Museum of Scotland
45	Old St Paul's Church
46	Church Hill Theatre
49	Bedlam Theatre
57	Royal Scots Club
58	Royal Mile Primary School
59	Edinburgh Playhouse and Studio
65	The Leicestershire Venue
73	Edinburgh College of Art
80	Pharmaceutical Society
82	Southside Community Centre
87	Inchcolm Island
93	James Gillespie's School
97	'Festival Place', The Mound
98	Marco's Leisure Centre
126	Theatre West End
131	Greyfriars Kirk
132	West Princes Street Gardens
A	Filmhouse
D	Edinburgh International Festival Office

CITY OF A
THOUSAND WORLDS
EDINBURGH IN FESTIVAL

OWEN DUDLEY EDWARDS

MAINSTREAM
PUBLISHING

EDINBURGH AND LONDON

To
Allen Wright
and
Philip French

Copyright © Owen Dudley Edwards, 1991
All rights reserved
The moral right of the author has been asserted

First published in Great Britain 1991 by
MAINSTREAM PUBLISHING COMPANY (EDINBURGH) LTD
7 Albany Street
Edinburgh EH1 3UG

ISBN 1 85158 398 X

A catalogue record for this book is available from the British Library

Typeset by Polygon, 48 Pleasance, Edinburgh EH8 9TJ
Printed in Great Britain by Mackay's of Chatham Plc, Kent

Contents

Mur tog Iehobhah féin an tigh
  Tha luchd na togail faoin;
Mur gléidh Iehobhah 'm baile fòs,
  Chaill luchd na faire 'n saoth'r.
Dhuibh's diomhain bhi ri moch-éiridh,
  San oidhch' ri caithris bhuain,
Bhi 'g itheadh arain bròin; mar sin
  D'a sheircin bheir e suain.
'Se Dia bheir toradh bronn mar dhuais:
  Mar oighreachd bheir e clann.
Bidh mic na h-òig' mar shaighde geur,
  'N làimh ghaisgich thréin gach am.
'S bu néarachd fear 'gam bi dhiubh sud
  A ghlac 's a dhorlach làn;
Gun ruthadh labhraidh iad sa' phort
  Ri 'n maimhdibh olc gu dàn.

SALM CXXVII

Except the Lord build the house,
  They labour in vain that build it:
Except the Lord keep the city,
  The watchman waketh but in vain.
It is vain for you to rise up early,
  To sit up late,
To eat the bread of sorrows: for so
  He giveth his beloved sleep.
Lo, children are an heritage of the Lord:
  And the fruit of the womb is his reward.
As arrows are in the hand of a mighty man:
  So are children of the youth.
Happy is the man that hath
  His quiver full of them:
They shall not be ashamed,
  But they shall speak with the enemies in the gate.

PSALM CXXVII

Antiphon.   May the Lord build us a house.

Response.   May the Lord watch over the city.

VESPERS, 3rd Wednesday

Preface

EDINBURGH IN FESTIVAL IS A CITY OF FAR MORE THAN A THOUSAND worlds each hungering for your arrival, in addition to the domiciles and refuges whose daily theatres perform for themselves. The Edinburgh Festival Fringe alone accounted for 9,000 performers in 140 venues last year. Add the productions and exhibitions under official Edinburgh International Festival auspices, the showings at the Film Festival, the performances at other Festivals in simultaneous celebration, and the dramas of press, administration, local government, city streets and who knows what, where, and the worlds mulitiply at a speed to make the most hardened astronomer or astrologer starsick.

What follows are reflections of and on some of these worlds as I discovered them, or *vice versa*, from 1974 to 1990 inclusive. I wrote or broadcast reviews or reports of public showings mentioned here, in almost all cases, but some of the worlds, while Festival-linked, were dramas without press or public ticket sales. I wrote about what I remembered, and without reference to any notices of mine given after performances; I then checked the files of *Scotsman* reviews to eliminate errors, when necessary correcting but not rewriting. The result is, I suppose, a dialogue with Memory, not an anthology of warmed-over reviews, and what I think now is in many cases the thought of a rather different person from that performance-viewer: I am old enough to be the father of the Festival-discoverer of 1974. But Memory has blazed some of those moments into strong if selective light, and I have tried to record some of the impressions, if not always the expressions, it burned on my mind. I found in rereading reviews for the first time since their appearance, sometimes since their composition, that I thought of the writer as 'he', more than 'I', sometimes with the feeling that he was bright, sometimes that I would like to kick him.

I have not quoted from my *Scotsman* reviews, although in one case I quote from a *Scotsman* review from Bonnie Lee, my wife, without whom there would be no book, and I would have nothing worth recording. For some of its issues, the files of the Edinburgh Student Publications Board's *Festival Times* have not survived, so far as I could discover; what I have found is due to the courtesy of my old friend Mary Gibson of the Board staff, and to the librarians of the Edinburgh Room at the Edinburgh Central Library on George IV Bridge, who have been indefatigable in hauling down enormous volumes of Festival programmes and publications. I have drawn on my *Festival Times* interview with Anthony Burgess, and I have also quoted in its entirety an article by Roger Savage, as timely now as when it was published in 1977. For his help, encouragement and professionalism then as now, I thank the Board typesetter Adam Griffin.

In the National Library of Scotland I am as always under the greatest of obligations to Margaret Deas, supervisor of the Reading Room, and to her staff, especially Polly Thomas, Sally Harrower and, above all, Dougie Matheson. The kindness of Stanley Simpson of the Department of MSS, housing the Festival archives, has been endless.

I have not had access to the files of the *Irish Times*, but I must record my deep gratitude to its Arts Editor, Fergus Linehan, for his friendship, support and inspiration over many years. The book contains far less of my Irish memories of the Festival than it did in an initial draft; but Irish preoccupations unbalance a book much more than I, as Irish-obsessed as any Irish scribe, first realised. Some day I hope to write an Ireland-into-Scotland memoir, and then I can pay my just tribute to Paul O'Hanrahan, the great Fringe Joycean reinterpreter, to Rosaleen Linehan's conquest of the city as Brendan Behan's mother, and to other noble cultural ambassadors whose diplomacy has worked such wonders.

Broadcast material I have not sought to have replayed, but Neville Garden, doyen of Festival presenters, has far outstripped any police force in refreshing Memory. I must record my gratitude to John Arnott, who painstakingly taught me so much, also to Bruce Young, David Jackson Young, Vivien Devlin, and many other BBC Scotland producers, to Chris Spurr, producer of BBC Northern Ireland's Festival programme and invaluable guide, to Catherine Smith, and to Marion Menzies, for superb Festival reviewing administration.

Mhairi Mackenzie-Robinson, Administrator of the Fringe, Tricia Emblem, Assistant Administrator, and their staff, were oases of charm, wisdom and aid in my various quests: Odysseus by comparison had an also-ran in Pallas Athene. I have not had to intrude on the Film Festival staff, but its Director, Jim Hickey, has met every request with his invariable warm support over the years. My obligations to Jenny Brown and the Book Festival are obvious, and so also, I trust, is my gratitude. In my University, I must thank Ray Footman, Director of Information Services, for his friendship, encouragement and assistance, and also for permission to reproduce Roger Savage's article quoted in part on the last page, taken from the Edinburgh University *Bulletin*. I want to say a special word of thanks to Bridget Stevens, and to the Royal Lyceum Theatre Club, and I thank the Royal Lyceum Theatre for hosting instructive conferences for the club. I also thank the speakers at those conferences. I would like to record once more my appreciation of the superb research work of Fiona Morrison, carried out for a book for Canongate (comparable only to Mainstream), *The Edinburgh Festival*, for which I contributed the text for Robbie Jack's invaluable photographs; I have generally sought to avoid duplication with that work, essentially concerned with the official Festival, but so thorough was Fiona's industry and so resourceful her spirit, that without having had to consult her, I found what she had done was of incalculable value for the present work also. I also thank many members of the Edinburgh International Festival staff not mentioned nor indirectly referred to in these pages: chief among them is Sheila Colvin, but also Roger Witts, David Palmer and Aileen Thompson and, on the present staff, Clive Sandground and Ann Monfries.

I thank everyone who appears in the pages of this book with the exception of Margaret Thatcher.

Many particular debts (of gratitude) are expressed in the text. But I have to thank very many good companions in covering the Festival: of those not mentioned here I would name especially Ewen Munro, Adam Brown, Hannah Aldgate, Jim Martin, Duncan Maclaren, Robert E. Stuart, David Johnston, Adam and Marianne Naylor, Ronan McDonald, Charles McFarland, and I owe on this as in so much else a particular debt to Rosemary Gentleman, of the Department of History, and former Rectorial Assessor on the University Court. Various colleagues and friends have proved excellent conversationalists on Festival productions, especially George Shepperson, Rhodri Jeffreys-Jones, Sarah Carpenter, Randall Stevenson, Nicholas Phillipson, Tom Morris, Nigel Billen, Alan

Taylor, Chris and Margaret Chambers, Jamie Donald, Ann and Bob Anderson, Kenneth Mackay, Angelica Goodden, Seán Ó Tárpaí, Brian Park, Hilary Koe, Elizabeth Koe, Neville Moir, Tony Axe, Sheila G. Coull, Jonathan Philbin Bowman, Fraser Grant, Chris Cook, Hayden Murphy, Bobby Small, Angus Calder, Sheena McDonald, Jean and Frank Bechhofer, Ronnie Mason, Michael Oliver, John Tydeman, Tim Willis, Gerald Roberts, and the late Martin Spenser. My mother-in-law, Elizabeth Balbirnie Lee, is a cause of gratitude beyond all powers of expression. So is my aunt, Elizabeth Wall.

I am grateful to Hamish Hamilton Ltd for permission to quote from *Peter Hall's Diaries*, edited by John Goodwin; to the late Walter B. Scott for the extract quoted from his 'Chicago Letter' (and regret that I never asked him whether Máire Ní Laoghaire derives from Mrs O'Leary's cow whose kicking over the kerosene oil lamp on 8 October 1871 burnt down Chicago); to Michael Grieve for three extracts from the poems of his father, Hugh MacDiarmid; and to Frank Kuppner for two verses from his *A Bad Day for the Sung Dynasty*, published by Carcanet.

No words of mine sufficiently thank my editor, Judy Moir, without whom this would have been an infinitely inferior book. I am deeply grateful to all the staff of Mainstream with whom it has been a delight to work. And my love and gratitude descend remorselessly on the head of William Kilpatrick Campbell.

This book was read in typescript and in proof by my daughter Sara, and was also read in proof by my daughter Leila, and by Roger Savage. They have saved me from innumerable solecisms. They have not deleted my allusions to them in these pages, even when they would have been happier without them, and these symbolise my responsibility for all remaining inadequacies or excesses. My good fortune in their support is incalculable.

Should the epigraph present any problems, then for 'the Lord' read 'Love'.

OWEN DUDLEY EDWARDS
University of Edinburgh
18 June 1991

Chapter One

The City Invents a Critic

Beginning of Oscar Wilde, *The Happy Prince and Other Tales:*

High above the city, on a tall column, stood the statue of the Happy Prince. He was gilded all over with thin leaves of fine gold, for eyes he had two fine sapphires, and a large red ruby glowed on his sword-hilt.

He was very much admired indeed. 'He is as beautiful as a weathercock,' remarked one of the Town Councillors who wished to gain a reputation for having artistic tastes; 'only not quite as useful,' he added, fearing lest people should think him unpractical, which he really was not.

PROFESSOR ROSALIND MITCHISON BEGINS HER MASTERLY *HISTORY of Scotland* by telling her reader to go and stand on top of the castle rock at Stirling. I am more demanding. Go and stand on the top of the dome of the Old College, heart of the University of Edinburgh, and metamorphose yourself into any bird save a swallow in order to do it. The Golden Boy, otherwise Youth bearing the Torch of Knowledge, is your companion. The gleaming statue may reflect the influence of Wilde's *Happy Prince*, published in May 1888. Walter Crane, who illustrated the book, was an associate of Fine Art Professor Gerald Baldwin Brown, who commissioned John Hutchison's statue, placed on the dome summit in or after July 1888. The Golden Boy may be a response to the Happy Prince, or to pre-publication news of the story from Crane; in any case, the story statue and the city statue are children of the same movement, born in the same year. Like the Prince, the Boy can see far across his city, especially when, unobserved, he looks around on all sides, and, like the Prince, he will have seen much he would rather not have seen. The Prince finds a swallow to fly on his missions against misery. The Boy just now gets you and me, and at the moment at least we are concerned with joy, celebration and Festival.

We stand for a moment which lasts from 1974 to 1990, the month being August: late August, stretching to early September for the first ten years, subsequently the greater part of August especially when the pre-Festival Fringe performances of 'week 0' are included. But the first Sunday formally inaugurates Festival and Fringe with the Festival

Cavalcade. And there it goes, two blocks north of here, sponsored by the *Evening News,* whose authoritative building, shared with its rival siblings *The Scotsman* and the recently-founded *Scotland on Sunday,* is a little more than a block from us, on North Bridge, west side, same as here at Old College on the South Bridge. We are on the corner with Chambers Street; across Chambers Street is the Festival Club, headquarters of the Jazz Festival which you can hear master-tootling any evening you want on payment of club ticket-fee, and a popular Fringe venue as well. One block down South Bridge and there is the old Tron Kirk where South Bridge ends, at the junction to High Street, part of the Royal Mile. Then down the North Bridge, past *The Scotsman* building: no, the reviews which sell so many tickets among the local punters who provide the bulk of Festival audiences don't go in that fine glass door, as a rule, but around the back, down Cockburn Street and half-way down the steps of Fleshmarket Close, and then into the little hatchway beside the staff door. An ominous street-name as destination for reviews, perhaps? Very old: two hundred years ago there was at its head (then on High Street) a huge alehouse of evil reputation where cockfighting was the performance art. The town councillor Deacon William Brodie lost heavily here but recompensed himself by meeting criminal acquaintances who joined him in burglary. Diagonally across from us you can see St Giles' Cathedral at the west end of High Street: just beyond it, the Tolbooth jail stood, famous from the long opening of Scott's *Heart of Midlothian*, and there William Brodie was hanged in 1788. Occasional plays about him surface on the Fringe, some better than Robert Louis Stevenson's.

North Bridge spans great open spaces, with the short east end of Princes Street Gardens below, just beyond Waverley Station. Then the Mound, curving up and around the Royal Scottish Academy and the Scottish National Gallery, where major Festival exhibitions have delighted and infuriated visitors on all manner of Art from Degas (1979) to Dada (1988). I was held in fascinated thrall by an elderly Dadaist while grappling with the remoter intricacies of his fellow-iconoclasts, which increased my sense of Dada as an intensely lovable crowd of perpetual innocents. Street performers outside preach everything from the old dawn to the new *angst* via reams of vastly engaging clowns, mime-artists, jugglers, musicians and, like the artists of the interior, exhibitionists. The ribbon of the Mound, winding upward over ground formerly cleared from the drained Nor' Loch to

14

make Princes Street Gardens, ultimately concludes in graceful homage to the Hall of the General Assembly of the Church of Scotland, the Festival's most majestic theatre since 1948, by turns everything from the Court of King Humanitie in the pre-Reformation pageant-play *Ane Satyre of the Thrie Estaites* (in 1948 and several subsequent productions) to Stevenson's *Treasure Island* adapted by Festival Director Frank Dunlop in 1990. West of the Mound is the mass of the Gardens, apexing at the Castle and ending in a Fringe venue and Exhibition Centre. And north of the Gardens, down Princes Street, on this first Festival Sunday, crawls the gigantic line of floats. Yes, Macbeth would not be the only one to ask if it stretches out to the crack of doom. After all, by 1990 there are 140 Fringe venues and 9,000 performers.

The crowd do them proud, provided the rain holds off. Surprisingly few shows are vulnerable to rain, its undependability betokening conservatism for open-air theatre; but their houses are. I once squelched for *The Scotsman* from the Assembly Rooms in mid-George Street (the next parallel thoroughfare north of Princes Street) to Walpole Hall in Chester Street (a few blocks below the West End) in the middle of a cloudburst without sight of a taxi or a sinner (often what James Thurber's schoolma'am would call the container and the thing contained), and on my arrival they had cancelled for want of audience. This they were entitled to do, as theatre convention permits cancellation if actors exceed ticket-holders, but I could not guarantee when the paper could send another reviewer in the myriad of review-demands, so they went on, both of them, well, in a nice little witch-hunt historical play. It is not the done thing to give an opinion before filing it, but mine was all the applause they would get, so I gave my most painful handclapping of that Festival and hugged them both. And then some gremlin in *The Scotsman* works held up my notice for ten days. And in 1975 there was a cloudburst over the Haymarket ice rink for the unhappy return to the official Festival of the Teatro Libero Rome who had dazzled all beholders in 1970 with their version of Ariosto's *Orlando Furioso*. Alas, their motor-car-bumping, Brobdingnagian, twentieth-centurying of Aristophanes proved as repulsive as a megamagnified butterfly, and at the interval about three-quarters of the audience fled to the doors. They looked in front at cascading sheets of rain, they looked back at torment unendurable, they hurled themselves into the city's most dreadful night. It was any storm out of that port.

15

Will the beholders take note of antics on the floats which particularly appeal to them? Some may, but for many the cavalcade is all of the Festival they want to see, give or take a few street-performers. Locals will go to great lengths to ensure good positioning while the procession wends its incredible way, and grandparents gallantly festoon themselves with wriggling descendants. There is enough momentum in the huge length to keep impatient infants happy; if some float is too staid, too stylised, or too incomprehensible, there will quickly be jugglers or clowns or mime artists or monsters or armoured knights or kings and desperate men or staged fairytale tableaux or cunningly upturned nursery rhymes or mad bands fighting or Japanese acrobats or drag acts or Dr Jekyll becoming Mr Hyde or Mary Queen of Scots getting her Head Chopped Off or Holmes and Watson or Jeeves and Wooster or Don Quixote and Sancho Panza or Burke and Hare or Deacon Brodie or the Devil Knows Who — the Devil Knows You, there he is, shoutin' at ye, that'll teach ye to slip my hand and run awa', Jimmie, he'll get ye yet one dark night, ach, shut yer blether, laddie, I was ainly jokin', why canna' ye behave yersel'? Whisht, whisht, there's a man makin' jokes, mebbe ye'll learn a new ane, it's aboot time. What? Whit's he meanin'? You'll never say that again, or I'll tell yer Daddy! The idea! As if the bairns hadnae enough dirty jokes of their ain!

I apologise. You're a bird on the Old College dome, not a brat in Princes Street. The Festival has incredible effects on the human age, reducing you to infancy, extending you to senility, all in a few hours. It was symbolised admirably in the 1990 Fringe by *Morning Has Broken*, a play by Tim Fountain about a young delinquent sentenced to voluntary work in an old people's home where he makes friends with an imaginative elderly lady (the production was a National Student Theatre Company entry and a great preachment of common ground between the generations). That kind of sensitive craftsmanship, capable of spanning six decades of age separation, says a great deal of the spirit of Fringe and even Festival. Even your recent embodiment, Jimmie, will go home with his grandmother in common conspiracy of satisfaction at their great day out, give or take the occasional smacked head. Mind you, the patience of those grandmothers, the way they look forward to hours of considerable discomfort, and their elation in the wild break in the convention of their lives, whatever they may say about it at the time, are great

16

tributes to themselves. How do I know? Neighbours' talk, eaves-dropping on bus conversations, reminiscences of students. It's not a particularly confiding city, but it is a city that ensures you know what it thinks.

Trying to cross Princes Street while that Midgard snake is bellying its way down the length of gardens, shop-fronts, crowds and police is, needless to say, impossible. In an emergency, get down to the railway station down the steps off North Bridge just at the side of *The Scotsman* where there used to be a striking, and frequently terrifying, exhibition by amateur artists (the terror by no means always intentional). Cut across Market Street into the railway station and down to the back between Platforms 7 and 1, and then up the footbridge taking you into the open, down to a sunken street under Princes Street and so to the top of Leith Walk just above the Playhouse where the Festival staged the great opera on international incomprehension, *Nixon in China*. To get from one end of Princes Street to the other, your only method, during the Cavalcade, is to take the half-hourly Glasgow train and drop off at Haymarket Station. (Yes, I know some idiot reviewing this book will say that I start by telling readers to begin the Edinburgh Festival by taking the train to Glasgow and, for all the good I do, I ought to have gone the whole way. Learn by doing, as John Dewey used to say.) You still have some mileage to make to get back to Lothian Road, roughly parallel to the Bridges and bringing you more directly into formal Festival territory, the grand respectable fastness of the Usher Hall whose somewhat stuffed-shirt concert-goers were so admirably shaken up by Frank Dunlop's throwing Weber's *Oberon* on the stage in 1986, with the diminutive form of its conductor Seiji Ozawa proving the greatest lightning-thrust warrior of them all, as he manoeuvred orchestra and actors in and around an entrancing maze of hurricane activity. The curse of the Festival has been a symbolic clamping of invisible doors before the multitude, conveying an élitism far above the ignorant heads of the masses. John Drummond, Festival Director from 1979 to 1983 inclusive, opened a grand campaign that Festival celebration was for everybody, and Festival culture was popular fun. Frank Dunlop continued the battle, and by choosing the two major points of élitist isolation, opera and the Usher Hall, he popularised them by integrating them, his own production of *Oberon* being a splendid exercise to show what supreme entertainment opera could be, how

17

lunatic quests of enchantment and entanglement could enthral in deliberate absurdity of plot, how virtuosic musical performance in undreamed-of conditions of complexity could fall in even more hypnotic captivation of his audience. Mind you, hearing Carlo Maria Giulini conduct Beethoven's Ninth ten years before took me far away from the repressive respectability of the Usher beer-magnate's benefaction which housed us, and the rapture it prompted is entirely my own business.

That is Shakespeare Square off the Lothian Road, turning into Grindlay Street, where the Royal Lyceum Theatre is fast becoming a people's palace in its own right, partly because of the present company's out-of-Festival encouragement of theatre-going for everybody, preceding opening night with a free performance. The Festival cannot fail to benefit from a theatre more and more ordinary Edinburghers now think of as theirs. The Drummond-Dunlop populism built on the enthusiasm for Everyone's theatre originally seeping out to the city from the Fringe, and Lyceum Artistic Director Ian Wooldridge justly capitalised on the Festival's new mood with notable results for the rest of the year. It remains for Festival and Lyceum alike to make a more solid contribution to new Scottish work. There have been some fine individual achievements, in some good cases preceding Drummond at the Festival and Wooldridge at the Lyceum, but we have a long way to go. You have to go to the far end of Grindlay Street, cross the road, down the steps and into the King's Stables Road, which becomes the Grassmarket at whose far end you find the Traverse Theatre, before you reach the natural cynosure of the aspirant Scottish playwright. You come up Candlemaker Row where you find the students' theatre, the Bedlam, sardonically dominating George IV Bridge, whose invaluable storehouses for playwrights and critics, the National Library of Scotland and the Central Public Library, incessantly feed such intellectual vampires as myself. Or if you are foolish enough to pass them up, you cross to Chambers Street west end. Or you can turn up to the stately pile of the University's McEwan Hall (another gift of the enlightened beerage), and beyond it the Teviot Row Students Union where the Fringe Club seethes in August, thronged with demonically energised sellers of showbiz at all hours of day and night. Time was when the Fringe Club was the latest drink during the Festival, but new licensing laws have relieved the pressure, so that now it seethes in greater comfort.

18

That can do to start with. Of course, I have not yet pointed you westward, where the Canongate above and the Cowgate below stretch their lengths down to Holyrood Park, whither the Fringe goes on Fringe Sunday for its Lark in the Park, or . . . Eh? Who do I think I am? Oh, very well.

I think I am a critic. If it moves, at Festival time, I review it. How I got like that is a story we will shorten. Born in Dublin, 27 July 1938. Father half-English half-Irish, Professor of Modern Irish History in University College Dublin. Mother wholly Irish, Cork, Celtic scholar, teacher, folklore-and-literature magician, my introducer to God knows how much literature, film, theatre and laughter. Both dead, but very much alive to me. Youthful experience as bookseller's assistant. Served Brendan Behan, who was cold sober and redolent with unrepeatable stories manufactured for my entertainment about highly respectable books in stock. Exit lines:

'And when may we expect *The Quare Fellow,* Mr Behan?'

'In October. From Methuen. Now, you listen to me. When that f . . . in' book comes in here, you stand in front of that f . . . in' door, and don't let one f . . . in' customer out of the f . . . in' door and say to each and every f . . . in' one of them "This is the greatest f . . . in' play that's ever been written and you're not gettin' out of this f . . . in' shop until you buy a f . . . in' copy." That's the way to sell a f . . . in' book!'

'It is, Mr Behan.'

We beamed at one another in mutual appreciation of our contrapuntal hypocrisy.

Common theatre enthusiasm of parents: Shaw. My theatre enthusiasm: Wilde. Family theatre enthusiasm: Shakespeare. (Thought, and still think, Micheál Mac Liammóir of the Dublin Gate the finest interpreter of all three I have ever seen.) Trained as historian. Researcher on Wilde letters for Rupert Hart-Davis, their editor. Brought proof copy to Mac Liammóir whose *The Importance of Being Oscar* put biography on the stage in a one-person show, incorporating the works, with astounding versatility.

'And so, my dear boy, you devote your energies and your life to this eternal quest perpetually pursuing musty books and dusty newspapers in remote archives and magnificent libraries to tear truth from the arms of time? How splendid! How admirable! How exemplary! How appalling! I couldn't do it for a moment.'

19

The Scotsman, 22 December 1884:

MR OSCAR WILDE IN EDINBURGH

On Saturday Mr Oscar Wilde delivered two lectures in Queen Street Hall, Edinburgh — the one in the afternoon, and the other in the evening. In his afternoon lecture, at which there was a fairly good attendance, Mr Wilde, with 'Dress' as his subject, desiderated the importance of costume following the lines of the human form, and, in order that an appreciation of the beauty of that form might be better cultivated and developed, he thought that children ought to be taught to draw from it, either from cast of Greek statues or from the actual living model. In this way the important matter of the proportion of the human figure would be learned; it would be learned, for instance, that the waist was a very delicate and beautiful curve — the more delicate the more lovely — and not, as the milliner fondly imagined, an abrupt right angle suddenly occurring in the middle of the person. (Laughter.) Going on, he referred to the effect of lines or folds in dress — the horizontal line apparently diminishing height; the vertical line apparently increasing it; and the oblique line imparting dignity to the carriage. Speaking of fashion, he said it was merely a form of ugliness so absolutely unbearable that it had to be altered every six months. (Laughter.) He denied that the changes of fashion produced variety; they only gave monotony, for every one adopted them. He had economy on his side, in the ground he took up in regard to dress. If his audience knew how much was spent every year on bonnets alone, one-half would be filled with remorse and the other half with despair. (Laughter.) He proposed no particular style of dress, historically or archaeologically, though there was hardly a nation of antiquity from whom they might not learn something in the matter. From the ancient Egyptians they might learn that the proper place from which to suspend the garments was the shoulder, and not the waist. Though, he said, in this connection, the hoop of past times did not survive, did not there linger to the present day that dreadful, that wicked thing called a 'dress improver'? (Laughter.) The Greek costume, he continued to say, was absolutely the most beautiful that the world had ever seen. In further remarks, he strongly animadverted on the practice of wearing high-heeled boots, stated that he did not admire the divided skirt as at present proposed, and advocated the use of wool instead of linen, as the basis of dress. Adverting, in conclusion, to male costume, he observed that all that could be said for it was that it was better than it used to be. He severely criticised the satin hat — 'an enormous glossy cylinder', he called it — and characterised a coat as a back without a front, and a waistcoat as a front without a back.

In the evening there was a rather meagre attendance. Addressing himself to the subject of 'The Value of Art in Modern Life', Mr Wilde employed his earlier observations in deprecation of the tendency to useless ornamentation which he held to prevail in the present day, as expressed, among other things, in the painting of flowers on vases and, worst of all, on mirrors, and in the reproduction of photographs on such articles as coal-scuttles. His main proposition was that whatever was beautiful must be useful — that whenever an article ceased to be useful it was ugly; and he argued that, as things at present stood, ornamentation was being made an enemy instead of a friend of art. Nature, he proceeded to say, was not the ideal of all art; it was merely rough material to the artist, and the mere imitation of it was worthless employment for him. Wherever art had become particularly bad, that had resulted from the selection of nature as the ideal; while, on the other hand, the best decorative art ever done in Europe was done by a people, the Mohammedans, who thought it a sin to imitate nature artistically in any way. The value of nature was the suggestions it gave; and it was attention to these suggestions in the way of 'effects' that he desiderated, and not so much running after 'facts'. He demurred to art students being taught to draw with a hard point to begin with — a state of things which, he said, had its reflection in the hardness of outline that characterised so many modern pictures — and he deprecated the tendency there was to make specialists of artists. One man, for instance, painted nothing but English cattle in a Scottish mist, another painted nothing but Scottish cattle in an English mist, and a third gave the public nothing but sheep by the sea. (Laughter.) He was not pleading for technical power in painting, his view being that where the *technique* of a picture was visible, the work was unfinished — that a work of art of any kind was not finished till all indication of the means by which it had been produced entirely vanished.

That was a Fringe event in Edinburgh in 1884 in what is now the BBC, as recorded by an unknown brother *Scotsman* scribe. Some of the themes Wilde picked out continue to haunt the Festival Fringe: the 'fairly good attendance', the 'rather meagre attendance', the evidence of audience attention and response given by laughter, the challenges to convention, the demands of a reordering of public taste, the iconoclasm, the sense of aesthetic vision, the faint and cautious allusion to Scotland. Wilde reflected his devotion and debt to his old mentor John Ruskin, as *The Happy Prince* would do, but he made no attempt of which we know to bring Scotland under specific fire for its aesthetic sins, as Ruskin had so forcefully done in the first of his lectures on Architecture and Painting delivered at Edinburgh thirty years before, on 1 November 1853. Wilde could not have alluded to the Golden Boy, but there is a nice moment of self-satire in *The Happy Prince* when, after trying to help his friend, the swallow, the statue loses his jewels and gilding. 'So they pulled down the statue of the Happy Prince. "As he is no longer beautiful he is no longer useful," said the Art Professor at the University.'

The swallow's initial delay in flying south was caused by his brief love for a Reed 'and he had been so attracted by her slender waist that he had stopped to talk to her'. It was winter when the swallow finished his tasks and died, as it was winter when Wilde saw Edinburgh. The Festival Fringe in the future might also find some prophesy in it:

> 'And here is actually a dead bird at his feet!' continued the Mayor. 'We must really have a proclamation that birds are not to be allowed to die here.' And the Town Clerk made a note of the suggestion.

Not that Edinburgh had any lessons to teach Wilde and my native Dublin in Philistinism. In 1958 the Dublin Theatre Festival was to stage plays by Sean O'Casey and Samuel Beckett, and a dramatisation of the Circe episode in Joyce's *Ulysses*, entitled *Ulysses in Nighttown*. The Roman Catholic Archbishop of Dublin, John Charles McQuaid, a reclusive figure of awesome power, announced he would not be able to celebrate the opening Mass if the Joyce play was staged. It was promptly withdrawn. Beckett, in artistic anger and personal loyalty to his old master, withdrew his play. O'Casey upstaged him by banning all of his own works from performance in Ireland. The Festival collapsed. I remember cycling past placards advertising the Catholic *Standard:*
'WE DON'T WANT JOYCE, O'CASEY OR BECKETT.'

Religion: Christian (Roman Catholic).

Graduate student, the Johns Hopkins University, Baltimore, Maryland, after undergraduate years at University College Dublin. Taught history at the University of Oregon, subsequently at the University of Aberdeen. Lecturer in History, University of Edinburgh, from 1968 until 1979. Reader in History there since 1979. Married Barbara Balbirnie (Bonnie) Lee, of Philadelphia, and of Staunton, Virginia, 1966. Three children, Leila and Sara, born 1968, Michael, born 1969. Mother-in-law, Elizabeth Balbirnie Lee, joined family when widowed, 1971. An enthusiastic amateur actress at the community theatre in Staunton, she encouraged her grandchildren in Liberton High School theatre. Leila in particular became a very impressive performer, in older parts, notably Madame Arcati in Coward's *Blithe Spirit*, which her grandmother had also played. Meanwhile on leave from Edinburgh in 1972-73, I met the Oak Grove Theatre and co-directed *An Ideal Husband* with the great father of the company, Professor Fletcher Collins, Jr, from whom I received my first practical education in theatre. I had also learned much from listening to my friend Roger Savage, who teaches drama in Edinburgh University.

The Oak Grove Theatre, as its name implies, exists within its own space and does not travel. But Fletcher's wife Margaret had created a touring company, Theater Wagon, which produced plays by the local authors, herself among them, where the Oak Grove worked with established material. The Collinses now talked with us about Edinburgh, as a result of which in 1974 I began my association with the Festival Fringe by becoming the licensee of a theatre. The space was known as the 'Cobweb', a basement in the Roman Catholic chaplaincy in George Square, provided by my eternal benefactor Father Anthony Ross, OP (later elected by students and staff of Edinburgh University as their Rector for 1979-1982). As the licence had to be procured before Theater Wagon arrived, I found myself knee-deep in plans — we had to clear arrangements, we learned, with the lighting authorities, the engineering authorities, the health authorities, the police, and above all with the Dean of Guild, who proved an education in himself. As far as I could gather he — or rather his permanent official — interpreted his mandate as the imposition of a series of quicksilver-changing regulations at whose purport the applicants made futile guesses and the whole thing resolved itself into a ghastly round game with petitioners ultimately collapsing in hot, red-eyed intellectual bankruptcy at which point the official would hand out some ukase for which no appeal existed. He favoured the

23

Venus-and-Psyche method of the apparently impossible task, and in dealing with me he waxed extremely eloquent on the iniquity of our having three exit doors. He insisted he wanted only two exit doors, and the third door was therefore illegal.

'You mean,' I said, 'that if there is a fire, and anyone saves their life by going through that door, they are breaking the law?'

'Exactly,' nodded the Dean of Guild's representative, apparently conceding a point in my favour for my evident perspicacity. He settled for the erection of a fire door at one entrance and I trailed my way back to Anthony, wretchedly feeling that this was but a refined method of kiboshing the entire enterprise. How could a busy penologist, historian and chaplain be expected to produce a fire door, and would he want to have his premises thus hacked around in any case? I should have had more faith in my Anthony. He listened to my morose report with the interest in analysis of bureaucratic pathology for which he was justly famous, produced some eminently gratifying reflections on the nature and preoccupations of the official in question, reached for the telephone, spoke a few sentences into it, and informed me there were three fire doors available to him in a back garden in Portobello and if we would pick them up and erect them, that would be fine. We did, and it was. Theater Wagon rolled in, re-rolled in the direction of Portobello — I recall the erstwhile Lord Goring showing a most unaristocratic acumen in door-raising — and we passed our subsequent inspections with happy hearts. They tell me the situation has been improved since then beyond all recognition. In any case, the relevant official, if so he may be termed, has retired.

Meantime, there was Milligan. That the Fringe was a swiftly mushrooming body of extraordinary heterogeneity was evident even to me, although my Irish antecedents have always felt anarchy as a more ambiguous epithet than its British users seem to intend. But anarchistic though its individual components might be, either in principles or in methods, there was nothing anarchistic about the methods of the Fringe administrator, despite a name so deeply identified with the immortal Spike. John Milligan was a towering presence, assisted by a moustache which would have moved the envy of the late Stalin who had tried something less successful along the same lines. To me, he was an absolute godsend. He combined a high idealism about the Fringe with a resolute insistence that the only way it could carry out its chosen destiny of revolt was by giving itself vital rules and sticking to them. He explained his methods to the meanest intelligence with a patience and courtesy combined with a riveting authority. One began association with him in hopes of doing the best thing for one's company; one continued it by not wanting to let Milligan down. The two activities not only did not conflict, it was not possible to see how they could conflict. He was integrity itself as regards any question of favour for anyone at the expense of anyone else. The inevitable ruthlessness of competition was held in check by Milligan's iron hand. The Fringe was supremely conscious of the disdain in which it was held by the official Festival Director Peter Diamand, and it was Milligan who ensured that the directorial snorts and sneers were made the basis of Fringe conviction of its own duty to pursue the best rather than the manufacture of chips on the shoulder or self-absolving grievance.

Some good theatre was coming through on the official Festival, but Diamand's spoiled darling child was opera, and hence the Fringe had a natural area in which to show its potentialities. Milligan did not rant, and he was in fact a cautious interviewee, but he set Fringe sights not so much on competition with the official Festival as in repairing the *lacunae* in theatre experimentation and production breakthroughs. *The Scotsman* had by now commenced its policy, under the inspiration and direction of Arts Editor Allen Wright, of rewarding Fringe worth and originality by Fringe Firsts. The Festival by contrast often had the look of establishment pure and simple.

Ironically, it was not until Diamand's successor, John Drummond (who completely reversed Diamand's anti-Fringe policy), put in his last year's great Festival theme of 'Vienna 1900' that the Fringe may fully have had the opportunity to recognise what Milligan had led, and by then it was under its second next administrator and few spared a thought back to Milligan. The 'Vienna 1900' Exhibition, allied lectures, and productions, testified to the 'Secession' movement and its impact on an atrophying Viennese culture. The Fringe under Milligan was a comparable 'Secession'. Because Milligan remained silent on many of the things he did believe in — Scots language drama, populist self-expression, agit-prop, left-wing radicalism and a conviction of the need to let the establishment get it in the neck as often and as variously as possible — he was much more effective than if he had hurled manifesto and statement with the profusion of his Vienna predecessors. He did not even need to proclaim 'Secession': Diamand had done that for him. He ensured that the protest could flourish by keeping itself within the unarguable legalities as far as reason could dictate. He could only give wise advice as to the best means of gaining production rights despite the lunacy in the Dean of Guild's office. But because of his training in deadlines, regulation requirements, and all the rest, the Fringe waxed large but disciplined.

The result was that the enemies of the Fringe were driven to expose themselves to fire rather than being able to count on the Fringe tearing itself to pieces or falling into pieces by its own lack of cohesion. Attacks on the Fringe usually took place on the Fringe's own ground where it could most effectively give battle. Milligan intervened in public as a rule when an intervention would be unexceptionable in the eyes of reasonable detached observers. It was not that he feared a fight in defence of the weakest link, but that his methods gave the weakest link every means for remedying much of its weakness. His famous succession of 'lists' of what productions looked like arriving and which ultimately did arrive, proved a boon to the press insofar as its representatives thirsted for a little cultural excitement. As for his leadership of 'Secession' or whatever one might term the Fringe's anti-establishment challenge, he did not need to speak it. It was evident in him, every inch of him, as he strode out on the first Sunday of the Festival and the first day of the official Festival at the head of the Festival Cavalcade.

Theater Wagon had been rather chuffed on receiving a gilt-edged invitation to the effect that the Board of the Fringe in general and Mr John Milligan in particular would be overwhelmed by the honour if Theater Wagon and friend, possibly even Theater Wagon and partner, but definitely only two human bodies in number, would assist by their presence at the festivities dispensed by the Fringe on Sunday afternoon on the conclusion of the Fringe parade. The function was one reputed to freeze the blood, since it consisted of casts and productions sweltering grimly in some hellish maelstrom whence they sought to exude hypnotic blandishments at members of the impartial press

26

whom it was hoped would then come and see their show with blazing headlines of approval.

If producers thought there was mileage from display of the costumes in their offerings, or if it was simply convenient to bring in major performers in the gear they wore promiscuously in procession, so much the better. We lacked the resources to enter a float in the procession beforehand, and it is a nice point whether or not a tableau capable of sustaining itself on the long haul up and back reduces theatre to still-life. There was, of course, the thought that stayed in the head of the resourceful Edinburgh director Sandy Neilson, a few years later when he staged Donald Campbell's *The Widows of Clyth*, a strong, heart-lacerating version of the lives of fisherwidows electing to remain in their Caithness-shire rural fastness instead of fleeing back to town when their men were drowned in one hideous accident. 'I thought of simply having the widows in their mourning black spinning or bread-making or whatever on the back of the truck,' said Sandy, 'and underneath them a large sign reading THE WIDOWS OF CLYTH FLOAT (WHICH IS MORE THAN THEIR HUSBANDS DID).'

But no legend for a serious new Scots play would flicker an iota of interest from the vulgar fraction of the press, sweating around the perimeter of Milligan's ball slurping *Cheateauneuf du Milligan*, while professionally on the lookout for something vaguely pornographic to titillate in image and condemn in print. Not many serious reporters were present, and those who were serious quickly became jaded without having reached one show as they found the leaflets slammed into their wine-dripping paws getting more and more numerous, more indecipherable and more detestable. Ultimately some reporter will murder a performer thrusting the leaflet that breaks the camel's thirst in place of the refill he sought, and the police will take it as another Fringe stunt. The reporter will complain about the meanness of his newspaper in not giving him expenses to cover cleaning blood off the suit.

That is to say, Theater Wagon sent *me*. I got rid of a large number of leaflets, not one of which brought a reporter to our doors. *The Scotsman* came, certainly, but that had nothing to do with Milligan's ball, which Allen Wright invariably spent sitting in his own office drawing up such reviewing schedules as were not already completed. *The Scotsman* review drew some punters to the Cobweb, so did the energetic poster-team from Theater Wagon, and so above all did the self-description in Milligan's list.

Theater Wagon did get one piece of publicity, however, although it was one whose value to the productions was minimal. Nevertheless it was an incident which is unlikely to be forgotten by any of the parties involved.

I was reached by a BBC radio reporter whom I knew, or rather, I think, I reached him. He was compiling a programme on the Fringe with the sounds of various groups in performance, which meant in souped-up versions of one or two moments supposed to take place in the course of performance. The producer (long since retired) seemed to be quite knowledgeable about Theater Wagon but had neither the time to discuss his knowledge nor to seek any addition to it. I may have sought to convey to him under the general head of who these people were that Fletcher Collins was the author of *The Production of Medieval Church Music-Drama*, and was leading his actors to Fleury Abbey after the Festival so that they could perform *Visitatio Sepulchri* as originally written by the local monks and not performed in Fleury for several centuries. So it was not altogether surprising that his fulfilment of a promise to get back into touch with me carried emphasis on Theater Wagon's musical interests; but the message came loud and clear that what would be required from them were folk items accompanied by their instruments. From what they had already seen of the Festival so *outré* a request was not in the least surprising, and in any case as Americans they were used to talk-shows in which authorities and performers were encouraged to discuss and portray anything with which they were not readily or even actually associated. But even they were surprised at what was wanted. It was clear that something like authentic folk fiddles were required. There may have been guitars, but I think guitars were seen as insufficiently authentic. Nobody liked to ask 'authentic what?' for fear of scaring away the publicity. It was concluded that what was sought was the genuine folk culture whence Theater Wagon came. Everyone, the producer assured us, wanted to hear the authentic tones of west Virginia.

So they presented themselves for their recording, and Fletcher found a fiddle and played it, something he had not done for years, and he was agonisingly flat, and the sound of their combined music was frightful, and then the interviewer asked Custer La Rue if she had spent all the money she possessed in order to come over to the Festival, and Custer, whose father was probably opulent enough to buy every ticket sold by Peter Diamand without noticing it, replied in her most magnificently poised drawl, 'Oh, no, A-a hayaven't spent hayalf of iyut,' and there were one or two more questions which seemed to have something to do with mining, which the group answered with what little knowledge of it they possessed, since mines have little to do with the Blue Ridge Mountains of west Virginia, and the feature formed probably the most excruciating segment of that Festival Round-Up and Theater Wagon bemusedly thanked me for getting them publicity.

It was several years before I discovered what had happened. One of the best ways for interest to be aroused in a show is by word of mouth, even more so in those days when reviewing was actually very sparse, and Fringe coverage from all but a few honourable exceptions was limited to offerings from the Traverse and the Oxbridge Universities. And word had certainly got around about Theater Wagon. People had seen the performances, and talked about them. While the University of Southern California made its frequent visits under Professor John Blankenchip, there were relatively few arrivals from the USA. The Oak Grove and Theater Wagon were based on a community which was far from wealthy by many American standards, but which was comfortably off. Some people had more, as did Custer, some had less. It was broadly based, not necessarily Virginian in origin — my own in-laws were immigrants from Pennsylvania, the Collinses were Yale graduates and the Pittsburgh-born Fletcher had arrived in the Blue Ridge Mountains via extensive folksong collection in North Carolina, and my late father-in-law had also been a great folksong collector around the country. The folk-preoccupation was in some ways stronger in Margaret Collins than anyone, and her play *Love is a Daisy* was a very entertaining satire on the absurdities of sophisticated sociologists seeking to come to terms with the truly remote folk-culture preserves in archaic Virginia. And *Love is a Daisy* had staged very well in the Cobweb. Did we but know it, the play had received its most signal compliment in that what it satirised had been taken to be what its performers actually were. And, inevitably, 'west Virginia' had been confused with 'West Virginia' so that the BBC took themselves

29

to have an authentic group of West Virginians who had sold all (or at least half) of what they had, had invested the proceeds in a theater wagon, had somehow made it amphibious, and had accomplished the ambitions of a lifetime in playing the fiddle execrably on the Fringe. If someone did enquire what the prodigal miners proposed to do with themselves afterwards, the information (if now listened to) that they were restoring the performance of a medieval miracle-drama to the town of Fleury which had given birth to it, must have set the capstone on the bewilderment of the producer. Margaret Collins was occasionally accused of writing in total innocence of the realities of human existence: in fact, *Love is a Daisy* would seem to have shown itself the Art which Wilde insisted was imitated by Nature. Edinburgh could not have more gloriously proved her thesis, that wizards of sound-recorders intent on gaining the authentic sound of folk culture believe whatever they want to believe.

Peter Allen of the University French Department was a dedicated Fringegoer, and an enthusiast delighting in sharing his enjoyment with friends. So he dragged me firmly along to what he was certain would delight me, probably on the Friday of week 0, immediately preceding that glorious and horrendous Sunday. What I got was Bradford University's production of *The Quest*, by Richard Crane, directed by Chris Parr (afterwards one of the Traverse Theatre's most successful artistic directors, winning outstanding results in his search for new Scottish material and authorship). It was at the Jesuit-owned Lauriston Hall, a fine long space, necessary enough since it had to be Arthurian Britain. *The Quest* reworked Malory and Tennyson, with an impish humour of its own, frequently making exactly the jokes every schoolboy wanted to hear about the Round Table ('Don't aggravate your brother, Agravaine'). It surprised me that Peter, a great exponent of modern French absurdism and the pillar of student French-language productions, should be so great a devotee of Crane, whose previous work, then unknown to me, was comparably dominated by variations on classical themes. I stupidly allowed Peter's immediate enthusiasms to make me lose sight of the long if not always visible loyalties: I knew more when I saw with what *élan* he later directed Corneille's *Le Cid* and Racine's *Andromaque*, but he is drowned in the Mediterranean and I cannot tell him how much I owe him.

The intimacy of the Cobweb had enabled Theater Wagon to make an audience believe in retrospect it had been in a sociologist-infested rural Virginia farmhouse, but Lauriston Hall had to do the work on our imaginations, all the more because Crane brought four of the major chivalric stories together in one sequence to work themselves out in successive dialogue quatrains keeping eyes skipping from corner to corner. *The Quest* would have made *Camelot* look like Camberwell, if it hadn't done so for itself. Galahad duly appeared in terrifying goodness, plunging the Round Table into a destructive and self-absorbed quest, savagely realised in the Knights' rushing forth to seek the Grail, striking down the ladies who impeded them. Lancelot's dismissal of Elaine might be expected, but the shock when Tristram struck aside Iseult was devastating. Tristram, ultimately self-revealed as one of Nature's bastards (far more than an oddly mystical Mordred), was a great performance by the author himself. Within a year, Crane married Faynia Williams, who took on the direction of his work. They continued the line of Fringe Firsts received by *The Quest* and by Crane's previous Fringe entry, a Brontë play, *Thunder*.

Sunday must have seemed *The Quest*'s golden day, beginning as it did with Harold Hobson's rave review in the *Sunday Times*, with Hobson's official Festival reports firmly subordinated well below his great and generous lead on the Fringe *Quest*. But on Monday when I looked in for some trifling piece of management business to the City Chambers, I saw a white-faced Crane and Parr piteously beseeching the amiable official on duty, Mrs McMullen. They became somewhat pacified by her reassurances, but amid all their distraught mien (Crane and his Tennysonian variations exuded contagious rhetoric) lay bewilderment.

The police, it appeared, proposed to close down their show, and they were at their wits' end to see why. But Mrs McMullen, it was evident, was not merely prepared to fight their cause, which her benevolence might not make too surprising, but to fight for it to the death. Trembling, the Bradford players cowered like some snake-hypnotised Andromeda as the lady of the City Chambers hurled her minions into the fray, tearing one magistrate from his sick-bed, grabbing another from the steps of an aeroplane, and with ultimate triumph thrusting an order to keep the hall open and in performance

31

into the very maw of the police. I learned little of this from Bradford at the time, for they were English, keeping themselves to themselves, and I thought it discourteous to intrude on their apprehensions, but Mrs McMullen was ready enough to talk to someone from the old country who had been, as he truthfully told her, educated by the Jesuits himself.

The police, it turned out, owed some of their recruitment to the pious but secret order formed in devotion to the House of Orange-Nassau, or at least to its most noted representative's Irish sojourn. The Jesuits remained for them a symbol of all they detested, being under suspicion of extra-mural activities to bring low the freedom, religion and laws of true-born Protestants. More specifically, the Jesuits had displayed a Jesuitical innocence in imagining that an entertainment licence, which their hall possessed, would do as a theatre licence, which it lacked. To plead unworldliness for the Jesuits would have moved the Orange mirth of the constabulary, and I blessed once again my Dominican friend Anthony, whose Highland origins in the Wee Free Kirk had told him what fires still burned in Scotland, and what other fires their attendants believed to burn elsewhere, and for whom. The Jesuits, like their tenants, were English for the most part. There was little sign of Protestant-Catholic hostility in the Edinburgh of 1974, but Mrs McMullen well knew that less than forty years previously a Protestant mob had stoned buses bearing Catholic schoolchildren, and she intended to give the heirs of that mob, however blue-uniformed, no cause to congratulate themselves on the humiliation of the Fathers of the Society of Jesus. 'One of the magistrates,' she told me, 'asked if there was any nudity or that, in the poor wee lads' show. I said, of course not, the Fathers would have no nudity in Lauriston Hall.' I assured her with perfect truth that any expressions of intimacy in *The Quest* were delivered with their male performers encased in suits of armour, or reasonable facsimiles thereof. I also complimented her on her work for a great cause which she aptly summarised: 'We couldnae have the Jesuit Fathers in the dock, or stop the wee lads' show.'

My life as a theatre critic began, curiously enough, because of a decision of Peter Diamand, although he remained, and I trust remains, Olympian in his unconsciousness of my existence. Diamand, or his assistant, Bill Thomley, to whom he relegated theatre, had decided on bringing over the Abbey Players from Dublin. With them came the chief theatre critic of the *Irish Times*, Seamus Kelly, from whom I received a summons to the Festival Press Bureau where I was introduced to a genial and most un-Diamand-like press officer, Iain Crawford. Kelly surveyed me with slight, very slight, softening of his cold eye, an eye that had stared down Captain Ahab of the *Pequod* — for Kelly, in God knows what transfiguration of his status as a critic, is immortalised on film as the second mate in *Moby-Dick*. (He occasionally reminisced about it: it proved to be one hell of a voyage, for they used an inflated whale which broke free in a storm and *Moby-Dick* was in fact filmed as the ship plunged in mad career across the Atlantic in quest of its errant performer in the title-role.)

Crawford was generous with his Festival's hospitality and Kelly spoke eloquently of the transformation in the Abbey players. He informed me that my orders were to be Fringe critic of the *Irish Times* during the present Festival. He would be occupied with reporting the success of the Abbey — he left me in no doubt that it would be a success, by the time his typewriter was finished with it, at any rate — and with some notice of Diamand's other productions. He waved a dismissive hand. These things, or rather this thing and those other things, would preclude his looking at the Fringe. But since he, Kelly, was in Edinburgh, people would want to hear something about the Fringe. It was right that they should. I might use my own by-line. He had, in fact, already filed his copy announcing that I would be taking up my command forthwith. And I was to keep my eye out for the Irish angle. (I had been writing for the *Irish Times* for fifteen years by then, but my dramatic criticism, while forceful, had been limited to coverage of the American Presidency.) The following year, in 1975, Crawford told me that, since Kelly was not coming over, I might as well report the Festival as well as the Fringe, if that was agreeable to my head office. I agreed.

I acquired a copy of a selection, and later of a full text, of Bernard Shaw's criticisms for Frank Harris's *Saturday Review* from 1895 to 1898. I reread them before each Festival.

Saturday Review, 23 February 1895:

> ? A play in ? acts. By ?. Opera Comique, 16 February 1895
>
> I am in a somewhat foolish position concerning a play at the Opera Comique, whither I was bidden this day week. For some reason I was not supplied with a program; so that I never learnt the name of the play. I believe I recognized some of the members of the company — generally a very difficult thing to do in a country where, with a few talented exceptions, every actor is just like every other actor — but they have now faded from my memory. At the end of the second act the play had advanced about as far as an ordinary dramatist would have brought it five minutes after the first rising of the curtain; or, say, as far as Ibsen would have brought it ten years before that event. Taking advantage of the second interval to stroll out into the Strand for a little exercise, I unfortunately forgot all about my business, and actually reached home before it occurred to me that I had not seen the end of the play. Under these circumstances it would ill become me to dogmatize on the merits of the work or its performance. I can only offer the management my apologies.

The worst thing I can recall having witnessed in the official Festival was in the later 1970s, when Sir Rex Harrison read a selection of Shaw's dramatic criticisms in St Cecilia's Hall. The script made its contribution to the disaster by running the selection into one almighty singleton, higgledying and piggledying all it chose to loot into the critic's Valedictory. Harrison read in the manner of a stenographer reading back the entire day's proceedings of the drafting of a Parliamentary Bill for the additional licensing of undertakers.

If you dislike the proximity of that 'read' and 'reading', so do I, but it makes its contribution if it faintly conveys the monotony of the proceedings. I could hardly say 'delivered it'. Nothing suggested, and nobody saw anything to suggest, delivery until he shovelled out the words: 'The younger generation is knocking at the door; and as I open it there steps spritely in the incomparable Max' after which Harrison turned the page with habitual heaviness and added 'Beerbohm' with all the confidence of an assistant executioner taking the precaution of an additional axing. There remained two lines more of Shaw ('Beerbohm' of course having been a condescending interpolation). Possibly the applause was induced by them, for one reason or another: 'For the rest, let Max speak for himself. I am off duty for ever, and am going to sleep.'

I did my duty to it on BBC Radio 4 *Kaleidoscope*, aided and abetted by a beloved producer, David Perry. I rendered my objurgation in the language I thought Shaw would employ.

If you were left-wing in my earlier years, you had an inferiority complex about workers. If you were Irish nationalist in my earlier years, you were required to have an inferiority complex about people who died for Ireland. James Connolly came into both categories, and, more admirable than either, was a great writer, thought-provoker, human libertarian, one who worked to remove inferiority complexes, not create them. His early life was passed in the Cowgate, where his family's hovel was crowded in amongst its fellows. He saw opulence parade its ostentatious way on North Bridge and George IV Bridge, and his father's — and, for a time, his — work consisted of collecting horse-dung and the excrement of other entities, and shovelling it into corporation carts.

It was a necessary function, but not one to be particularly proud of. The same may be said for reviewing Rex Harrison in St Cecilia's Hall, also in the Cowgate. For once I could look Connolly in the eye with the job done, and then we threw down our shovels and walked away. The only pride in a thing like that is that the atmosphere is a little sweeter when the work is done. All youthful critics, certainly myself when I started being one, congratulate themselves on their demolition work as though it was something of incomparable glory. In fact, even when most necessary, demolition work degrades and dehumanises its operators. If it has to be done, the place where it is really needed is when some wealthy and successful audience-attracting name is giving a dreadful performance in supreme contempt for those who have paid himself and/or his material the compliment of saving up a few pounds to witness them. After I had spoken my piece on the air the *chatelaine* of St Cecilia's, Sadie Aitken, looked at me at our next encounter with the reserved congratulation of an austere housekeeper for a successful detergent:

'You didn't like Harrison?' There was honey as well as gall in the transparent falsehood of enquiry.

I said I had not liked him.

'Aye.' Sadie brooded, a little Jeremiacally.

I said that he had been twenty-five minutes late. She snorted.

'You didn't have to pour hot black coffee into him both days after he had had his lunch at the George.'

There is something about the word 'George' which suggests gluttony on a level other and even pricier establishments cannot offer.

Shaw is said by Michael Holroyd (who performed most honourably in a symposium in St Cecilia's a few years later) to have been partly animated by a kind of jealousy of Henry Irving's ascendancy over Ellen Terry, whom Shaw entertained himself by loving from the audience, cascading with letters, and never meeting until many long years had gone. It was true that I had loved Harrison's wife Kay Kendall from the stalls when she came to Dublin to play Elvira in Coward's *Blithe Spirit*. We learned later that her ethereal shimmering presence transcending frontiers of life and death actually foretold her own death from leukaemia. A few years later I saw her in the film *Once More With Feeling*, made in 1959 when she really was dying, and marvelled at its professionalism. She acted right down to the end.

Which is more than her husband did.

From P. G. Wodehouse, *The Inimitable Jeeves:*

> 'She is very wonderful, Bertie. She is not one of those flippant, shallow-minded modern girls. She is sweetly grave and beautifully earnest. She reminds me of — what is the name I want?'
>
> 'Clara Bow?'
>
> 'Saint Cecilia,' said young Bingo, eyeing me with a great deal of loathing. 'She reminds me of Saint Cecilia. She makes me yearn to be a better, nobler, deeper, broader man.'

Grace Kelly must have enslaved me just before Kay Kendall did (my Kendallatry deriving from stage presence, not films), that is to say, in *Rear Window* (1954) and *To Catch a Thief* (1955), both directed by Alfred Hitchcock. But Grace Kelly killed what was left of my Romeotics stone dead when she married Prince Rainier of Monaco, largely because he was a stamp in my collection or had possibly been abandoned in a swap. On the other hand at the age of forty I owed something to soppy sixteen. If I were to sneer at its secret obsessions, it had no doubt ample reason to disapprove of what I had become. So the least I could do was to seek admission to Princess Grace Kelly at St Cecilia's as she read the flowers of American poetry. And the *Irish Times* absolutely insisted on it, even if I had to climb up on the skylight of St Cecilia's Hall and hang myself on the Irish angle. But Iain Crawford had nothing for me. Normally courteous and resourceful for any enquiry I might raise, his present situation was hopeless: every ticket to spare had been devoured in the snobocratic interest, and what the free list of Beautiful, Beautiful People had not snapped up, the voracity of the city fathers had gathered into their maw. A seat at Grace Kelly's feet might be guaranteed to charm away the doubts of district councillors as to the cost of *Carmen* or whatever budget-busting opera had been called up by Diamand this year. The *Irish Times* might represent the land of Grace Kelly's ancestors, if not precisely their place on its sectarian divide (or, as Irish delicacy put it, the foot with which they dug), but my cornucopious Crawford had for once to limit himself to advice. I could try for an interview (after all, she and I dug with the same foot, even if the paper didn't) and in the slim event of success she might get me into her performance that way, in fact she almost certainly would. No performer could imagine for one minute that an interviewer could continue to exist on the planet without seeing them doing whatever they were doing in whatever the interview was about. And I arose from the Festival Press Bureau to the National Library in order to work out the exact method of addressing a Serene Highness of Monaco according to the *Almanach de Gotha*. The address was by no means the only part of my letter which could be termed Gothic.

Her Serene Highness vouchsafed me no reply. This, while disappointing, did not leave me any the more contemptuous of my affections at soppy sixteen. I certainly believed that she had every right to come, perform and depart, without a word to ladies and gentlemen of the press, if any. A performer is entitled to absolute seclusion from the press if it so desires, provided it performs. And I could well see that my pompous little embassy while innocuous on its face, gave her no guarantee that I would not prove to be a *Paris Match* photographer seeking to trap her in some unspecified way. Indeed Crawford told me of one Finnish photographer who was offering £300 for a ticket, presumably for stronger reasons than ancestral piety or nostalgic calf-memory.

And then, when hope seemed not only dead but buried twenty-four

years deep, Michael Grieve of Scottish Television found me a ticket
from his institution's allotment, some recipient having had to decline
at the last moment. Michael and I had met in 1969 when I first covered
the Scottish National Party and he, hearing I had had to take a double
room in the absence of a single one, asked me in our first breath of
greeting to give half my bed to another nationalist, stranded there at
Oban without accommodation. I had contributed to a three-author
work on *Celtic Nationalism* along with his father, otherwise Hugh
MacDiarmid (whom I did not know when we wrote though we had
met since). I had been delighted about this immediate insistence on
Michael's part that I was a comrade-at-arms with a common code, and
now Scots brotherhood was as usual doing more for me than Irish
royalty. So back I went to St Cecilia's Hall, to enter with whatever
diminished hopes and attic-stored dreams into some cultural
communion with the former fine foil of James Stewart and Cary
Grant.

The faintest breath of forewarning, like the flick of a cold wind, was
the sight of the programme. That the Princess would be supported by
Richard Kiley, a US musical-comedy celebrity, and Richard Pasco,
the English classical actor, mattered little. She was out of training, she
needed to breathe, they could take up the slack, and they meant
nothing to my nonage or my newspaper. But the list of American
authors to be read was headed 'Anne Bradsheet'. The programme had
no doubt been proof-read hastily at the last moment; half of the ticket
crisis had been induced by the lateness with which details arrived,
Crawford had said. (Had not Conrad Wilson of *The Scotsman*, who
combined music criticism of the Festival with supervision of its printed
music programmes, once passed 'fancy lands forlorn' as authentic
Keats?) This blunder must be annoying to Her Serene Highness.

Alas, her opening words of introduction made it all too clear her
Serenity was entirely untroubled by it. Anne Bradsheet the customers
were told they would get, and Anne Bradsheet the Princess told them
she now gave them. But if Grace Kelly, now rattling off the mildly
banal lyrics of Anne Bradstreet (1612-1672), famous as the first
British American poet, knew no more of their author than she was
told in the script, then this was not a collection of her favourite
American poems, as stated, but simply a job for whatever charitable
purpose or otherwise. And all must depend on her use of the
material, not on her feeling for it, which she patently did not possess.

38

And what she did she did with wooden conscientiousness. There was no question of Harrison's cynical greed and sloth: Grace Kelly, returning to the stage for one occasion after twenty years, was ready to do what she was told. But who was to tell her? Her illiterate script-writer? Her equally bemused companions? We had come to behold our pale goddess of cool, clear intonation and Nordic-Irish purity; we were present at a decent, confused, rocking-horse rendition from a Philadelphia Momma grabbing the first book that might hold the kids or, maybe, raise a dime or two for a worthy cause.

About one-quarter of the audience disappeared at the interval. The remnant possessed their souls in patience as the balance ran the gamut from the ponderous to the pedestrian. I went out at the end, thinking of Alfred Hitchcock and the great man that he was, who could drag immortal performances out of the most unpromising Irish-American dough (in all senses). As I slunk into the darkened Cowgate to keep a rendezvous with my Rhadamanthine typewriter I could not reach the Golden Boy, beaming so far above me. But my foot made one swift movement, and the ghost of Peter Pan fled howling back to the Never-Never-Land.

From Hugh MacDiarmid, *A Drunk Man Looks at the Thistle* (1926):

> *The munelicht's like a lookin'-glass,*
> *The thistle's like mysel',*
> *But whaur ye've gane, my bonnie lass,*
> *Is mair than I can tell.*
>
> *Were you a vision o' mysel',*
> *Transmuted by the mellow liquor?*
> *Neist time I glisk you in a glass,*
> *I'se warrant I'll mak' siccar.*
>
> *A man's a clean contrairy sicht*
> *Turned this way in-ootside,*
> *And, fegs, I feel like Dr Jekyll*
> *Tak'n' guid tent o' Mr Hyde. . . .*
>
> *Gurly thistle — hic — you canna*
> *Daunton me wi' your shaggy mien,*

I'm sair — hic — needin' a shave,
That's plainly to be seen.

But what aboot it — hic — aboot it?
Mony a man's been that afore.
It's no' a fact that in his lugs
A wund like this need roar! . . .

The best lighting that ever I saw at the Edinburgh Festival was provided by God. The Golden Jubilee of *A Drunk Man Looks at the Thistle* was duly celebrated in St Cecilia's by Tom Fleming declaiming the entire thing in the afternoon, before the old man himself, his wife Valda, their son Michael, his wife Deirdre, Norman MacCaig and an illustrious audience. The oval chamber, Robert Mylne's, has a clear and uncomplicated light in the early afternoon, but as the sun moves westward, the shadow lengthens. Tom Fleming, tall and commanding in any work he undertakes on stage, slowly becomes gigantic against the white wall. Who the narrator of *A Drunk Man* is, remains much less easily defined than who he is not: he is not Christopher Murray Grieve, the man, nor Hugh MacDiarmid the poet (two entities from time to time sharply differentiated even in their views by Grieve), and what he says will not always reflect either of them. He is more a voice that Grieve, outside MacDiarmid, wanted MacDiarmid to release, and that MacDiarmid brought out as the one voice but in several different, confluent epiphanies. But the drunk man is drunk, and hence begins with limited preoccupations and sometimes conflicting prejudices which elbow up against one another and, as the great poem continues, the drunk man becomes increasingly sober, with corresponding alterations in his vision, and in St Cecilia's Hall the increase of sobriety meant the increase of the shadow. The fears and hopes, now muted, now thundered by Fleming, became starker and more austere in the waning light, and the brooding, enlarging silhouette dominating all now as a ghost, now as a threat, now as a warning, above all in its implacable insistence on a human spirit without which all design must fail. MacDiarmid was at once almost savagely individualistic, and his poetry showed a highly conscious celebration of the great and unknown voices of Scots literature down the centuries before him, from whose vocabulary he built his poetic language. So that shadow might be Fleming's, or the drunk man's, or MacDiarmid's (Grieve's leonine head dominated the first rows, remaining alone visible within the audience as the hall grew darker and darker), or it might now be the shadow of one of the pursuers of Tam o' Shanter, or of the wizard Michael Scott entering Branksome Hall in the last minstrel's fearful climax, or of the *Doppelgänger* of James Hogg's justified sinner, or of Mr Hyde, or of a surviving Pict from John Buchan who, for all his resolute Unionism, was the first major voice in British letters to hail the literary and linguistic achievement of the young MacDiarmid. And at last Fleming brought the epic to its end, and stood like an exhausted Thor finally delivered from his Midgard Snake whom he had battled so long — Circumjack Cencrastus, as MacDiarmid liked to call the Nordic animate global cincture — and the old man arose, and in that high, wonderfully modulated voice which brought its own music into each separate syllable, said that when he had completed a sound recording of *A Drunk Man* he felt it had gone away from him, and now Tom Fleming had brought it back. And Tom Fleming had brought a bottle of whisky to present to his great poet, and nothing would do the old man (instead of drinking it at home as Tom intended) but to ask his friends to the dressing-room below. Thomley was among them, looking wretched, as he knew the Festival should have produced the whisky instead of the artist paying for it and the poet standing it, and that the Director should have been there as he would be for any opera in a foreign language other than this one but he had not perhaps realised how eerily operatic, not to say Stravinsky-Auden rake-stopped-in-mid-progress the dialogue had been between variously Drunk man and his legionary Shadow.

And God said 'Au Revoir'.

The old man did not believe in God, and had frequently said as much, but he had written very splendid poems which had everything to do with God — prayers when you think of them, although he often seemed more concerned to pray for humanity to understand God than *vice versa*, which only showed that the old man knew theology was the ignorance of Man. Has anyone done more to show God's omnipresence despite Man's self-centricism? It was no wonder that 'GRIEVE, Christopher Murray' had set down as his *Recreation* in *Who's Who* 'Anglophobia', holding from his cosmic understanding that England eclipsed Scotland from the universe and the universe from Scotland when the Scots were not doing it themselves in Pavlovian colonialist response. He wanted an international Scotland, and complained that Edinburgh's idea of an international Festival was a provincial acquiescence in what seemed like a safety-measured cultural dosage. He was the true focal-point of the revolt against cultural caution which the Fringe at its greatest coherence might express, if it knew the meaning or even the existence of MacDiarmid, which much of it did not.

At the end of the 1978 Festival the old man died.

The new Festival Director, John Drummond, taking office in 1979, had a MacDiarmid celebration in St Cecilia's Hall, which I scripted and directed. Sandy Neilson gave the lyrics, diatribes and elegies the sinewy subtlety with which the Scots language broadens human understanding, and of which he reaffirmed his mastery a few years later in his solo performance of 'St Luke's Gospel' in the Lorimer translation into Scots (the words of the Devil alone being in English, since he is in that context a sophisticated metropolitan). But the most memorable revolution of the MacDiarmid evening was caused by the beautiful Lewis voice of Dolina Maclennan reading *Island Funeral*. Originally published in MacDiarmid's travel volume *The Islands of Scotland* (1939) (whose weakness is its evident dislike of the Shetlands where he was living unhappily at the time), the poem was not a favourite among MacDiarmid's friends. But in the strange blend of plain humanity and a half-hint of the preternatural which Doli's intonation gave it, the whole poem was transformed, and suddenly what MacDiarmid meant by the music beyond words in island speech was revealed in his words as spoken in that voice.

Drummond was there, as was most fitting, for he had shown himself as an enthusiast and critic in exactly the proportions I needed. He put his finger on the script at one point and said, 'That's where you're going wrong.' That was all. He was perfectly right. It got the thing on the rails again. He was alleged to pack in more words per second than any human currently known to science but, as supervisor of a script, he did more with five words than I would do with five thousand.

One story from the green-room only. I had included, Drummond had approved, and Sandy and Doli had read in their scripts a certain poem. We liked its words, its meaning, its atmosphere, its elegant variation on Shakespeare, its intimacy, and what we took to be its wit. And when the actors read it for the first time to me in rehearsal, we

42

three fell helplessly to the ground. Up to then, the two Scots readers had silently absorbed the last line as perfectly reasonable and explicit Scots; Drummond and I had separately been impressed by the crucial word's obvious derivation from the Latin root *facio* 'I do' here used in the sense of 'make'. Try reading the poem out loud yourself when you are alone:

COUNTRY LIFE

Ootside! . . . Ootside!
There's dooks that try tae fly
An' bum-clocks bizzin' by,
A corn-skriech an' a cay
An' guissay i' the cray.

Inside! . . . Inside!
There's golochs on the wa',
A craidle on the ca',
A muckle bleeze o' cones
An' mither fochin' scones.

'I bet he did it deliberately,' gasped Doli, wiping her eyes. 'He could be a *wicked* old man!'

John Drummond, equally helpless when we read it to him, concurred in our shattered expression of intent for its removal. Revolution we intended, but nobody had the nerve to bring the blush of modesty to the cheek of St Cecilia.

Drummond said afterwards that a continental friend had complimented him on an Edinburgh celebration of a poet one-quarter of whose quoted poems and prose consisted in abuse of the town. The friend said he could not imagine one European city in which this would have been the case. Drummond was delighted. So were the Grieves. Sandy, Doli and I felt we had done, on the whole, what the old man would have wanted us to do, and that our love for him would stay with us forever.

The cornet solo of our Gaelic islands
Will sound out every now and again
Through all eternity.

I have heard it and am content for ever.

Allen Wright reviewed it for the *Irish Times*, generous about strengths, constructive and incisive on weaknesses. It had been very good of him to do it, in the midst of his generalship of *The Scotsman* Arts army, as I knew very well in asking him in my *Irish Times* lieutenancy. For I was now also a private soldier in his army. It had happened like this.

Edinburgh University possessed the largest student publications board in these islands, which had played a significant part in cartoon and journalistic warfare in resisting and in part reversing the monopolistic tendencies within the University administration. It was closely associated with the student rectorships of Jonathan Wills and of Gordon Brown (later MP and at present a leading light on the Labour Front Bench). It had inflamed the great debate on Scottish identity (which would culminate in 1979 in the referendum narrowly favouring Scottish devolution) with a massive *Red Paper on Scotland* edited by Gordon Brown. It had also started, among many other things, a little paper called *In-Fringe,* under the leadership of John Forsyth, the sardonic, idealistic Board manager. In 1974 this hard-hitting expression of the spirit (but not voice) of John Milligan gave way to *Festival Times*, which sought to embrace the entire Festival in its coverage but tried too much with too few resources. In 1975 that was revived under the best editor of its seventeen-year existence to date, Michael Worton, a graduate student in French of quite incredible charm and industry, and remarkable critical capacities joined to a wide cultural range of expertise. (He is now a leading luminary in University College, London.) Peter Allen was his Fringe editor, Forsyth his film editor. I had been co-opted on to the Board, firmly told by Forsyth that this was on my merits such as they might be without reference to my faculty status, and through a series of accidents found myself acting Chairman of the Board for the summer. In practical terms this meant availability for filling in unexpected *lacunae* in the paper's coverage. In the event, I wrote nearly half of the first issue.

Michael was an editor who radiated confidence and inspired much devotion, and some of his *coups* were sensational, such as an interview with Rudi Nureyev by the late Tony Firth, then Controller of Programmes for Scottish Television, as the *Festival Times*'s representative. Tony threw himself into the thing with delighted zeal, as desperately anxious to win the approval of the editor as any first-year student: it was in fact a superb piece of work, concluding:

44

FT: It has been very good of you to give us this interview, Mr Nureyev.

Nureyev: It has.

I forget almost everything I did, apart from the moment when Michael, after three or four virtually sleepless nights desperately seeking to finish his last editorial — or was it his first? — collapsed over his typewriter and I eased it away from his sleeping form and concluded the piece. I knew his opinions fairly well by then, and the printers were due in a couple of hours. But we had a column on the Festival critics, mostly aimed at the pretentiousness of visiting gurus from London, in which 'Nicholas Bottom' in each issue pompously analysed the claims of several for the award of worst critic of the year. (It was ultimately given to Benedict Nightingale of the *New Statesman*.) In the course of this I had necessarily to examine the case of Allen Wright and stated that there was nothing dramatically bad in his writing, and indeed little that was dramatic at all since parents of children, however fractious, could be guaranteed their immediate slumber on a reading from the Arts Editor of *The Scotsman*. And no doubt I thought it was very funny. Eighteen months later Allen Wright, whom I had never met, asked me to fill in for a few weeks as TV critic of *The Scotsman*, and while I was doing so, told me he had asked me because he had enjoyed so much what I had written about him. I remember vividly the gentle but firm way in which later he worded a just rebuke when I had failed to keep one column up to standard. I applied for a place in the ranks of his reviewers for the next Festival, 1977. That was a man I wanted to go on working for.

Going to work for *The Scotsman* drew me much more heavily into the Fringe and, while Allen Wright was always ready to send reporters to what they might ask for, it became increasingly evident to me that most instructive results would follow throwing myself completely in his hands, all the more when the massive grey head would look down and a Puckish eye look up, and the Arts Editor would shake his head and say, 'You won't want to go to', or 'It wouldn't be fair to you to ask you to go to'. That, as he well knew, was an irresistible challenge. He once sent me to a one-man rock concert which I reviewed in the style of Henry James to the gratification of the performer's admirers.

45

Chapter Two

Diamands Aren't Forever

Edinburgh Festival August 12th to September 1st 1984

FRINGE

Recollection of a BBC TV report of Wimbledon Tennis Championship:

> *BBC commentator (concluding his orgy of results guesstimation):* But we won't know until the last ball has been served.
> *United States tennis star Pam Shriver as guest commentator:* Or, like we say in the US, 'the opera isn't over till the fat lady sings'.

WHEN IAIN CRAWFORD BROUGHT ME INTO FESTIVAL CRITICISM, it meant that my prime target, in his eyes, must be the opera. That year the lead opera was Mozart's *Le Nozze di Figaro*, officially produced by Sir Geraint Evans, modestly describing himself as 'co-ordinator of a group of singers, or friends, who have teamed together to work out the production'. His friends included Daniel Barenboim, conducting the English Chamber Orchestra, Dietrich Fischer-Dieskau playing the Count, Teresa Berganza (Cherubino), Heather Harper (the Countess), Judith Blegen (Susanna), John Fraser the designer, and the Scottish Opera Chorus. Evans was Figaro.

Those last three words are the key. Opera was then at a turning-point in Britain, performing the same evolution and revolution Garrick had achieved in play performance two hundred years before, moving from staged declamation to realisation of the theatre in all its aspects. The music and singing in Geraint Evans's *Figaro* were a vital concomitant of the work as drama, not simply something greater than movement on stage and essentially outside it. The talent of the librettist Lorenzo da Ponte is ludicrous when measured alongside the genius of Mozart, but da Ponte had behind him the genius of Beaumarchais, in the play of 1778, with the opera first performed in 1786. Fear of Viennese censorship led da Ponte to mute the revolutionary message of Beaumarchais who had been fired by his involvement in the American Revolution to expose insolent claims of aristocracy over the persons of productive people exploited as *droit de seigneur*; for instance da Ponte deleted Figaro's final diatribe against all varieties of aristocratic privilege. Evans therefore had to consider a Figaro controlling the action, or rallying his forces when it seems likely to overwhelm them, and yet with high irony fuelling rather than dampening his anger. Figaro is the combination of commentator and manipulator, having to comprehend in order to control the complex of human interactivity. It was a part made for an actor-manager, but one less attuned to his own apotheosis than to the maximum deployment of the capacities of his team: and Geraint Evans worked his Welsh magic on the production, on Figaro's movement of his fellows, on Figaro's own richly haunting voice. It was not simply that his range flowed from irony to passion; the irony restrained the passion, and then the passion conquered but was matured in the irony. He was at once a great producer, a great singer, a great actor, above all realising the character of Figaro as an actor-producer. The revolutionary fires of Beaumarchais were banked, but beneath the banking they burned.

Geraint Evans got the utmost out of his cast, which is not to say that his cast had his manifold capacities. Dietrich Fischer-Dieskau is a singer, not an actor, and he frankly hammed, notably in apparently hammering his thumbnail in an attempt to surprise Cherubino in his wife's apartments. But in its way this did the work, even Beaumarchais's work. The Count was a bad actor, in a false situation, where he sought to betray his wife, his former benefactor, and his servants whose fidelity merited more than his infidelity: the Count, in brief, was the sham Beaumarchais was declaring the promises and pretensions of aristocracy to be. Looking from the stalls at Fischer-Dieskau hopping up and down, the magnificent voice was all that remained to tell us that this self-created marionette was what Raymond Chandler would call something that had once been a man. The lusty teenage Cherubino, mezzo-soprano, is obviously female: but if Teresa Berganza was hardly likely to deceive Sherlock Holmes as to her sex (as Irene Adler, another prima donna, had proved able to do), her movement, lightness, sheer embodiment of youthful innocence and folly, lent the needful illusions. Her exchanges with Figaro in the *Non più andrai* passage in act one were an exquisite counterpoint of her fear and his irony, and Berganza's femininity actually pointed up the absurdity, and the tragedy, of this delicate little butterfly of boudoir and bed, striding out in the majesty of war surely destined to crush and break it.

Peter Diamand's first press conference in 1975 was a denunciation of the failure of the city to give him an Opera House, and for this purpose he duly paraded Geraint Evans to point out that more ambitious operas were beyond the Festival's scope if restricted to the King's Theatre. But Evans must have seen the absurdity of such a platform for such a cause. His *Figaro* was what, after all, had brought his presence down for the Count (for he certainly was performing servant once more to Diamand's Almaviva), and the King's had been ideal for the production, holding its ironies and intense emotions seething in small space, where a larger stage must have detracted from the acting performances. If Sir Geraint doubted if the ideal way to cajole the City Fathers was directorial castigation of this vintage vinegar, he kept those doubts locked in his wise Welsh heart: Figaro would use other methods to cajole. But the city clearly meant nothing to Diamand save as a location for opera, and having no further call on his affections, he proclaimed its worthlessness for failing to rise to his occasion. His manner demanded all other urban needs should be swept aside for his Opera House; he tacitly, even explicitly, brushed off the fact that the long-bruited Opera House had been initially projected as part of a Festival complex also involving theatres. That the complex had been shelved *in toto* now seems a decidedly mixed curse, while such buildings as the University jimcrackery on the ruins of the once-beautiful George Square, or the Stalinoid St James's Centre, conserve Edinburgh architectural taste of the 1950s and 1960s. But Diamand was inflexible: he had hyped for them, and they had not advanced, he had sung for them (or, more happily, he had got Geraint Evans and others to sing for them) and they had not built. There was nothing but talk, he said, and a hole in the ground. His feelings when the hole in the ground was occupied in the early 1980s by the Fringe Circuit tents are fortunately not on record, for that was after his Directorship, the longest in Festival history.

The irony of the lost Opera House continued to dominate opera chatter, and yet Diamand operas owed some of their success to the intimacy of the King's. He would, presumably, wish to be remembered above all for his *Carmen. The Scotsman* headlined it 'A CARMEN TO JUSTIFY ALL FESTIVALS', a somewhat unhappy capitulation to the Diamand thesis that grand opera was the sole art-form on which Festival success must hang or be hanged. But the same article by Conrad Wilson declared the success of the 'dusky-toned' Teresa Berganza was partly indebted to her performance hall. Small was beautiful. Perish the thought that such reflections were intended to give aid and comfort to what the operamaniac Bernard Levin styled 'the mean burghers' of Edinburgh, a city he claimed to love but loved so remotely as to misattribute the parts demolished by the said burghers in conspiracy with University vandalism. Mr Levin (and the Beautiful, Beautiful People) apart, the laments for the Opera House that wasn't may have had an undertone of anxiety as to what dreams might come if Diamond ever got it. Grand Opera ate its inordinate fraction of the Festival grant greedily enough in the King's; God alone might guess what proportion of it Diamond would demand for the productions he would conjure up in a full-scale Opera House. Meanwhile, *Carmen* gave enough for the Beautiful, Beautiful People to rave about, whether they brought a special and profound expertise to bear on their delirium or whether, in the happy phrase of Frank Forbes of the BBC, they 'wouldn't know Bizet from a bull's foot'.

Figaro in 1975 had won my heart from the stalls, but *Carmen* in 1977 I saw from a box, Iain Crawford kindly making the most for me of the later date of performance appropriate for an *Irish Times* wrap-up. A box at the King's has its own peculiar charms, the most macabre being the view of the audience languishing below like endless hordes of halibut laid out on fishmongers' slabs. Perhaps it brought us nearer the spirit of Covent Garden.

'Carmen,' observed Teresa Berganza, in a letter to Peter Diamond printed at the head of the programme, 'is no common prostitute.' This she certainly did not mean to have her translator say, however persuasive the thesis. She had settled on the part as that of a respectable feminist gypsy for whom Don José, it turns out, is unsuitable. 'The tragedy begins when Carmen first notices Don José. Immediately she senses that he is of a different order and, as we know, she is right: a man without identity; a victim of every kind of complication and problem, be it religious, social or within his own immediate family . . . a man without fortune. In Mérimée's work we are presented with a person who, even at the hour of his death, is incapable of accepting his own responsibilities.' How far Placido Domingo sympathised with this view of the character which Piero Faggioni's direction would thrust upon him is a nice point. He sang divinely, but he performed with a somewhat diminished, hunted air, not so much as a man without identity as a man with an identity which this was not. Berganza's respectability drew back even from Carmen's fellow-nomads: 'When she is later pursued by the law she can find no alternative but to work alongside the smugglers. Carmen *will* give herself, aware of the consequences of such actions' — (*sic?*) — 'but, at the same time, she *demands* from others what she, herself, has given' (*sic!*). After all this, she herself demanded, and got, the presence of Peter Diamand at every performance, be his other Festival commitments what they might: he was evidently cast as her off-stage duenna. For the rest she declared that 'in my interpretation of Carmen I shall be trying to put across to the public an impression of the Spain of that period. Both Mérimée and Bizet were misled through their own lack of knowledge about this country, something which later criticism has done nothing to correct and which has led to a profusion of naturalistic productions, to an imagined "tourists' paradise" which never was, and never can be, Spain.'

Whether she was outlawing or extolling naturalism seemed to have eluded her interpreters: anyhow, the Boys Choir of George Watson's College for the sons of gentlefolk was decoratively gathered on stage in the guise of street-urchins in dubious keeping with their parents' social aspirations. If the spectacle of the junior Edimburgeoisie going native in Spain was intended to detouristify *Carmen*, it hardly succeeded. On the other hand, it undoubtedly ensured some deprettification of the opera, which was all to the good.

The Festival and production directors had given Berganza her head, to which the hype had duly gone, but she was hardly to blame for the major incongruity. Escamillo was played by Tom Krause, whom Conrad Wilson termed 'dangerous' and 'sombre-toned'. True enough: the man was the spitting image of Richard Nixon, only recently removed from the public eye by his resignation in consequence of the Watergate affair. When he strode to the footlights to declaim the Toreador song, it was disturbingly unprefaced by 'my fellow-Americans'. If the bull gored him, the bull it was that died. This may seem unduly facetious: presumably people who resemble Richard Nixon are nevertheless entitled to practise their professions. The trouble was that the dark ambience seemed to shadow Krause. Escamillo should have given him the redolence of confidence to surmount his unfortunate physical associations, but it deepened them. Most of the cast were uneasy in their French, over which quite a few expletives had probably been deleted. The production compensated by shading the chorus into what were termed the appearance of Manet paintings, *'Déjeuner sur l'herbe'* presumably not among them: where

53

Manet was felt to dovetail into the Berganza demand for the true unBizet Spain I cannot say.

What remained was an immensely powerful performance from the London Symphony Orchestra under the inspired baton of Claudio Abbado, who threw a rising, blood-churning, nostril-flaring inevitability of doom into the work. The whole dramatic force of the opera found its greatest expression in the music — apart from Berganza herself. And whatever she thought she was doing, she did it magnificently. It may have been difficult to see how either of her suitors could summon up the nerve to proposition her, but within herself she radiated the bewitchment of Carmen. It was in a sense a closed Carmen: she communicated stronger in anger than in love, save for love in the abstract. But she encapsulated mystery and fatal force. She actually struck something much deeper than a siren-note: she was the harbinger, agent and victim of destruction as magnet rather than pursuer. It seemed impossible that this creature of wonder and terror could have been the captivating, Puckish Cherubino of two years previously. Cherubino had been a pawn; this was a queen who had never been a pawn at any stage in her devastating progress.

Nevertheless I did not apply for a ticket the following year, 1978: Diamand's repetition of Berganza's *Carmen* was a fairly deliberate statement of his priorities at the expense of all else, and I left him to them. But I attended his last press conference, which was Grand Contemptuary. As a style, it did not build opera houses, but it blasted budget-balancers' bitchings over Bizet. He began in his good English, whose Dutch inflections were almost an additional purity of speech:

> I have read the repörts of the prress on the Fesstiväl, and I have freequently found myself conclüding that the prress and I have not been prresent at the same Fesstiväl event. The prress äctually knöws very little about what häppens in the Fesstiväl. *Hjeh.* Miss Bergänza on the day of her ärrival in Edinburrgh was discovered to be suffering from a thröat infection. I at once summoned the leading thröat specialist from London and hee prronounced her unable to take part in any rrehearrsäls. Förtunately, a löcal young lady quite familiar with the rröle of Carrmen very gällantly stepped into the brreeach and substituted in all rrehearsäls. Änd it was äll rright on the night. Not one worrd of this ever leeaked out to the prress. *Hjeh!* . . .

Roger Savage, 'After Diamand', *Festival Times*, 1977, no. 4:

Some suggestions to the next Director of the Edinburgh International Festival (Heaven help him) arising from the name of the circus he will be running when Mr Diamand retires in 1978.

EDINBURGH FESTIVAL

In the popular mind this phrase means the 'official' Festival (your Festival) plus the Film Festival, the Fringe and Tattoo. The popular mind would be amazed if it knew the chilling distances between some of these organisations. As elder brother, so to speak, could you not take steps to draw the family closer together? (It will be a red letter day when an offical Festival Director publicly embraces the Administrator of the Fringe and stops thinking of him as a walking threat or a standing insult; and it is a long time since Sir Thomas Beecham conducted the massed military bands on the Castle Esplanade.) Applied specifically to your own circus, *Edinburgh Festival* is an interesting contraction because it can mean two different things: a festival IN Edinburgh (Korean puppets, Peruvian actors, Mongolian string quartets, Nigerian dancers and Tasmanian clowns brought together within piping distance of the Royal Mile) and a festival OF Edinburgh (a celebration of the life in art of one city and its nation). Which do you intend it to mean? Hopefully both simultaneously.

EDINBURGH INTERNATIONAL FESTIVAL

The short form of the proper name of your show. Each word raises issues. *Edinburgh* is the home of the Festival and it might help a considerable number of Edinburghians to accept that the EIF is not merely an autumnal cuckoo in their nest if Edinburgh was your home too, if Mr Festival was a seen and esteemed local figure from October to July (which does not mean you should not, if you want, have an office in London, New York or Timbuktoo and hold a Transylvanian passport). *International* has meant predominantly 'European' and 'American' in the Festivals of the past. How good if you could change that! After all, now Europe has become a united states, to be truly international must be to go beyond Europe (and beyond the other united states as well). Your presiding genius should be a citizen of the world with a pronounced Scots accent. As for *Festival,* the mind boggles at the thought of Edinburgh truly *en fête*, but the boggling would be reduced if you could woo greater and greater parts of the population into festiveness. Edinburgh is a city rich in tensions. Your challenge is to make as many as possible of them into tightropes on which you and your festive-performing bear can turn cartwheels.

EIF OF MUSIC AND DRAMA

is traditionally the full title, and that deserves breaking down too.

OF MUSIC

Apart from the occasional recital, music in the Festival has tended too much to be Western art-music since Bach. There should surely be much more Western art-music of the fourteenth to seventeenth centuries, art-music of other civilisations and folk music from all over. Mozart-to-Mahler rules OK? No, it's not OK.

AND

Much virtue in 'and'. Not 'attended meekly by' or 'followed limpingly in the rear by' but 'in equal partnership with'.

DRAMA

If a great orchestra is giving half a dozen official concerts, then the half dozen performances given by an official drama company should be expected to be as good, i.e. to have the same zest, tingle, finesse. This has not always been so in the past, perhaps because Mr Diamand's penchant for Continental Grand Opera (a splendid beast but a spendthrift one and *not* the undisputed lord of creation) has not left much behind in the purse for plays without music. If it is indeed a money matter, then you should put your money where your aesthetic is, and either make a lusty woman of drama or require the Festival Society to drop her from the title. As for the sort of drama to be played and the players to play it, there should be enough stimulus in the rich conjunction *Edinburgh International Festival*, reading 'Scots' for 'Edinburgh' but not reading simply 'European' (and certainly not 'English') for 'International'. One does not have to be a member of the SNP to feel that try-outs for and fugitives from London runs should go to the bottom of your list of preferences, though one would be prepared — indeed eager — to make exceptions for both of Britain's mega-companies, especially of the so-called National Theatre (you know, the London one), which might well be compelled by law to make a three-week progress to the North British capital every Festival.

Peter Diamand's festivals have revealed some glittering peaks of Western high culture: the art of Stockholm and Sofia puppet theatres, for instance, Grotowski's *Akropolis* and Ronconi's *Orlando,* Tito Gobbi's *Gianni Schicchi* and Prospect's *Edward II*, Stravinsky danced by the New York City Ballet, and the Abbado-Ponelle *Cenerentola*, Giulini conducting Beethoven, Boulez conducting Elliott Carter. We hope you will reveal other such, but please also make the EIF more festive, more international, more Edinburgh.

I think John Drummond read that article: from the first he paid great attention to the *Festival Times*, and to Roger Savage, who accepted his invitation to join his panel of advisers on drama. (He asked me also; I refused, being too promiscuous a reviewer to hold with the hare and ride with the hounds — anyhow, I am not much of a man for committees, preferring casual encounters. Roger reviewed little, and was peerless when he did — and was ruthless in refusing conflict-of-interest assignments.) Certainly Drummond acted as though the 'After Diamand' article was his agenda, though I know enough about committees to appreciate the difficulty of giving full weight to each agenda item.

Drummond never took a house in Edinburgh, though he gave serious thought to it; I recall in his last year taking him to a small Grassmarket pub run by my friend Peter Fraser, with a folk group led by Dougie Matheson of the National Library performing, and he was almost in tears at his enjoyment of this other Edinburgh he had never known until the eve of his departure. The London office was retained, although the justifications for its pre-eminence dwindle yearly. Any case for retaining it in more than branch status remains at bottom a confession of inability to emancipate ourselves from the parochialism of London-centrism, a mental condition very hard to break. The advances of modern communications and Drummond's own widening of the Festival frontiers along the lines Roger proposed — lines Frank Dunlop extended in directions Drummond had intended to go, had he remained — make a London organisation base as absurd as it is contemptible. Not everything worked as Roger had hoped. The National Theatre came with the York Mystery Plays, in Tony Harrison's version, in 1980, and left most comers in raptures at the resources of South London players pretending to be medieval actors pretending to be Judaean nomads, brilliantly mingling the theatrical and religious implications of the Assembly Hall if not in a form its original founders would have wished. The National also brought pre-London productions, but this turned very sour as it forbade London journalists to cover its Edinburgh work and in 1981 returned from the Edinburgh Festival première of Tom Stoppard's version of Nestroy's play of shopman and boy assistant *On the Razzle* only to announce that the subsequent London opening was the première, and Stoppard, whose rise to eminence derived from the Edinburgh Fringe production of *Rosencrantz and Guildenstern Are Dead*, signed the

57

published text to the same effect. Subsequently the National Theatre priced itself out of Festival reach. The Royal Shakespeare Company also returned with *Henry IV* Parts One and Two, with a former Edinburgh University drama star David Rintoul as an unusually kingly Prince Hal.

Drummond, like all directors, is remembered for what he did: not that he was robbed of hopes of bringing John Gielgud in *King Lear* in 1980 when my choice as the greatest living actor decided against returning to that well whence he had drawn such magic, or that he never obtained the outstanding Scottish contemporary play (other than the Traverse *Animal*) for which he negotiated so hard and so long. A slot was held for such a production in 1982, and its cancellation by the company at a late date forced Drummond to move a late-night entry, Peter Ustinov's play on the rehearsal of Mussorgsky's uncompleted opera based on Gogol's *The Marriage*, to a main slot. He had not seen it previously, unwisely relying on an assistant with little of his *flair* for spotting theatre breakthrough, but the disaster would have buried itself quietly had it not been for Drummond's entirely unmerited misfortune in his efforts to encourage new Scottish theatre. I remember as I took my seat in the Lyceum stalls before *The Marriage* hearing a confident Scottish voice, probably legal, bestowing approval on an ancient tribute to the author-director-star by its appropriation: 'Well, we should certainly enjoy this. Ustinov would be entertaining if he merely read the telephone directory!' And I heard it at curtain-fall, almost strangled into a scream: 'Why in God's name didn't he read the telephone directory?' My own embarrassment was now considerable, as I was scheduled to interview the great man the following morning for the *Festival Times*. I was no more ready to bring up the subject of what the press had unanimously declared a Festival disgrace besides a private grief than I would have been to intrude what Wilde would term the family skeleton into the family prayers; Ustinov from time to time made faint and courteous attempts to steer the conversation in its direction, and I headed him off like the faithful hound pulling its master back from the invisible cliff. He was very kind, and followed me into all subjects, nonsensical and otherwise, and to my uttermost delight actually did his great magic before my eyes of shimmering into an entirely different face, becoming President Giscard d'Estaing. It was absolutely unearthly, and completely convincing; he did it again at a public symposium at St Cecilia's that afternoon when the shimmering transformed him into a retired military gentleman on the Arts Council, and should anyone ask me if I have had spiritualistic experiences, I can now reply in the affirmative.

1982 must have been Drummond's most unhappy Festival, as for other reasons it was certainly mine. There was much he brought to melt the frozen reproach: the London Early Music Group in the Queen's Hall performed Italian music from the age of Monteverdi, and that morning was followed by a late-night Monteverdi Choir in St Cuthbert's Church culminating in the Scarlatti *Stabat Mater*, and Puccini opera was performed for the first time at the Edinburgh Festival with an inspired Scottish Opera *Manon Lescaut* rendered in grand period re-creation only to be depressed in the fourth act when Manon's death in the desert was apparently relocated in a lunar landscape, thus self-baptising as Moony Lescaut. The Sankai Juku company made street appearances culminating in three members hanging upside down for almost a day outside the City Chambers; but Allen Wright was nonetheless moved to opine at the Festival's conclusion that John Drummond should join them there in penance for *The Marriage* and for the American Repertory Theatre, another product of his ill-chosen talent scout. Their offerings were an indifferent *Sganarelle*, and a *Lulu* adaptation from Wedekind transposed, motels and all, into present-day New York, of a joylessness far beyond despair. Its director, Lee Breuer, and the company's director, Robert Brustein, were no longer on speaking terms when called on to fulfil an appearance commitment on contemporary American theatre at St Cecilia's, and all of Drummond's diplomacy was required to bring them before the awaiting public on the same platform. Their dire contributions were offset by a knowledgeable and instructive Frank Dunlop, then undreamed-of as Drummond's successor within two years, and a Chair galvanising the lumpen intellectuals into some semblance of professionalism in a performance of masterly resourcefulness from *The Guardian*'s Michael Billington.

And Roger, bicycling to an event on my behalf for the *Irish Times*, was knocked down and run over by what he subsequently termed two old dears, making a purblind turn on Melville Drive, bounding the Meadows, who in their horror then stopped the car dead on top of him. He was literally smothering to death when his cries brought providential assistance from four nearby footballers who lifted the car off and extricated him. His incredible resilience sustained him in the hard days that followed; anything less festive than my own spirits as I did my reviewing duty I could not imagine, save the daily reward his fortitude gave me; in fact he kept Festival by his gallantry while missing so much for which he had longed. He did it so well that even now some of the worst days of my life appear in retrospect lightened by the smiles through his pain. And if I recall the chills of horror at the realisation of the two deaths he so nearly obtained, my gratitude for his salvation from both melt them also. He zealously turned our talks into Festival-talk, winnowing my trivialisation into positive reaction, grinning at concomitant absurdities, sending me to this and that for which he was so fitted to be the ideal audience. The highest expression of his incredible range of human and cultural understanding in that series of visits was, I suppose, reached when he advised me on what I would do — not what I should do — when I attended Britten's *Noye's Fludde*.

It was performed in St Mary's Episcopalian Cathedral in Palmerston Place, with Sandy Neilson's finest scriptural music in speaking the Voice of God, William McCue as a lovable and courageous if frequently bewildered Noye, and Linda Ormiston as a strongly feminist Mrs Noye. It was an inspired manipulation of the resources of comedy to create awe, grief, wonder, and a sense of the sublime. The growing tensions at Mrs Noye's refusal to join her increasingly panic-stricken husband, her long-protracted and ultimately effected forceful removal within the Ark, the laughter becoming horror as her gossips were swept away, dreadful all the more in their comicality to the final doom, the ringing crack she indignantly landed on her pathetic husband's face, and the terrible, fluttering, dwindling hope of the raven, were all ventures into theological mystery, and all broke down any ordinary critical observation into storms of the heart. The magic of the thing was that no episode in biblical history is more famous, with resolution more certain than that which is so unquestioningly doubled as pious story and infant game; and yet the abiding emotion was fear for the destruction of the Ark. The genius of Britten in enlisting the audience for singing participation made so much of this possible, and so even more did the desperate vulnerability of the characters. 'And you will sing "Those in peril on the sea",' said Roger, 'and you will cry buckets.' And I did. I suppose I would have done so anyway, but its cathartic effect in making me express my sense of nearness of death, and the hopelessness of confronting it without the moral support of God, released all the terror and gratitude seething within me in the previous days. That it ended in comedy, even unintentional comedy, was also vital for me. I could giggle weakly, internally, at the simpering dove: it was only appropriate that the first creature to reach security should be so ludicrously pleased with itself. It was even more appropriate that the great rainbow raised by the chorus from assorted schools should be known thereafter as 'Cameron's Rainbow', being the creation of Cameron Wyllie, our former pupil, then English master in Daniel Stewart's and Melville, whose own pupils among others were each contributing their mite to the promise of future hope. The sheer happiness of grief in *Noye's Fludde* was the best thing I could have received.

Yet one reservation on the above description must be made. It is all quite inadequate. Music simply does not produce anything satisfactorily translatable into words. I was overwhelmed by it in emotional forms far deeper than speech of any kind can convey. Somewhere far beyond any kind of verbal expression, Britten found me, as my friend knew he would. So does any good musical performance at the Festival or anywhere else, which is why I have so little to say about music. I remember at Diamand's last Festival listening to Sir Georg Solti conducting Mahler's First Symphony; beside me was an agreeable colleague, with whom my meeting was accidental and my relations pleasant but not close. At one given moment we turned, looked at one another, smiled and looked back at the Usher Hall stage. We had both said everything that there was to say. The everything was pretty ecstatic. It was certainly enhanced by the charm of her smile. I saw Drummond after that concert: his eyes were like stars. Sometimes one word can say something, but not more than one word. In 1990 the opening concert was conducted by Seiji Ozawa with Mstislav Rostropovich on the cello for Dvořák's Cello Concerto, followed by Brahms's First Symphony. The word was 'Freedom'. Any elaboration would be self-destructive.

The breath of freedom was omnipresent in Edinburgh in 1979 as John Drummond entered on his kingdom and immediately ended the cold war with the republic that is the Fringe. Thus he showed that the

Festival, while he controlled it, would be 'our' Festival. The joint press conference with Alistair Moffat the previous year had already affirmed common concerns in an atmosphere of mutual respect. To begin his first Festival, Drummond went further. The opening concert in the Usher Hall, symbol within symbol of the Festival at its most self-conscious élitism, would include among the performers Andrew Cruickshank, eminent in his own right but here specifically recruited in his capacity as chairman of the Fringe Board of Directors elected from its members. It combined the statesmanship and chivalry normally characteristic of John Drummond.

Andrew Cruickshank (1907-1988), Aberdeen-born and profoundly Scottish, not least in his manic enthusiasm for Kierkegaard, had won a place in almost all Scottish hearts with access to television by his performance as the crusty, resourceful, wise and tartly benevolent Dr Cameron in the famous *Dr Finlay's Casebook*, a series based on A. J. Cronin's characters and employing the Holmes-Watson formula of remote-wisdom linked to accessible-innocence. Cruickshank did his work so well that viewers might be pardoned for thinking Cronin (and Conan Doyle too) had him in mind in conceiving an elderly general practitioner. Callendar was for long pointed out, or pointed to itself, as the original of the series location, 'Tannochbrae'. Much of Cruickshank's success had been in London, which meant that he ideally united the Scottish base of the Fringe with its cross-border clientele. In 1974 he was asked to accept the Fringe Chairmanship, vacant since the death of the first Chairman, Lord Grant, the Lord Justice-Clerk, that distinguished judge having been killed in a car accident in 1972 a year after the office had been founded. The Fringe had known its business in putting an eminent Scottish judge at its titular head, what with constant attacks by puritan demagogues and threats from licensing bureaucrats, but it felt secure enough now to seek a Scottish candidate from the high realms of London theatre success whither so many of its present and future members so longingly aspired. Cruickshank accepted the offer, placed before him by Fringe Administrator John Milligan, Vice-Chairman Michael Westcott, and Andrew Kerr, Secretary to the Board. In the words of Alistair Moffat in his book *The Edinburgh Fringe*: '. . . since 1974 Cruickshank has given to the Fringe the length and breadth of his experience in the theatre. And, in a sense, he has given the Fringe to his profession with an evangelical fervour. He believes in the Fringe as a lifeline of new talent to the theatre, and as a unique form of arts organisation which ought to be exported more widely than it is.'

Naturally, Milligan, and subsequently Moffat (and after them the great-hearted Michael Dale and then Mhairi Mackenzie-Robinson) continued actually to run the Fringe, with invaluable back-up and wisdom from Westcott and Kerr, but Cruickshank made characteristically ebullient appearances at Fringe Boards, and brought momentary blessed peace to the horror of the Fringe press party by an oration of welcome ranging in his manner from Kierkegaard to Dr Cameron. He looked his seventy-odd years by 1979, but he was still in the fullness of his powers, having played John Anthony in the National Theatre revival of John Galsworthy's *Strife* the previous November and being on the verge of rehearsal as Rosenberg in Peter Shaffer's *Amadeus* to be performed at the same address. Peter Hall's *Diaries* mention that at the end of the National Theatre strike, settled in late May, Cruickshank 'said with ringing authority that all National Theatres had to have their strikes, their revolutions, in order to reach maturity'. Drummond had no evident cause for anxiety about his symbol of reunion. The chief anxieties were probably felt by broadcasters faced with the duty of pronouncing the name of the BBC Symphony Orchestra's conductor for the opening concert, Gennadi Rozhdestvensky.

The main item on the opening concert was Stravinsky's *The Rite of Spring*, in formal celebration of Sergei Diaghilev, the theme of the Festival, and in informal celebration of the Festival's new freedom. It was to be preceded by Prokofiev's *Chout*, in which Cruickshank was to narrate. But Cruickshank was unable to be present at rehearsal. By this stage Drummond was ready to maintain his symbol if he had to fly a helicopter himself bearing the narrator to the roof of the Usher Hall. No problem, he insisted; he would stand in as narrator in the rehearsal himself. (The ease with which Festival Directors arrange for substitutes for leading performers at rehearsals must freeze the blood of Fringe directors, frenziedly rehearsing to the last moment with desperate self-reassurances that a Bad Dress Rehearsal means a Good Opening Night.) The final rehearsal went like a dream, Drummond carrying out his work, as he carried out every other performance thrust upon him, faultlessly and inspirationally. On the night, therefore, the massive countenance of the Fringe Chairman in full evening dress (and therefore actually suffering the television-light temperature afflicting every performer on stage) looked down on the Beautiful, Beautiful People, doubtless madly reminding themselves that he was a Distinguished Performer at the National Theatre, with never a thought in their minds for *Dr Finlay's Casebook* or the Fringe. The view from the audience, somewhat obscured by floral decorations in front of the stage with which the philanthropy of eager, elderly votaries ruthlessly festooned it, was happily enriched by his majestic form as he rose to deliver his first words, 'This is the story of a fool, who fools seven other fools . . .', and his rich brasswind smote the remotest corners of the hall with every explosive 'fool'. The Beautiful, Beautiful People made zealous efforts to look intelligent.

Rozhdestvensky proved a conductor of force, and the contrivance of Prokofiev's buffoon made its way happily through the first three scenes. But before the appropriate moment when further narrative was required, Cruickshank suddenly trumpeted to his feet with the urgency of an elephant apprising his wives of sudden danger, and fought the BBC Symphony Orchestra to a standstill. Rozhdestvensky retreated under remorseless fire, and we were into the fourth scene however prematurely. But if Cruickshank had won the battle, Rozhdestvensky had every intention of winning the war. As the fourth scene concluded, the baton thrust down and across to Cruickshank with all the vehemence of a fisherman gaffing an enormous salmon. At the interval the Beautiful, Beautiful People were frenziedly assuring one another of their certainty from the first publicity that this was to be expected from the folly of recognising the Fringe.

In Frank Dunlop's opening year, 1984, Andrew Cruickshank made a formidable contribution to *The Thrie Estaites* as an Abbot, silent during most of the play, but suddenly thunderous, sulphuric and menacing, in defence of the Church establishment and its iron retention of benefices for which the incumbents lacked any spiritual vocation. Roy Hanlon as the Bishop harrying reformers had been a strong and cunning diplomat, but Cruickshank had the work of revealing the much harder, much more hidden, obduracy of ecclesiastical corruption. He was awesome, a monument of selfishness masquerading as piety, and this time there was no sign of under-rehearsal.

Had anyone known it, John Drummond in 1979 featured not only the Fringe Chairman, but also his successor. Cruickshank was followed in the Fringe chair by Dr Jonathan Miller, whose first public

64

appearance at the Festival had been in the late-night revue under official Festival auspices, *Beyond the Fringe*, in company with Peter Cook, Dudley Moore and Alan Bennett. Undoubtedly Drummond's policy of good relations with the Fringe helped the republican ranks to turn to an illustrious figure whose leading Edinburgh credentials were more of official Festival than Fringe variety, and of these the most illustrious was surely Miller's production of *La Traviata* for Kent Opera, beginning in the King's two days after the opening concert. It proved an admirable rationalisation of opera, with Jill Gomez showing every sign of imminent tubercular death, and the accent of the entire production towards the probability of the events on stage. The self-sacrifice of the Traviata is not a particularly incredible idea; indeed Miller, as a doctor, would know well that death, imminent within weeks, erodes human realism. It was proved possible to grieve with admiration at the tragic purity of Gomez's performance while becoming seriously enraged by the folly of Alfredo, instead of having to dispense with all personal involvement save the aesthetic. And two years later Jonathan Miller was a Drummond Festival guest once more, in the Television and the Arts Conference final session. Three years after that, Cruickshank retired, Miller was drafted, and I was telling Fringe Administrator Michael Dale he might expect to find a horse's head in his bed, Miller having taken office in the aftermath of his realistic *Rigoletto* in New York, for which the Mafia were said to have put out a contract on him. If the Mafia had arrived, Michael would have reasoned with them, and would quietly have saved Miller from them, and would himself have been killed by them: Michael is like that.

Sir Peter Hall, Director of the National Theatre (London), diary, Wednesday, 22 August 1979:

> A long weekend at the Edinburgh Festival. It was strange moving so quickly from the glossy prosperity of Salzburg to this hard Scottish city. Yet in some ways I prefer Edinburgh — it has a freedom, a lack of constraint, which seems good.
>
> I saw the two productions of the Georgians (they do not like being called Russians), the Rustaveli Company, who are the sensation of the festival. *Richard III* is a freewheeling adaptation which I didn't much

admire, though its vitality, and its life are unarguable. Their production of the *Caucasian Chalk Circle* I enjoyed much more. The boring socialist prologue is cut, and the whole thing is presented as a frank entertainment with a narrator and a piano player who are man and wife circus performers. Ramez Chkhikvadze gave both Richard and Asdak: he is a great ham, but a great liver, and a great actor.

This company are much influenced by Brook in their freedom, their eclecticism, and their embracing of rough theatre. But I have never seen acting like this before. Actually it comes down to national temperament. The Georgians are Latin, emotional, sly, cool, very humorous. They don't stamp and roar. They are not intense, not cosmic, and they are certainly not Russian. They seem to mock everything, which I like.

I preferred the *Chalk Circle* simply because it released Brecht's wonderful fairy story as a popular entertainment. Ideology and politics were out of the window. *Richard III* was, I thought, a liberty, a cartoon: nothing to do with Shakespeare, his world, or his play.

You begin by celebrating freedom; you end by complaining about a liberty. Sir Peter, a friend and successor of Lord Olivier, may have felt restraints in sanctioning liberties taken with the play his predecessor had brought to its widest audience via the cinema, albeit with liberties of its own such as 'improvements' from Colley Cibber, interpolations from *Henry VI* Part Three, drastic cuts from major roles other than his own and picturesque additions to that. Yet there was a kinship between the Olivier version and that presented by the Georgians at the Royal Lyceum Theatre in Drummond's first year. Whether or not the Georgians had been influenced by Peter Brook, they would certainly have had available to them the ideas of Bernard Shaw, in good USSR standing, as expressed in his review of Sir Henry Irving's *Richard III* at the London Lyceum, collected in his *Our Theatre in the Nineties* and republished in Shaw selections, originally appearing in the *Saturday Review* for 26 December 1896:

> The world being yet little better than a mischievous schoolboy, I am afraid it cannot be denied that Punch and Judy holds the field still as the most popular of dramatic entertainments. And of all its versions, except those which are quite above the head of the man in the street, Shakespeare's Richard III is best. It has abundant devilry, humor, and character, presented with luxuriant energy of diction in the simplest form of blank verse. Shakespeare revels in it with just the sort of artistic unconscionableness that fits the theme. Richard is the prince of Punches: he delights Man by provoking God, and dies unrepentant and

game to the last. His incongruous conventional appendages, such as the Punch hump, the conscience, the fear of ghosts, all impart a spice of outrageousness which leaves nothing lacking to the fun of the entertainment, except the solemnity of those spectators who feel bound to take the affair as a profound and subtle historic study.

Shaw went on to argue for Irving's having played it as Punch, and the film certainly suggests Olivier played it as Punch (or played Irving as Richard as Punch), but there can have been few interpretations so thoroughly Punchian as that staged without translation by the Rustaveli Company in their own Georgian language. Characters were established by hurling the names of prominent personalities at their performers more or less at the outset, with scant concern that 'R-R-R-R-Rich-mond' was thus introduced about four acts too early, and thenceforward matters took their tumultuous course on lines tolerably recognisable to anyone acquainted with play or film. The widowed Lancastrian Queen Margaret and the dying Yorkist King Edward were the most obvious puppet-figures from marionette-show, with fine employment of Jack-in-the-box. But Ramez Chkhikvadze was triumphantly Punch from start to finish, with echoes of all evil puppet-kings from the mummer devil to Jarry's Ubu Roi, the family resemblances here expressing themselves involuntarily rather than intentionally (surely Stalin and his successors would have discouraged study and performance of *Ubu*). He conspired, gibbered, snarled, writhed, bullied, overawed, dissimulated, panicked, defied and died as King Punch in every movement and gesture. These Festival memoirs may seem short on mime, but mime had its greatest Shakespearean moments in this gigantic leap over language barrier.

Thus began John Drummond's five-year evangelisation of foreign-language theatre on the Edinburgh Festival stages. Georgia was an inspired choice with which to link Scotland and a very wide world. Sir Peter's alertness to the Georgians' dislike of being termed Russian he could comfortably have analogised to the people among whom he saw them perform. Or perhaps the correct word is 'uncomfortably': that he found the Rustaveli *Richard* 'a liberty' may have derived in part from a feeling that this was no way to treat a classic in its own country. But they were not performing it in Shakespeare's country, as Shakespeare would have been the first to stress. Drummond had found a means for Scotland to translate its own self-consciousness into identification with other cultural unities striving to assert their national identities against the arrogance of alien metropolis. If you want to be Scots, he was saying, then be Georgian! Hugh MacDiarmid, a celebrant of Georgian-Scottish links, would have enthusiastically agreed.

1980 brought Polish in Kantor's *Wielopole Wielopole*. 1981 produced the National Theatre of Rumania's version of Terence's *Girl from Andros*, Amphi-Theatre of Greece in Pieros Katsaitis's *Iphigenia in Lixourion*, and Theatre de la Salamandre in Racine's *Britannicus*. 1982 showed Rome's Cooperativa Teatromusica in Pietro Metastasio's *L'Olimpiade*, and Sardinia's Akroama in Lelio Lecis's *Mariedda*. Sometimes there would be simultaneous translation (as there had been with the Rustaveli *Chalk Circle*), sometimes not. In any case, many members of the audience preferred to dispense with the equipment, and trust to the stage. What was happening was a new form of theatre apprehension, Drummond inviting his public to lay aside their fears and inhibitions about foreign languages, and allow stagecraft to work its own magic. After all, nobody yet demanded simultaneous translation in an opera, and these performers transmitted their art with far more generous reliance on spectacle and movement than any opera. Frequently the material conscripted the sympathies of the audience by stressing the actors' comparable problems with barriers of time. *Britannicus* was staged by twentieth-century actors deliberately setting themselves in Racine's own time to portray his Neronian drama in terms which would show its preoccupation with comparable intrigue and treachery at the Court of Louis XIV. *Iphigenia* was an early eighteenth-century extravaganza about the staging of a tragedy from the fourth century BC on a theme supposedly set eight centuries earlier. Sometimes the production would derive from a well-known base, such as *Mariedda*'s origin in Hans Andersen's *The Little Match-Girl*. But whatever the encouraging dramatic obstacles to be leapt, or the thematic common ground to encourage, Drummond's foreign-language imports were invariable successes; his delighted audiences emerged with some dazed notion of invigorating swimming in unfamiliar water with the Festival Director's hand supporting their collective chin. Word of mouth and ecstatic reviews brought in punters never likely on their own to attempt any drama other than Anglophone, and Edinburgh seemed to ring with cries akin to 'Come on in, the language is no trouble, and the play is perfectly fine, you can ride on the actors!'

John Drummond's last Festival in its totality eclipsed even the great four years he had filled with such riches before it. He had declared Festival themes for each save the third — Diaghilev for 1979, the Commonwealth for 1980 (bringing among other wonders the Australian Wildstars, a radiant galaxy of dancers, and the Canadian celebration of the World War I flying ace Billy Bishop), and Italy in 1982 (above all in the ballet-puppet Compagnia Marionettistica of Milan's Carlo Colla e Figli whose 170-year-old *Prometheus* and twentieth-century *Cenerentola* (Cinderella) achieved beauty, tragedy and laughter with delicacy enviable by any live company, and so transported the audience into puppet-thought that the appearance of the puppet-masters for curtain call seemed a terrifying Brobding-nagian vision). But the theme of Vienna 1900 brought another city and another time setting down so firmly on Edinburgh 1983 that many of us vaguely convinced ourselves we walked and listened among the turn-of-century Viennese. The great Glasgow Citizens production of Karl Kraus's *The Last Days of Mankind* in the Assembly Hall reached out to its audience so thoroughly that the floor at least became silent participants in the apocalyptic remorseless exploration of central European humanity hell-bent on verbal self-destruction. The second major play was in Hebrew, from Israel's Haifa Municipal Theatre (whose high cultural achievement mocked the Israeli proverb 'Make money in Haifa, spend it in Tel-Aviv, and then pray in Jerusalem'). Yehoshua Sobol's *The Soul of a Jew* was similarly preoccupied with doom and last days, this time the last day in the life of Otto Weininger, a Jewish philosopher who rejected his faith and his people, embraced anti-semitism and anti-feminism, and tortured himself in his con-troversies with Zionist friends until he finally committed suicide on 3 October 1903. Although Hitler would later make capital of Weininger's *Sex and Character*, the play was a profoundly pitying portrayal of the renegade whose tragedy almost sang its dolorous message in the language he scorned: the sheer music of the Hebrew speech time and again induced abandonment of simultaneous translation from the thronged seats in the Assembly Rooms.

At the heart of the Festival was the great Exhibition, created by Peter Vergo (famed for his *Art in Vienna 1898-1918*) in the Queen Street National Museum of Antiquities of Scotland. Here was history translated into visual force and strength, conveying, for instance, the power of the reforming anti-semitic Mayor Karl Lüger, the threat of the pan-Germanist George von Schönerer, the communications explosion featuring and enraging Karl Kraus, the new wisdom of Sigmund Freud, the conventionalism of Viennese art and the rich challenge of its Secession movement and the later revolt against that, Charles Rennie Mackintosh's Scottish Room here recreated as it originally appeared for the Secession Exhibition of 1900, and some of the richest art treasures of Vienna's Schönbrunn Palace. A series of outstanding lectures, two per day, on the life and culture of Vienna 1900 placed due emphases on such fundamental forms of cultural exchange and challenge as café society. Hamburg State Opera brought two works from the Viennese composer Alexander von Zemlinsky, both based on Wilde, *Eine Florentinische Tragödie* and *Der Geburtstag der Infantin*. Brückner, Mahler, Schönberg, Berg and Webern dominated the Festival music. Never before or since has a Festival so astoundingly interlocked its variety of arts in celebration, and as each supplemented its fellows, Vienna 1900 was here. And then Drummond was gone.

Frank Kuppner, *A Bad Day for the Sung Dynasty* (1984), IV, verse 354:

> There are forty-three poets here travelling in a ferry
> Designed to carry six passengers safely across the river;
> One cannot help wondering whether this administration
> Is as sympathetic to literature as it claims to be.

Queen Elizabeth, daughter of the 14th Earl of Strathmore and Kinghorne, consort of King George VI, was one of the founders of the Edinburgh International Festival in 1947. Her patriotic spirit, which had played a significant part in the maintenance of British morale through the worst days of the Second World War, rallied enthusiastically to the idea of a Festival intended to preach cultural reconciliation and rebirth for a world crawling painfully out of the ashes of the war and the holocausts of Nazism. The success or failure of the first Festival trembled on a knife-edge, and the Queen's patronage was unquestionably one of the decisive factors in making it a permanent event. She brought her husband and her daughters to various events in successive years, and after she was widowed in 1952 she continued to attend many Festivals as the Queen Mother, as did her daughter Elizabeth, now Queen. The Festival to this day sports their names as its patrons, but a quarter-century has now elapsed since their presence at any event. From 1965, Princess Margaret occasionally visited the Fringe Club, or saw an exhibition on the main Festival. Prince Edward performed with the Cambridge Light Entertainment Society on the Fringe when he was a student at Cambridge, and dealt with Fringeperformers' perpetual nightmare of accommodation by putting up the cast at Holyrood House. He has since become a patron of Jeremy James Taylor's National Youth Music Theatre. The Fringe is not conspicuous among friends of monarchy but the Prince's modesty and enthusiastic team spirit have made him well liked.

The presences of Queen Mother or Queen are no longer necessitous for Festival survival, but could make a good deal of difference to the future of the Arts in a hostile climate. The principle is simple enough. When James Young Simpson pioneered the use of chloroform in midwifery, the gigantic social task of persuading women to accept it, and, more particularly, their self-centred husbands to permit it, was enormously facilitated by Queen Victoria who sensibly eased the hideous pangs of birth in her last parturition by the use of chloroform. A Queen's leadership can make important converts to support for vital social reforms and cultural evangelisation. But that leadership is no longer there, apart from two lines of print, as far as the Festival is concerned.

It would seem that the mistake was that of the Festival Council when, instead of following their previous pattern of choosing the assistants of successive Directors, they reached out in 1961 beyond the confines of their founding father, Rudolf Bing, whose Glyndebourne Opera Company had produced himself and his two heirs; the new choice was George, Earl of Harewood, cousin to the Queen. Lord Harewood boasted much experience as opera impresario, but his kinship is unlikely to have been absent in the attractions of his candidacy. If a closer connection with the Festival's Royal patrons, already generous in the time they gave it, was one of the objects of the appointing committee, their ambitions had a dramatically ironic fate. Lord Harewood resigned in 1965 having fathered a child outside his marriage, following which he was divorced and married the baby's mother. The Profumo affair and its peripheral associations in 1963 had whetted the public appetite for scandal, and the Royal family would seem, after the Harewood resignation, to have shunned an event inviting recollection of a family member who had provided fodder for salacious tittle-tattle. It is hard not to sympathise with Lord Harewood's Royal cousins; any mention of scandal in a Royal context invariably set on foot a chain of speculation, as steamy as it was probably groundless, concerning more eminent figures still.

But any such decision may also have been expedited by another factor. Critical comments in the late 1950s had alleged snobbishness and élitism in the Queen — in retrospect an unfair charge, if unfairly answered by private vicious assaults on the critics, and particularly unfair to the Queen Mother who had shown no élitism in visiting bombed dwellings where her encouragement had been badly needed — and in the mid-1960s advisers to the monarchy on its image would seem to have encouraged more down-market interests. Simultaneously the Festival became more opera-obsessed, these being the Diamand years, and the growth of the Fringe was in part a reaction against the social climbers in perfect evening dress who so vigorously exuded the aura of a Festival where the élite meet, Fringetranslated as where the effete bleat. The Fringe and the monarchy, it would seem, came to the same conclusions about the Beautiful, Beautiful People, viz. that they were boring snobs. But when Drummond and, after him, Dunlop extended the frontiers of the Festival to make it truly an event showing that culture was entertainment for everyone, and Drummond's first formal press appearance was in tandem with Fringe Administrator Alistair Moffat, the Fringe in general was ready to end the war. Drummond invited the Cranes to the official Festival with their adaptation of *The Brothers Karamazov*, and the great Polish dramatist Tadeusz Kantor, originally brought to the Fringe by Richard Demarco; and indeed inaugurated his régime with two plays under Traverse Theatre production — of which one, Tom McGrath's *Animal*, directed by Chris Parr with movement direction by Stuart Hopps, was in itself a great frontier-breaking work depicting the reaction among a colony of non-speaking apes (played by the bulk of the cast) into whose satisfactorily self-contained lives the incursion of humans proved a symbolic disaster. There were drawbacks. The Beautiful, Beautiful People, few of whom would have been seen dead at a Fringe show unless it contained an aspirant relative, began to chatter about apes and Cranes as though they had known them since before Darwin and Lorenz. But the Fringe has survived Festival blessings without much loss of its radical spirit, and while the Beautiful, Beautiful People are still secretly doing their damnedest to bring back the snob-opera days of their Harewood and their Diamand long ago, the Festival has not yet abjured the Drummond revolution. The monarchy has good reason to come in from the cold.

But if the monarchy remained immune to the attractions of the Festival, the circumstance in itself invited the attention of one visitor who missed few opportunities to usurp regal functions. The place of cultural interests in the priorities of Mrs Margaret Thatcher does not seem high, and her administration certainly gave little encouragement to any such thesis. But an opportunity of making a state visit was another matter. It was true that the presence of the Prime Minister was not particularly likely to increase the ticket sales for the rest of the Festival and Fringe, which the Queen Mother and the Queen had known would follow when they played their important parts as patrons. The Prime Minister does seem to have had another motive.

The Thatcher years were marked by a consistent erosion of support for the Tories in Scotland. Seats which had been Tory since 1918 fell to their enemies as Scottish hatred of Thatcher grew and grew. The Prime Minister herself was possibly of more significance than any other single factor in expediting this process. Her class-conscious rhetoric, her hostility to community sense, her vaunted delight in ignoring the referendum result of 1979 where a majority of Scottish voters had favoured a Scottish Assembly, her encouragement of lieutenants telling Scots with every additional electoral result against the government that Scotland wanted and would get more Thatcherism, her insufferably patronising manner sedulously suggesting the great lady amusedly making friends with the village idiot, her illiterate allusions to Adam Smith as some sort of Scottish tribal totem, her lordly if picture-postcardish pronouncements on Scottishness as something she of all people was fitted to define, her rabid militarism, her ferocious and most expensive defence of secrecy in government, her poll tax passed first for Scotland in a Parliament with overwhelming opposition to the measure from Scottish representatives in utter indifference to the parliamentary obligation of consent of representatives to their constituents' taxation — it is difficult to single out any one of the reasons above the rest in Scottish hatred of the lady. But the fact itself was all too well known, especially to the collapsing Tory party in Scotland.

73

But Thatcher could never accept the idea of her own unpopularity in any part of her dominions, still less that of its certain place in the destruction of her party fortunes. Her answer went farther than that of her lackeys: Scotland wanted not only more Thatcherism, it also wanted, must want, could not exist without wanting, more Thatcher. In vain even her most servile Scottish creatures sought to divert her. Having won the 1987 General Election with three in every four Scots against her, she announced her intention of becoming a Festival event. Her by now desperate Scottish Ministers seem to have fed every possible neurosis among her security staff to ensure she would not appear, only to result in her unstoppable advent being shrouded in spectacular secrecy. At least it would limit the electoral damage of her presence to fairly small numbers, and avoid some thoughtful remarks from Fringers on her policy of cultural pernicious anaemia. Nobody had seemed to worry about security precautions when her Minister of the Arts, Lord Gowrie, came to the Festival a year or two earlier to give a press conference and meet Fringe prizewinners, although his resignation — coincidentally — was announced the next day. No greater precaution than a quick smile to acquaintances attended the Secretary of State for Scotland, Malcolm Rifkind, as he slipped into his Festival concert hall seat for the classical music he loved so devotedly and so unostentatiously. But, for the Prime Minister, something on the lines of Ceaucescu meeting the public seemed to be required. A list was drawn up of those whom she wished to meet at a Saturday morning reception under Government auspices. The commands were delivered in the small hours preceding, once she had arrived on the Friday evening and taken her seat in the Usher Hall where the Pittsburgh Symphony Orchestra was performing Beethoven's Eighth and Ninth Symphonies. Her entourage had thus the leisure to speculate on the appropriateness of the choral *Ode to Joy*, with its rapturous salutation of love and friendship, but they were content that she knew the works, saw no offence in them, and found them appropriately regal fare.

The response to the commands varied. The Beautiful, Beautiful People were ready to scratch each other's eyes out to get them, and it may be hoped that those who were disappointed initially were accommodated at the eleventh hour and fifty-fifth minute as it became clear that not every invited guest was prepared to sacrifice leisure, comfort, rehearsal, business, family or friends on no more notice than

74

a few hours, possibly with disturbance of sleep occasioned by the reception of the Prime Ministerial despatch riders. M. Rudolf Nureyev, due to perform the Saturday matinée of his *Homage to Les Ballet Russes and Diaghilev* in the Playhouse Theatre at 2 p.m., absolutely refused to pay homage to anyone other than Diaghilev, Stravinsky, Fokine, Benois, Massine, Bakst, Nijinsky, Bolm or P. Puthyk, and left it to the *ad hoc* Paul Revere serving him with his command to make such use of it as seemed appropriate; but M. Nureyev was appearing under the auspices of the Ballet Théatre Français de Nancy which had no grant from HM Government to forfeit.

But for those persons of significance in British bodies of artistic interests, there was no such freedom as that enjoyed by M. Nureyev. Their specific institution might or might not be in receipt of government aid, or, as the Thatcherites liked to put it, 'public money', but no British institution of artistic concerns dared wantonly to alienate a Prime Minister whose arm, when enraged, was known to be long. Little though the Government did for the arts, nobody dared give it encouragement to do even less. The Artistic Director of the Festival, Mr Frank Dunlop, was of course present and correct. The Fringe Administrator, Ms Mhairi Mackenzie-Robinson, was presiding over the annual general meeting of the Fringe Society, but leave it she must, and security insisted that no public explanation could be given. The Director of the Book Festival had to leave Lady Antonia Fraser and Ms Dorothy Dunnett, two authors about to meet the public, to consume their coffee in the Roxburghe Hotel where the visiting chairperson, not on the Book Festival staff, managed to convince an amiable management that his signature on the bill would be honoured despite his unofficial status. And so on and so forth. I cannot say whether the Berliner Ensemble, then appearing in the King's Theatre in a production of *The Caucasian Chalk Circle* of icicle-sharp clarity, were commanded and obeyed, but if any of their number were present, ample opportunity would have been furnished to them for the scrutiny of alienation under traditions other than those of their master Brecht. Those present, when questioned later, said that the lady had been graciousness itself, and had spoken much to many of them. As to whether they had been able to say anything to her, they were courteously evasive. She then sped northward to her titular Sovereign at Balmoral, where such information as she vouchsafed on the Edinburgh Festival did nothing to encourage a Royal return. But the Prime Minister was quite delighted with her Haroun al Raschid conquest of the Festival. She arranged to have her appointee as Lord High Commissioner to the General Assembly of the Church of Scotland invite her to its deliberations in Edinburgh next May so that she might speak to it, told it that she was greatly honoured to have been invited, and stated she was deeply grateful that it had now asked her to address it. Among other things, she said '. . . for, when all is said and done, a politician's life is a humble one'.

Chapter Three

Booked, with Accomplices

The
Edinburgh
Book Festival!

From Anthony Troon, Book Festival, *The Scotsman*, 24 August 1983:

> *Brutalisation was behind another event, when horror writer James Herbert was hilariously interviewed by Owen Dudley Edwards. After a learned discussion involving giant rats and castration by garden shears, the two men turned to the fact that both were reared as Roman Catholics.*
>
> *In fact, Herbert revealed that he was intercepted once by a nun of his acquaintance, who asked what kind of book he was working on. 'Well,' he said, 'it's about Catholics.' 'It's not going to give us a hard time, I hope,' she declared.*
>
> *Some months later she asked how the work was coming along and was told it was taking a long time. 'Ah, well, ye see,' she said with undisguised pleasure, 'it's just the will of God.'*

THE BOOK FESTIVAL. TERROR. PLEASURABLE TERROR, CERTAINLY, but still terror. No hiding in an audience now, except for events I cover as a critic. No anonymity, no gratifying sense of unimportant importance with eyes and ears on the stage and identity cuddled within until the late-night duel with notes and typewriter. Much worse than speaking or lecturing in public. Then the stomach butterflies, certainly, or else the worry that things will go wrong because of over-confidence symptomised by no stomach butterflies. But those things I live with as my occupation at university, however much in class lecturing I worry before and after that my material does not go across so as to excite listeners into reading and reflecting. Debating, when I have to do it, again not a new problem but the old devils to beat. Debating was my one sport at university, and in 1959 Osita Godfrey Agbim of Nigeria and I won the *Observer* Mace. I debated once in the short-lived Radio Festival, short-lived in Edinburgh at any rate. It was daunting, but made much less so by the warmth and encouragement of the organisers, who were as hot to encourage participants from outside professional radio ranks as their brethren in the Television Festival were cold.

I spoke to the Television Festival once, about a historical documentary on the Spanish Civil War made years before for the Inter-University

Film Consortium by Paul Addison, Tony Aldgate and myself. A hostile audience, annoyed at the interruption in their incest, but here the very hostility, admirably symbolised by the guard dogs on the perimeter of the fastness I had to penetrate, was its own stimulus. I knew who they were, and that they would not like me. That was easy. The next year, outside Festival time, I had to form one of a panel of historians and politicians speaking about two television histories of Ireland on Ludovic Kennedy's *Did You See . . .* programme. Just before we went on, Mr Brian Wenham, then high in the councils of the BBC, told me smoothly that if I did well he would perhaps be able to get me an invitation to speak at the Television Festival. I said that I had spoken to it the previous year. He did not seem to be listening. He looked as if he had been listening when the programme was over, for I had said a hard word or two on deliberate misstatements within the BBC item, misstatements transmitted in the knowledge of their falsity but supposedly justified by the exigencies of programme-making. 'You attacked our programme,' he hissed, a famine of TV Festival invitation in his eyes, all the more gratifying since once is enough to breach those familial ranks. Few virtuous moments are more gratifying than the rejection of a bribe one does not want.

But the Book Festival is welcoming, as much so as the Radio Festival, and Jenny Brown and her staff appeal to one's honour, not against it. The responsibility is the greater. To make a mess of a chairpersonship or interviewship is to let down a beloved institution and a beloved team. It is not a simple matter of performing: you may wreck the show by performing brilliantly, if you do it at the expense of your guests. It is them the audience has come to see, and if they disappoint the audience, you are only a slight substitute and the fault may well be yours, should be considered as being yours whatever the palliating circumstances. It is not a matter of controlling the audience. As head of debates, or Auditor of the Literary and Historical Society of University College Dublin, I had to control private business in a house much of which had been visiting neighbouring hostelries, and all of which was alert for any sign of weakness in the chair. Those were hard lessons, but they made me unafraid of any future comparable houses elsewhere. But the Book Festival audience would be sober and civil, and if there were to be disturbers of the peace, that would be an exciting challenge and one I knew. The problems are much more deeply related to the guests. Will their opening statements go on too long? Will they be too short? Will they be too introverted? Will they be intractable for discussion? Will the several guests prove less easy to relate to one another than the wise programme planners had believed? Will I be too warmly kid-gloved? Will I be too hard-hitting, and spoil the thing by creating an ugly atmosphere? Will I stay with the speakers too long and not go to the house for discussion early enough? Will I go to the house too early and risk not one or two dryings-up of discussion requiring conservation of further prepared questions, to be orchestrated in the light of what guests and house have said — but a multitude of dry spots, in which case I have taken the thing too close to the rocks?

In fact the house at the Book Festival is the main insurance I have found. It wants a good session, and is usually prepared to work for it. If I am holding the thing too long among the guests, a hand is likely to go up, or perhaps a reproachful voice. I have no problems of national identity: one of the most rewarding things about living in Scotland is the constant assurance that Scots are ready to welcome outsiders who want to think of Scotland as home, provided they mean home and not simply an area for exploitation or a sojourn intended to conclude with return to a supposedly superior place. I am fully permitted to be Irish as well as Scots, provided it is not obsessively Irish, or Irish to the exclusion of Scottish concerns. The English visitors at the Book Festival are normally courteous and conscious of being visitors, not of asserting their mastery over an outlying province. Should they attempt the latter, the house can be relied on to disprove the legend of taciturn Scots. Americans are normally bathed in an aura of amiable fascination, and are very quick to praise the freedom of discussion, superiority of the occasion over a mere selling device, and so on. European continentals have usually some constructive comparative points to make. What I have to worry about is me.

Thanks to the house and the organisers, and indeed to many of the distinguished guests, I don't think I have made a mess of a session so far, but there have been moments when a cold trickle of fear has made its ugly way down my spine. There was, for instance, the episode of James Herbert, in the Book Festival of 1983.

A cold trickle of fear was, in its way, most appropriate to James Herbert, whose vast reading public expects precisely that reaction to his work and is unlikely to be disappointed. Had circumstances been otherwise, perhaps I could have told him of my symptoms, elicited his gratification at the predictable reaction to him however unexpected its location, and maybe inspired his greatest horror novel of all to be entitled *Festival*, or possibly *Book*. I was supposed to discuss horror fiction with him, a proceeding for which my idle reading had left me somewhat overprepared. As I saw it this was not simply intended as a 'Meet the Author' session. The Book Festival evolved from John Drummond's idea of a Word Festival-within-the-Festival which he set up in 1980 under Frank Delaney, when some highly significant discussions on aspects of the Word ensued. And there were other sessions, such as that involving Kingsley Amis, where the larger themes disappeared while the author talked about himself and his work. The Book Festival had also partly arisen from the dedicated work of organisers of 'Meet the Author' in various guises over the years and usually outside the Festival — and here for once let me quote from my writing at the time, in a *Festival Times* piece, where I noted its debt 'to the tireless activity of Judy Moir of the Scottish Publishers Association supplying the vital Scottish nucleus for its work, to that most noble and humane of children's writers Joan Lingard who has given so much of her dedication to literature in the vital contribution she has made here, to the quiet charming efficiency of Mary Baxter who has fostered so much cultivation of the love of books in Scotland now and for many years' — and in the Book Festival's evolution the names of Ainslie Thin the bookseller and of Alan Taylor the reference librarian (now literary editor of *Scotland on Sunday*) should also be joined. But the Charlotte Square Book Festival, as I well knew in this its first year, could not justify itself as glorified 'Meet the Author'. Larger issues, issues in depth, issues celebrating the literary traditions as well as new challenges to them, must surely be raised.

I had been supplied with several of James Herbert's books, which I had devoured with interest although with some sense of repetitiveness of theme. He had begun in 1974 with *The Rats,* involving immense destruction of human life by a plague of rats master-minded by a King Rat. He had gone on to *The Fog*, again chronicling impressive disaster, this time from a mysterious darkness with monstrous powers of inducing madness in whole populations. There was an undoubtedly impressive passage in which the entire town of Bournemouth walks into the sea. James Herbert had gone from there to further disasters, occasionally revisiting the rats, but becoming more interested in apparent doom-figures haunting humanity, as in *The Survivor, The Jonah,* and, most recently, *Shrine,* in which a Bernadette-of-Lourdes figure proves an agent of evil. This all seemed to have enough material to give us a cheerful session plumbing the horror-fiction of the past, ranging over Mr Herbert's inspiration therefrom, examining what new directions he sought to take in it and felt others might profitably pursue or were pursuing. I revisited a few old friends, more as an act of piety than for revision, and then I was ready.

I wonder if the audience contained any followers of the game of cricket? I was in the situation of a slow bowler, sending in every device he knows. James Herbert was in that of a careful batsman under orders to stonewall, and he stonewalled practically everything I sent him. H. P. Lovecraft, M. R. James, Bram Stoker, Robert Bloch, Ray Bradbury, Conan Doyle, Sheridan Le Fanu, Flavia Richardson, Oscar Cook (the bowling began to get a bit wild) — he may have heard of one or two, but all would seem to have remained closed books to him, and books he evidently had every intention to keep closed. We may have got somewhere on Orwell's rats in *1984,* though I doubt it. Orwell was certainly useful in one respect — it is very seldom he fails completely on invocation — in that his horror of the rats and use of them as the means for the final breaking of Winston Smith evidently arose from personal experience, and on this James Herbert was certainly ready to speak so far as he himself was concerned. He had grown up in fairly deprived circumstances in the London East End, and he had a vivid memory of seeing rats, and observing them. As I recall he was not possessed by Orwell's sense of personal nausea, but rather was intrigued by the thought of the potential effects of rats let loose on a much wider (and much less deprived) area. I alluded to the giant rats in *Gulliver's Travels,* and in Wells's *The Food of the Gods.* I brightly mentioned the story of the plague of rats directed by a King Rat in the Communist scientist J. B. S. Haldane's fantasy work for children *My Friend Mr Leakey.* It had been a Puffin and had therefore enjoyed a wide circulation during Mr Herbert's youth. He stated he knew nothing about it. His austere, dark, grim countenance began to acquire a slightly hunted look which advised caution.

So I threw my old friends to the winds while cherishing the vain hope that Ambrose Bierce, whose fate has been unknown since his disappearance in Mexico in 1913, might enter the tent and take over, thus proving whether or not Mr Herbert would remain immune to the impact of the past masters of horror-fiction in every circumstance. We talked about James Herbert. On this subject Mr Herbert spoke eloquently, and the bowling became somewhat mechanical in its turn. We progressed from rats to fog, and I complimented him on his obliteration of the population of Bournemouth. He relaxed a little. Mercifully no obvious literary antecedents came to my mind, Lovecraft's meditations on the amphibious practices of the people of his imaginary Innsmouth having been ruled out. I forget whether I tried on him the old one about 'Portsmouth for the continent, Bournemouth for the incontinent', which in the context might have invited analogies with coals to Newcastle. Anyhow, if I did it proved unproductive. James Herbert took the work of James Herbert very seriously, and showed no signs of stimulation by frivolous chestnuts. Even that aspect of the literary past, those antecedents of the Word, remained closed to us.

Oddly enough we finally struck pay-dirt not with what I read, but with what I was. It emerged that both James Herbert and I shared an origin of what is termed 'cradle' Catholicism, although he had left his in the cradle. He believed that his *Shrine*, with its hard words on the dangers of Lourdes cults, might prompt the anger and possibly even the condemnation of the Roman Catholic authorities. In brief, he at least resembled certain former practitioners of the art of writing, and indeed present practitioners of that of Fringemaking, who knew the advantage of a little ecclesiastical disapproval. Accurately, if somewhat maliciously, I assured him that *Shrine* did a great service to the Roman Catholic Church, which was fully alive to the dangers of diabolic intervention in cults of supposed apparitions, and should welcome thoughtful reminders of those dangers such as he had now put forward. Indeed, I saw a theological future for him. He accepted this, a little grudgingly I thought, possibly with the suspicion that I might be taking the Archangel Michael out of him. Anyhow, we parted with civility if without affection, and the audience, which had now acquired, by what I hoped was less painful experience, an indication of Mr Herbert's conversational preferences, put a few questions on his work. These were efficiently answered, and we dispersed, secure in the knowledge that whatever about the larger issues, the Author had been well and truly Met.

It was comforting, if also slightly galling, to know that the issues were not falling by the wayside elsewhere in the Book Festival. John

Drummond did great execution on Robert Lacey, best-selling author of *Monarchy*, demanding to know what value there could be in a proposed biography of Princess Diana, who had after all had a life of no significance until her marriage: his suitable qualification to this unquestionable thesis was 'no disrespect to Princess Diana', the words 'no disrespect' forming one magnificent syllable in his characteristic *Flying Scotsman* delivery. On the other hand James Herbert, if self-obsessed, was actually concerned about the content of his work rather than its success. Interviewers with Jeffrey Archer found it much heavier going than had I with Mr Herbert, in their desperate efforts to dissuade the magnetic needle of his utterance from swinging back to his constant asseveration that his *Kane and Abel* had sold 25,000 copies. Some years later I heard that Mr Archer was unable to tell *Scotland on Sunday* who was the father of Cain and Abel.

Anything strike you as slightly odd about the foregoing? Quite right. I am being a little gentleman, as defined by Nurse Wilks in Wodehouse's *Meet Mr Mulliner*: ' A little gentleman must always take the blame.' By proclaiming the fact, I promptly lose the status, but Shaw was very clear that no critic can be a gentleman, so that's all right. Of course I am not alluding to my brief encounter with James Herbert, but to the misapprehension under which I began it. The billing was perfectly clear as to James Herbert being present to discuss horror fiction, and was so before I was offered the chair. But no blame seems to me to attach to Jenny Brown, who had taken over the Directorship of the Book Festival very late in its inception, having previously been a deputy. Initially the Director was a Beautiful Beautiful Person (male) from London, who, as the Victorians used to say of their maidservants lacking the specifications desired by female employers or possessing those desired by male, 'did not give satisfaction and departed'. It is a permanent tragedy of Edinburgh's schizophrenic situation of an ex-capital aware of its Scottish status yet perpetually persuading itself a capital outlook demands mirroring itself in London miniatures, that it will appoint London smooth-talkers to positions for which they are unfitted and for which Edinburgh locals, usually women, are admirably qualified in what the post actually needs. So Jenny Brown worked wonders in a short time, not the least of its anxieties lying in sorting out problems left by the activities of her predecessor. To the hype merchants infesting so many London publishers' public relations offices, many of them industrious in every particular save that of reading the books they publicise, little distinction may exist between securing an appearance and defining the form it is to take; and to the happily departed Beautiful, Beautiful Person, equally unable to distinguish between an intellectual discussion for a Festival and the physical presence of an author ('Himself. Not a picture.'), no necessity proclaimed itself as to the definition of such distinctions. James Herbert and I would have been spared much anxiety had he been previously absolved from the status of discussant of horror fiction other than his own. On the other hand, the audience would have lost many a good giggle, to judge from the sounds which floated into my reddening ears as name after illustrious name crumbled into the putrefaction of Poe's M. Valdemar under Mr Herbert's gaze.

From Jenny Brown, *Edinburgh Book Festival Official Programme 1989*, 'An Off-the-Shelf Carnival from Cover to Cover', *The Scotsman,* 11 August 1989:

'Lectures are a new feature with lectures by Gore Vidal. . . .'

Jenny Brown is an angel, and the most efficient since the Archangel Michael, and the only other notable case of my being forced into instant (intellectual) brief-changing in presenting a Book Festival guest was entirely the doing of the guest. As I was, and still am, prepared to sing the praises of that particular guest to any audience, however hostile in principle, whether in this world or in the next, I simply recount the incident in a spirit of gratitude for the exercise. It happened in 1989 and the guest was Gore Vidal.

Philip French was a BBC 3 talks producer as well as *arbiter elegentiarum* on *Critics' Forum*, and I was thrilled to the gills when he put up my name for a twenty-minute appraisal of Gore Vidal's *Lincoln* on its first British appearance, in 1984. I had been very impressed by Vidal's *Burr*, admiring its high craft as a novel built on hard research and shrewd speculation. The historical novel, it seems to me, can perform a particularly useful function in working out in a fictional setting ideas deserving serious reflection but needing to deploy parts of the past which formal history cannot reach. What *Burr* did was to look at the development of high politics in the United States from the American Revolution to the Jefferson Administration (1776-1809) through the eyes of the democratical patrician Aaron Burr in recollections communicated in the Jacksonian 1830s. Its critics seemed to me to have missed the point: the usual complaint was that Washington was not like that, Jefferson was not like that, etc., which ignored what historians should be alive to above all others, that these were Burr's Washington and Burr's Jefferson. The Jacksonian setting was realised with sufficient credibility, though even that was seen through a narrator. Vidal had worked well with such of Burr's papers as remained. Undoubtedly he took a schoolboy pleasure in putting iconoclastic observations in Burr's mouth, such as Washington's shifting to ease a boil on a buttock (thus endowing the Father of his Country with a medical ailment also suffered by Marx), or Jefferson's unintentional near-suicide with his much-vaunted invention of a bed raised to the ceiling: the real Burr would probably have been equally iconoclastic, and much less amusing. But the great principle was that of inviting readers to rethink conventional, 'consensus' judgments on the American past, which is what all students of history are supposed to be trained to do. Hence in my most severely academic go-to-meeting hat, I rejoiced in this Vidal and sought for more whence that had emerged; *1876*, which followed, was a little anti-climactic if one knew the period: it was forceful and absorbing, but any recital of the leading established political facts of that year (of the Presidential election won by the Democrats and awarded to the Republicans) is so iconoclastic in itself that the constructive iconoclasm of the earlier work could not be repeated with any element of surprise. The fine detail and vigorous broad brush-strokes which had brought Jacksonian New York into such clear vision were admirably evident in the sequel. So I awaited *Lincoln* with impatience, devoured it with fascination, and set to work on my script.

To my delight Philip French liked the script, and while it was probably twice the length required — for I had simply sent him my overflowing discourse apologetically leaving decisions on its truncation to him — he wanted it to have a further life of its own. He made masterly cuts for broadcast, as usual doing wonders in paring down my convolutions, but felt the full text as revised to our satisfaction should interest Anthony Thwaite, then joint editor of *Encounter*. The broadcast duly took place. Mr Thwaite, whom I had not yet met, was indeed a receptive host for the proposed text for print. And then, when it was in the printing press, mysterious telephone calls from copy-editors at *Encounter* began to reach me. Mr Melvin Lasky, long-standing co-editor, disliked the piece. By editorial convention he left the book section to his co-editor. But suddenly he was quoted as demanding radical changes, most of them prejudicial to the high praise heaped on Vidal. It was indeed evident that he preferred not to publish the essay at all.

I had known of the *Encounter* scandal in the late 1960s, when my friend Conor Cruise O'Brien, having analysed its partisan pro-American stance on Cold War and related issues, drew blood on the question of its backing from the CIA. *Encounter* vehemently denied any such link which was also denied by members of its parent body, the Congress for Cultural Freedom, the economist J. K. Galbraith being particularly forceful in his rejection of the charge. Then the investigations of Senator Eugene McCarthy revealed that the Congress was CIA-funded. *Encounter* was publicly shamed, less for its partisan stand despite its proclamation of objectivity (the partisanship having been shown clearly enough to those with eyes to see) as for its lies and those of its Culturally Free overlords. One co-editor, Professor Frank Kermode, resigned. The other, Melvin Lasky, remained in place. Of its former editors one, Stephen Spender, convincingly and ashamedly now professed his ignorance; the other, Irving Kristol, made no such profession. It was clear enough that the CIA had operated with a 'front' editor, innocent, and its own editor, implicated. But all of this had happened long, long ago, and the CIA funding had vanished.

Philip French had no doubts that the journal was now to be taken at face value; neither had Conor Cruise O'Brien, who had in fact recently published work within its pages himself. But the copy-editor innocently remarked that Mr Lasky had been concerned about my article, because it had received an adverse judgment from Mr Norman Podhoretz, now a high priest of the New American Right as fully as Mr Irving Kristol. I said that if Mr Podhoretz disliked my article, it was open to him to send a letter in rebuttal to the editors, who might publish it if they saw fit, but that Mr Podhoretz was not an editor or in any way publicly stated as in the employ of or holding a consultancy from *Encounter* and that therefore the relevance of his views eluded me. It appeared that Mr Lasky might have cleaned his overcoat, but still retained ominously leopardine spots: secret hands still pulled strings at *Encounter*.

In the event, Anthony Thwaite made a strong stand on behalf of the article he had accepted, I agreed to minor changes which made no alteration in substance, and the piece appeared. Gore Vidal's British publishers, Messrs André Deutsch, quoted a line from the article on subsequent Vidal dust-jackets.

Gore Vidal wrote me a charming little note, and we met after he had come to Edinburgh for a non-Festival appearance some years later. He, it turned out, was rather touched that I, as a historian, felt so enthusiastic about his work; I, as a teacher, had reason to thank him on behalf of my students as well as myself. What I in the audience saw of him on that platform made it clear that nobody would be wise to presume on his benevolence. (Some years previously, he had done fairly terrible execution on Malcolm Bradbury on the South Bank Show, with a wicked deployment of official benevolence, allowing the East Anglia professor [whom I otherwise know as a superb teacher and most assured public performer] to tie himself in post-structuralist knots while the author genially proclaimed *himself* a simple soul only desirous of telling a straightforward story.) Nevertheless my first sight of him in action in Edinburgh was a gentle affair, as his interlocutor, Allan Massie, was cautious about any introduction of the political theology of the New English Right, to which he was elsewhere incessantly committed. Gore Vidal toyed with his sword only once, and then did not unsheath it; Allan Massie for a moment was slow to reply to a *riposte*, and Vidal, kindly giving him time to collect his thoughts, was reminded of his campaign for Senator from California against Jerry Brown, when in answer to one of Vidal's unanswerable points Governor Brown would reply 'Be that as it may . . .'. Vidal suggested that Massie might care to adopt the formula.

I read the next two volumes of his 'biography of the USA', *Empire* and *Hollywood* (the latter, as yet unpublished, supplied by Deutsch in typescript for use in the Book Festival interview). Both made rich use of social history, and both had as a theme the subversion of truth by the communications media, the press in *Empire* and the infant movie industry in its successor. Once again there was his refreshing reappraisal of many historical figures, handled with mastery and realism.

I was not to interview Vidal: I was to introduce him. On the big night I therefore enjoyed myself hymning the historian within the novelist, and the audience in the great tent seemed ready with Amens. Occasional trucks broke the rhythm of my discourse as they made unwanted voyages around the stately historicism of Charlotte Square, but it simply gave time to draw breath. Vidal had spoken at an earlier Book Festival session that day; but I was then still in a train returning with my family from holiday. So I spoke my piece with warmth, all the more because I resented the meanness of political enemies secretly stealing his just rewards. I perorated, introduced Vidal, and subsided with a happy exhaustion into my chair. Vidal beamed on me with the air of a worldly bishop entertained by the antics of a likeable if slightly daft curate, remarked, 'Go on, go on', and turning to the audience said approvingly, 'I could listen to this all night', and then to my horror unleashed the words, 'I'm tired, so if you don't mind, I think we'll do what we did this morning, and handle the thing by questions'. I was out of the chair into which I had sunk with the speed I would have shown had Vidal simply produced a bradawl and sunk it into my hinder parts. And a sea of expectant faces gazed up at me, and me without one prepared question.

In retrospect it was really delicious. There was I, who had asserted over the insidious wiles of the New American Right that Vidal was the master of the unexpected, the seminal challenge to complacency, the great galvaniser of historians out of their armchairs and into the arena, and now in proof of the last process I was Exhibit A. I knew that the best way to send the temperatures of the meeting back to 0° was to come clean and say I needed a moment to respond to a welcome but unexpected invitation. The house would be disappointed and embarrassed for me, I would be letting Jenny Brown down, however justified my ignorance of what was about to happen, and I was possibly likely to throw Vidal badly since underneath the self-assured manner there had been a definite plea for assistance. Moreover, he was, I knew, grateful to me, and would not want to put me in an impossible pickle; he obviously had no objection to gently disconcerting me, but he clearly assumed I had seen his interview that morning with Melvyn Bragg and would naturally be able to go on from there. So I went on, beginning a sentence whose end I was frenziedly thinking out as I allowed comforting academic pomposities to spray from my lips in necessary camouflage. I think it had something to do

90

with the novelist using history with advantages of invention, while being invisibly shackled by limits on that invention dictated by things which could not have happened. Somehow the ghastly sentence writhed its way to its unpredestined conclusion — you never did like me, John Knox — and the ball was back in Vidal's court. After that, it was happiness unalloyed for me. All he needed was a stimulus, however idiotic, and he was off. He considered the point, threw a few backhanders to his unfavourite historiographical critics, raised a few examples from problems he had encountered, and took at least five minutes to do it in admirably mingled hilarity and education. And I brought out my next question with every air of its composition in an academic rarity so remote as to imply antiquity almost to the point of decomposition. This was dealt with by Vidal, the audience now responding to his quips with such enthusiasm that the roar of the crowd was warming me up as thoroughly as him. For anything that might follow, I had little to do but build on our exchanges. I recall one moment with rather smug satisfaction, pedantic as it was:

Vidal: My picture of Lincoln is entirely composed of impressions in the minds of others. I never once show the reader events through Lincoln's mind.

Self: Never when he is awake. But you do bring the reader into his mind when he is dreaming about his own lying-in-state after his assassination.

Vidal: You know the book better than I do.

Mind you, he damn nearly got me again at that point. I had to whip out another unprepared question very fast. I grinned at him affectionately, and supplied it.

Be that as it may, I will always look back on the interview as one of the most therapeutic experiences the Book Festival has given me. Gore Vidal concentrates the mind wonderfully: besides, it was excellent exercise for my back.

My adventures at the Book Festival on Saturday, 22 August 1987, with Lady Antonia Fraser and Dorothy Dunnett were blighted at the outset by the Prime Minister. The Thatcher hijack had removed Jenny Brown, leaving as our only escort Lady Antonia's youngest child Orlando, who wanted my opinion of a Fringe production in which he was involved. With his assistance, I had to march my guests from the Roxburghe Hotel to the major tent, taking care to have none of them killed as we braved the traffic merging from George Street into the ever-rolling stream bearing all its victims away in the circumnavigation of the green Square commemorating George III's Queen Charlotte (no omen for scintillating literary discussion, as the diary of Fanny Burney bears unhappy witness). Then down the planking into the Square, and oh God, was I taking them to the right tent, would we intrude upon some children's competition in which I would be mistaken at best for the White Rabbit or the Mad Hatter while Dorothy Dunnett would be expected to understudy the Duchess ('and the moral of that is . . .') and Lady Antonia Fraser, the Queen of Hearts ('off with his head!' — mine, naturally, for misleading them)? It was probably Orlando who saved us, resourceful, obliging and fleet of foot. I am persuaded the rain dripped down, but this is probably a pathetic fallacy invited by the presence in Edinburgh of the Director's abductress: permit me the recollection of squelching my way in before a large audience, seating the ladies with elephantine grace, and observing Orlando's tactful self-obliteration as we entered, and he found some obscure audience fastness.

But, as Don Marquis's Mehitabel so admirably observes, wotthehell wotthehell, or, in the lines of the poet Kuppner

> *The traveller stops to read the placard by the road:*
> *'All pessimists found in this forest will be killed, slowly';*
> *After looking around for a few seconds,*
> *He strides resolutely forward, with a bright smile.*

The covered awning around the Book Festival tents increased an illusion of a wood in which I had felt such ineptitude for the finding of trees. Enough. As always, the crowd, whatever individual Upas trees it might prove to contain, was collectively my reassurance. I dived into introductions, attempting to mingle entertainment with information, bright-smilingly. These distinguished writers were well known for historical fiction in the case of Dorothy Dunnett, and non-fiction in that of Lady Antonia Fraser. But today we were examining their work in the *genre* of thriller. Lady Antonia had written several thrillers on a television investigator named Jemima Shore, possibly descended from Edward IV's celebrated mistress Jane Shore. Dorothy Dunnett had written several thrillers about a yacht named *Dolly* and her owner who rejoiced in a name sacred to those of us experienced in the changing of infants' nether garments, Johnson Johnson. (I may not have said that, but I wanted to: I had been gripped to the little Dunnett volumes, outstanding for their understanding of the professional hazards of their different heroines of culinary, medical, beautificatory, or whatever, training, but I frequently found disbelief unsuspended by that unfortunate baptism of the hero.) I said a few words about locations, the Fraser books' British, the Dunnetts' far-flung. No doubt I also blethered about distinguished literary antecedents: neither Dorothy Dunnett nor Lady Antonia bore the slightest resemblance to James Herbert.

How would the guests respond? Dorothy Dunnett I had chaired before, though she seemed if anything to have made herself more diminutive, more self-deprecatory, almost Miss Marplish, than I could recall from our first meeting in 1982 for the book-launch of her *King Hereafter*. I was not surprised, therefore, though slightly dismayed, that she played it for contrast: her opening statement was read at first with almost a hesitating monotone while depicting a Morningside wifie given to interrupting her household duties by an absurd fondness for scribbling fictions. But I lost my dismay rapidly: the momentary hesitation vanished, the voice became much more rhythmical and indeed musical, and if she really wanted to disguise herself as somebody infinitely insignificant by comparison with the blonde, beautiful goddess on my left, I knew it for formidable debating tactics. Marpling is a fine weapon with which to camouflage against an adversary, and I had found it sufficiently effective in my time. It has no restrictions of age or sex. Meanwhile she was evidently enjoying herself by sending her own formidable scholarship and craftsmanship up rotten, while giving excellent advice on how to write thrillers.

Dorothy Dunnett was very wrong if she thought — but, oh, how *could* such a sweet elderly lady have thought any such thing? — that she would thus disconcert her far more widely known rival (rival? inadmissable word in such benignity). Neither Marpling from a colleague nor poltroonery from a chairperson made the slightest impact on the generous mouth, the strong cheekbones, or the clear eyes of Lady Antonia. She embarked on her own discourse in a brisk no-nonsense tone. I had mentioned her character Jemima Shore. She was glad I had made it clear the name was 'Shore' because she was consistently annoyed by persons who thought the name was 'Shaw' when they heard it on television. (She may briefly have lost her chairperson and most of her audience on this: neither in Ireland nor in Scotland is there much inclination to pronounce 'Shore' as 'Shaw'.) She dealt with the business of thriller-writing, as she apparently dealt with most things, efficiently, confidently, and insouciantly.

I had not met Lady Antonia before, although I had known her father, Francis Aungier Pakenham, seventh Earl of Longford, at very occasional intervals over the past thirty years. And I had observed his brother Edward, the sixth Earl, head of the less illustrious theatre company in the Gate. The Pakenhams were a long line of Anglo-Irish magnates, generally characterised by imperviousness to dissent from their opinions. In 1815, Major-General Sir Edward Pakenham had moved resolutely from an impregnable military position into a wholly vulnerable one, thus enabling the future President Andrew Jackson to win the Battle of New Orleans. The theatre Earl was known to stand democratically in front of the stage when his company was on tour repeating 'programmes, sixpence each' in a voice of confident resonance easily drowning the actors until on one occasion an infuriated member of the public handed him a £5 note and annexed the lot, whereupon Longford pocketed the note, went out, and returned with a further pile, stationed himself at his old point and resumed 'programmes, sixpence each'. The sixth Earl of Longford was Protestant like all his ancestors of record in Irish history; his successor was a famous convert to Roman Catholicism. I admire Frank Longford, whether or not I agree with him, as a man of genuine spiritual conviction, perfectly ready to face and magnificently ignore ridicule in the furtherance of any crusade he sees as God's work: his attempt to win one of the Moors murderers to salvation was ludicrous to many, heroic to me. With memories of the Irish Censorship Board, not to speak of the Philistine onslaughts on the Festival, I was less enthusiastic about his obsessions about pornography, but I had no doubts as to its resolute and extremely exceptional sincerity. Lady Antonia's brother, the historian Thomas Pakenham, I saw once, presiding over a discussion on an historical paper in which the chair was apparently wholly convinced that all the audience wanted to hear was his demolition of what he took to be the inaccuracies of the paper. Nothing of what I now saw in the present representative of the Pakenhams suggested she would defend herself inadequately against

94

any criticism, or that she would require any protection from the chair. She was of course vulnerable to comment if comment became personal: she was a vigorous participant on TV in the late 1960s and early 1970s as a Roman Catholic wife and mother, but had been divorced in 1977 and had married the playwright Harold Pinter. The ancillary ramifications had been complex.

Nevertheless, when the blow struck, I was hardly ready for it. The chair had kicked around a few questions inevitably touching on Jemima Shore, and hence also Johnson Johnson. Then I threw the discussion open to the house. The tone of the very first voice held a warning: it was menace, veiled in insolently thin civility. The questioner wished to ask both ladies about their identifications with their detectives. Did Dorothy Dunnett like to go to the places whither she sent Johnson Johnson — the West Indies, Ibiza, Canada? These were, in general, most enjoyable places whither to travel, and it would be natural for Dorothy Dunnett to wish to go to them. Dorothy Dunnett most charmingly responded that she usually chose a place where she had not been, and put her next Johnson Johnson novel in it, and after the book was completed went there herself for a holiday. The questioner thanked her — having served notice of a dual question, he was fully entitled to present its second half — and asked, did Lady Antonia like to do the things Jemima Shore liked to do? (Lady Antonia in her opening remarks had quoted one headline on Jemima Shore, 'MISS MARPLE BEDS THE WORLD', and said it was a bit of an exaggeration but that if it was all right for James Bond to have all the fun, why was it improper for a woman?) I stretched the bright smile to its uttermost — the Cheshire Cat was surely a safer identity for me than Rabbit or Hatter — and assured the questioner heartily that Lady Antonia could not do what Jemima Shore did, since Jemima Shore attends a coroner's inquest in Scotland in *The Wild Island* and Scotland didn't have them. The next moment the executioner's axe almost severed the Cheshire cat's head from its invisible body once for all.

'Congratulations,' hissed the infuriated damsel, entirely unaware of rescue from any peril (thank Heaven), 'you have just won the award as the thousandth person to point out that mistake to me!'

'Thank you very much, Lady Antonia,' beamed the Cheshire cat, arching its recovered body into an almighty cast culminating in the point of a right claw reaching for salvation to the top left-hand corner of the tent as far away from the recent questioner as possible, 'and now the next question, please, from that gentleman up near the roof.' We had no further problems, and her ladyship thawed into some graciousness, and Dorothy Dunnett remained very sweet, and after a very lively but wholly literary session, we closed.

The indignant feminist of either sex may well enquire, what justification did I have to usurp Lady Antonia Fraser's right of reply? If she was invited to discuss her private life and was ready to do so, or alternatively to inform the questioner accurately of his loathly character, this was her business. I am not prepared to concede any superiority in feminism to such a critic. My concern was not with Lady Antonia — her family resemblance to redoubtably insouciant Pakenhams, her whole manner as hitherto revealed, and her present biographical subject of Boadicea, gave ample warrant for her capacity to face out any attack, however repulsive. But I was not prepared to allow a discussion on thrillers to go sour for an audience who had paid their money to investigate unlooked-for corpses, hairbreadth escapes, incisive detection, unfamiliar locations.

And the audience contained Orlando. I had arranged with Orlando that I would meet him before a performance of the play in whose production he was involved at its location, St Columba's-by-the-Castle. So a few days later I made my way up the Lawnmarket, skirting the might and height of Edinburgh Castle with its green-festooned, almost sheer rockfall to the Grassmarket so far below, and thence down the first yards of Johnston (not Johnston Johnston) Terrace, and down a few stone steps, in through a rusty iron gate under refreshingly luxuriant branches. I enjoyed James Pembroke's play *Rat-a-Tat-Tat* with its sophisticated intricacies of modern bohemian upper-class life, and made a few criticisms which may have been of some use. But it was a little before Orlando conducted me into the theatre that I ventured to contradict him on some point, to which he gave immediate assent.

'Well,' I said, startled, 'you are the first Pakenham I have met who accepted a contradiction.'

'Perhaps,' said Orlando, 'that is because I am a Fraser.'

From Anthony Troon, Book Festival, *The Scotsman,* 26 August 1983:

> . . . Updike has been upstaged. The guilty party was Anthony Burgess whose dissertation yesterday on the relationship between music and literature was a masterly piece of stagecraft that kept his shirt dark with perspiration and his audience in such a state of bemused admiration that they couldn't think of anything to ask until it was almost too late.
>
> Burgess plumbed literature to unearth some motifs that could be expressed musically. Then he played on an electronic keyboard that sounded like a steam calliope suffering from injudicious immersion in the Mississippi.
>
> In the end, however, his message was that music has no intellectual meaning. 'If the writer sits down and writes about violence and immorality he feels a sense of guilt. But music says nothing immoral, it says nothing about sex. Write music and you end up feeling clean.'
>
> Music, he said, meant nothing but tension and release. Any meaning we imposed upon it was brought from outside. Clearly, literature was the greater art.

My business with Anthony Burgess was that of an interviewer for the *Festival Times.* We had met during the Festival 'word' symposia in 1980, introduced by Richard Ellmann in the lobby of the George Hotel as Burgess waited for transport and Ellmann and I were pushing off to talk about his great biography of Wilde then in the making. They were an interesting contrast against the background of raw red plush: Ellmann on his feet, his lips drawn back in affectionate laughter, Burgess seated, nodding, frowning, cigarillo-smoking, each of them shooting gnomic lines in light-hearted instalment of a perpetual argument about James Joyce, Ellmann tossing out symbols, Burgess replying with linguistics, Ellmann's receding hair uncovering a mighty dome on which the light reflected, Burgess's long, light wave forever falling over his left eyebrow and occasionally twisted away with a head-rear only to fall once more. I would live to see Dick Ellmann's face crunched down and twisted in pain as he tapped out messages to me on a machine to transmit words he could no longer speak as the deadly motor neurone disease tightened its hold, his body wasted to a fraction of its former unconscious dominance. He was one of the best and wisest men I have ever known.

But when Burgess and I met again, in the Roxburghe smoking-lounge, Ellmann was so far as we knew healthy and strong, and we opened in a mutual exchange of his praises. We swapped a few of our own: Burgess had been very kind about my biography of Conan Doyle in *The Observer*, and I had been greatly fortified by his support for some of my speculations as to the importance of sound in the choice of fictional names as possible evidence for missing biographical data. We were also united in the conviction that Conan Doyle was a fine craftsman whose success with Holmes had induced a snobbish critical neglect of his works. And then I, too, had been a member of Burgess's lecture-audience, and took a professional pride in saluting my superior in my official calling. As Tony Troon, one of the finest Festival wordsmiths among our brethren, amply testified, it upstaged John Updike — it upstaged us all. Its art was the absence of art; he used not a trick of the trade. The delivery was swift and staccato, paradox wielded with the dexterity of his old Manchester University teacher A. J. P. Taylor, but without Taylor's air of contrivance. Burgess shot his ideas out, speeding from his mind to those of his audience, eyes flashing, hands ready to thrust out in probably unconscious emphases.

Did I want a drink? I did not: I had given up drinking during Festival time. He nodded vigorously. 'You're right. That's right. They're always trying to thrust drink down the throats of us writers' — 'us writers'! *Et in Arcadia ego* — 'to get us to make fools of ourselves. It slows us down! It gets in the way of our productivity.' He drank very little himself, and it certainly did not get in the way of his productivity, whose variety and intensity is mind-reeling. I commented on his lack of 'art' in lecturing. He said he had taught himself to avoid epigrammatic, 'fine' writing, and learned to speak from his immersion in the written word, and so his noteless lectures stemmed from his writing, constructed on the same discipline which had cost him considerable pains to achieve. He had started because of his love of languages. He had become convinced when in Malaya that he could not make that experience real without knowledge of the Malayan language. 'Maugham lacked that. Conrad lacked it.' He wrote his trilogy on Malaya to set down what he had learned from the country by knowledge of its languages. He had no idea it would begin the literary work of a lifetime. It meant that he leaped a frontier at which so many other writers paused, observing: he observed too, but from both sides. I mentioned Greene as an obvious literary frontiersman. But he did not much care for Greene's writing, which surprised me. He smiled, and talked about the natural conviction of a born Catholic that a convert never quite understands the religion. He is not a practising Catholic. 'But you can't get rid of it! I don't know if God exists but, if He does, He has a great sense of humour.' I remarked that St Peter, founder of the Papacy, was chosen because he was the stupidest of the Apostles and therefore the one whose inadequate grasp of what Jesus was saying would be most representative of humanity. Vigorous nodding. 'It all shows God's splendidly sardonic sense of humour.'

Lips pursed, little cigar forming longer and longer ash, hand impatiently through falling lock, we got back to Greene. 'His use of Catholicism is a kind of literary device to explore the problems he wanted: the dilemma of *The Heart of the Matter* is bogus and contrived.' I don't think I mentioned the Greene short story, *The Hint of an Explanation*, which is my real point of theological fortification from Greene. I wish I had. He passed on to Waugh. He prefers Waugh to Greene; he even admires *Brideshead Revisited*, whose reduction of Catholicism to some awful final exclusive circle of snobbery gives me the heeby-jeebies. Burgess was ready enough to assist my teeth-setting-on-edge on that point: 'He wanted to appear an aristocrat, socially, politically, and theologically. And, of course, he wasn't one. He came from a strong businesslike background — publishing, for God's sake!'

We settled back in our chairs, and thought about publishers, and laughed.

That was a very Lancashire remark. There is nothing professional north country about Burgess, nothing of the revived stage-northerner of J. B. Priestley or (God save us!) Harold Wilson, but that kind of clincher blasts through the attempted sophistications of the south, above all poor old Waugh's posturings. The contrast is even stronger in Burgess's businesslike friendliness. Class self-adjustment, class differentiation, status deployment simply have no place in him. We were there, we had enough in common to need no time-wasting. I am too much of a chameleon in most of my life. Perhaps partly as a legacy of debating, I observe the setting my interlocutor arranges for me; I inhabit it, I judge when and how much to disarrange it, and for what purpose (usually trivial or for passing effect). I needed none of these things with him, and played with none of them. He was what he was; I had a shot at being what I was. I may even have succeeded. I thought I did.

'But *Brideshead Revisited*,' continued Burgess, 'is a very careful theological work, about the Four Last Things, Death, Judgment, Hell and Heaven. I liked the television version. I saw it from start to finish, without a break, and without the music, which is distracting. It got rid of the problem of visualisation which defects the work of the author and interferes with the assimilation by the reader. The theology emerges even more strongly from the book once the problem of visualisation is over.'

His own first creative work was in music. He had recently been trying to put Joyce's *Ulysses* to music. 'All hell broke loose during the recording for transmission, which I insisted should take place in Dublin. The musicians from Radio Éireann said that the work was blasphemous and immoral — Joyce's work more than mine — and wouldn't play it. Finally the producer had to call in the union to compel the performers to return to work. So they said "We'll play it. But we'll play it badly." Play it badly. God knows they did.' I hate English voices trying Irish accents, convinced of their success, abysmal in their failure. Burgess's Dublin accent was perfect. I told him so; he shrugged, he should be able to do it, he is partly of Irish — and partly of Scottish — descent. Dublin? The cigarillo smouldered; he now had me on one as well. 'A terrible place. I love it, but what a place! "What's all this business, Mr Burgess, about saying this man Bloom was a Jew? Sure we had no Jews in Dublin in 1900." A sort of quiet anti-semitism, I suppose, not positive, but asserted by denying they existed when they did.'

The books on display at the Book Festival are new, and newness is the name of the game in publishers' hype. Today is perpetually enslaved by tomorrow; yesterday has to make the most of its few chances. The new books made Anthony Burgess think of the old ones he loved and thought deserved immortality, and which were being forgotten. *Augustus Carp, Esq. by Himself* he thought an extraordinarily funny book he wished someone would reprint. John Fothergill's *An Innkeeper's Diary* was another one which diverted and educated a generation of intellectuals. Burgess had fought for Rex Warner's *The Aerodrome*, and it had been reprinted, and he had just received a telephone call that it was to be filmed. Eric Linklater, now, was a fine example of a writer in danger of being forgotten. *Poet's Pub* was a splendid book; he remembered that it had been the second Penguin to be published. Suddenly I saw a nineteen-year-old Burgess,

100

eagerly responding to Allen Lane's new publishing venture in 1936 with its monthly tensome of sixpenny prints. It had given him lifetime friendships with books he would not let be forgotten now. 'It is a constant fight to keep good authors from oblivion.' A pause. 'Well, I may be forgotten myself, and not so long from now.'

We wandered back to *The Kingdom of the Wicked*, the novel he was writing on the Christians after Christ's death. I mentioned Robert Graves's *I, Claudius*. 'I remember reading it soon after it came out.' (It was first published in 1934, when Burgess was seventeen.) 'For that time it was hot stuff. Graves drew much more than he indicated on Suetonius and on Tacitus, certainly not to the extremes in their description of Roman Imperial families — things no novelist can justify, and yet presented as fact in their accounts. I am having a lot of trouble with Josephus, trying to reconcile his account with what seems reasonable to credit. Josephus played it so that he could be on both sides, with the Jews he came from, and the Romans who had assimilated him. It wasn't very heroic, but it was surely fortunate he did so, for where would we be without him, especially myself trying to show how events in Judea interacted with events in imperial Rome? And there was interaction of that kind. Pontius Pilate was a creature of Sejanus. Herod Agrippa was a friend of Caligula. When someone sneezed in Rome, Judea caught a cold.' He nodded in reinforcement.

He makes use of the historians partly because they are among his great books, which he reads for pleasure as well as use: Livy, Tacitus, Holinshed. He took up Xenophon when asked to write a film on the life of Cyrus the Great for a cousin of the Shah, and naturally got down to work on the *Cyropaedia* discussing Cyrus's youth and education. But then the Shah's cousin was killed in the revolution, and the film scrapped, so Burgess remained with Xenophon for pleasure.

On *The Kingdom of the Wicked*: 'What I look out for are things which didn't explain themselves in the Acts of the Apostles. Why did the disciples other than Peter fade out of the story? What on earth happened to them? Did any of them backslide — probably some did. Apocryphal legends and narratives on which so much tradition has been placed are almost entirely worthless. Keep asking the questions. Why do the Acts say nothing about Paul's trial in Rome? Was there a trial? Was the subject dropped because it all proved very unimportant and the case was thrown out? And why was Stephen singled out as the first martyr? I'm sure I have this right, and Stephen was a Greek. That means that the whole thing was going beyond the Judean community of Jews, and that was dangerous, and so Stephen was singled out both for death and as a cult.'

'You said in your lecture that Paul was an epileptic.'

'Yes, I can't see any other satisfactory explanation for his vehemence on both sides, and his falling down on the road to Damascus. I can see all the pointers to Peter's stupidity. He could never master languages. It was all very well to begin with Pentecost and the gift of tongues, another example of God's very sardonic humour. Afterwards Peter always had to have an interpreter. And that ridiculous business of being crucified upside down, so absurd and essentially misunderstanding a response to his own conviction of his unworthiness to follow Christ's example. Crucifixion, all of those thousands of crucifixions of the Jews by the Romans, of course the real point of it was the obscenity of the thing. Suffering, yes, but above all obscene suffering. The body naked, none of these loincloths, and the nail jutting out below the crotch like an artificial penis in erection.'

'In some ways,' (I wrote for the *Festival Times*), 'Burgess is a very Catholic writer indeed. I had never heard such a sense of blasphemy of the thing, blasphemy towards humans, blasphemy towards Christ. And then he turned to the subject of Judas. "Poor bastard. He suddenly got it all wrong." I suggested that Judas, from whose perspective nothing was known, might have been directed by Christ to follow him. "Quite possible. And then, the fatal mistake of despair. A tragic figure. My God, he's a tragedy." His eyes were alive with pain. Self-destruction, he and I were told when we were young, is the supreme rejection of the Creator. In a novelist of Burgess's stature and preoccupations, I suppose, there must be something of that Creator. His sense from above of what constitutes humanity. His pain at human rejection. And his humour.'

102

Chapter Four

I Like a Murder . . .

From the Film Festival Brochure 1980:

Brothers and Sisters

>*UK 1980. Dir: Richard Wooley. Prod: BFI Production Board/Keith Griffiths. Script: Richard Wooley. Editor: Mike Audsley. Photo: Pasco McFarlane, Russell Murray. Sound: Alf Bower. Cast: Carolyn Pickles, Sam Dale, Jennifer Armitage, Robert East, Elizabeth Bennett, Barry McCarthy, Barrie Shore. 96 mins., colour.*

>*The BFI's biggest budget feature to date.* Brothers and Sisters *eludes any easy categorisation as either art film or straight commercial cinema and sets out to find its audience in both camps, with a fusion of soap opera, television style and more experimental elements. On one level it is a thriller, posing the enigma of who killed Jennifer Collins, a prostitute. But in closely examining the lives and lifestyles of the suspects — among them two brothers: one a middle-class intellectual with liberal principles, the other a professional soldier and a right-winger — the plot becomes a springboard for an investigation into the relationships between men and women on a wider scale. Both brothers betray their standards and the murder of the prostitute is used to highlight their own sexual hypocrisy. This shift into the arena of sexual politics poses the murder mystery in quite different terms: all men are suspects and the clues lie in looking and learning from how men treat women.*

I LIKE A MURDER. I LIKE A MURDER WHETHER IN PROSE FICTION, verse, trial report or film. I am less enthusiastic about it as play on stage, but it can be quite agreeable. I am perfectly happy if it chooses to make significant social comment, or judicious psychological analysis, or finely judged legal points. I am in fact enthusiastic if it invades the higher reaches of human intellect and uses its own *genre* as parable, or metaphor, or some other challenge to conventional attitudes.

The quotation above is a perfectly fair, if slightly enthusiastic, description of *Brothers and Sisters*. After it was shown at the Film Festival in the session restricted to participants, the writer-director took questions. Solemn enquiries followed on certain other technical points whose articulation might be expected to reflect well on the artistic consciousness of questioner and respondent. It was a comfortable discussion, all the more for its rarefied tone. But I was sufficiently concerned about one point to make a last attempt at its resolution. I was not a regular participant in the Film Festival, but I had been given press credentials for this session, required for *Critics' Forum*, and for anything the *Irish Times* might want. I raised my hand and, in response to a courteous signal, my person.

'Whodunnit?'

'Wha-a-a-at?' The urbane directorial voice was almost a squawk.

'Whodunnit — well, did it? — I mean, the murder, well, you don't say, do you? It looks like the bohemian brother, and then it looks like the respectable brother, but we aren't told. Who do you think was the murderer?'

He looked at me in horror. He wasn't contemptuous, merely appalled.

'I haven't the faintest idea.'

I don't think anyone even said 'Well, on that note . . .'. We all dispersed, rapidly. I fancied that some very dubious glances flickered in my direction. Philip French, walking me towards the coffee-room, grinned happily.

I always loved visits to the Film Festival, a welcome and exciting interval in the normal theatre diet, with the wide ante-room in the Filmhouse happily proportioned for business and rendezvous, the zealous efforts at efficiency from beleaguered youthful helpers generally conveying their own enjoyment, the enticingly diplomatic corridor to coffee-room and bar, Film Festival Director Jim Hickey's warm smile, Philip French, tall and bespectacled and gleaming-domed and plunged usually into some fascinating citation of film history, occasional glimpses of other film critics affectionately held in mind above all the bearded red countenance of BBC Scotland's Ian Agnew happily gurgling over mutual reminiscence or feeding me some ludicrous anecdote of the Festival, *The Guardian*'s Derek Malcolm earnestly brooding over some reprehensible development in the film-world or delightedly discovering some further unexpected tug on his Scottish ancestral roots, the urgent sudden departure of the troops into some viewing for which they would loll in some of the most comfortable cinema upholstery obtainable in these islands, the eyes radiating on the screen holding for the nonce its audience in reverential silence for all the hidden mutiny in felt-pen cyphers spider-webbing notebooks in darkness, the bliss in the wonder of giant moving images no perpetual exposure can ever quite rob of its miraculous proof of a triumph of the century, the orgy of coughs and rustles after conclusion reminiscent to me of nothing so much as a Catholic congregation in my childhood piously signifying its previous temporary cessation of sound and motion during the Canon of the Mass, the huddles in dissection of the recent epiphany with most participants probably unconsciously holding themselves in attitudes eerily reminiscent of the postures lately paraded before our eyes.

Critics' Forum had to tailor its viewing times to the schedules of participants, and Philip French often had to arrange for a separate viewing for our item, when we would file into an almost deserted auditorium. 1984 brought one such viewing, as I recall, for the movie *Company of Wolves* based on Angela Carter's Gothic yet realistic variation on the story of Red Riding Hood. I was able to bring my daughter Sara, which would not have been possible at a regular for-the-critics showing in Film Festival when ticket allocation was necessarily limited by the huge demand from the Film Festival participants. Neil Jordan's great film should require no exposition here, beyond a reminder that it proved a searching and sensitive exploration of the sexual awakening of a young girl expressed in a terror of wolves becoming a welcome, the great influx of wolves into her house in the final stages of her dream, moving from images of menace into great playfellows, with culmination of the transformation of the form of play they implied. Earlier passages translating wolves into vigorously realised sexual manifestations were distinguished by their mingling of almost scientifically clinical detail with horror-film technique of high sophistication.

The movie, quite ludicrously, was restricted to persons of eighteen and above; Sara was sixteen at the time. No voice was raised with enquiry as to the whereabouts of her birth certificate or other evidence, and very rightly too, as it turned out. For when the film was concluded she found herself surrounded by the *Critics' Forum* representatives apprised of her age. What we all wanted to know was, how authentic was the film in its purported realisation of awakening sexuality of a girl in her early 'teens? Only one of us had ever been a girl in her early teens, and that had been some time ago — in fact, the only woman critic was not, I think, present at this showing. Sara briskly ran over the main points of particular interest, commented on their effectiveness, and vigorously hailed the powers of the film in realisation of its intended theme. We stood around taking notes for a minute or so. Philip French subsequently lacerated the Film Censorship Board's age restriction in his *Observer* column, all the more because it excluded those persons to whom its appeal must have the greatest authenticity. As Sara remarked, considering the sexual garbage customarily rated as suitable for teenage viewing, it took a very twisted mind or set of minds to proscribe work so unusually sane and sensible in its exploration. Her response was that of a schoolchild who had just witnessed an exceptionally intelligent teacher at work. I had something of the same reaction to Angela Carter when I had to interview her some years later at the Hay-on-Wye Festival; there was a relaxed magisterial air heightened by her grey hair, but its length suggested a strong retention of the memory of her own senior schoolgirl status, so much so that at the end of her powerful reading I saluted her happily, 'You're a brick, Angela.' I apologised for this *bêtise* after our session ended. 'I expected it,' she smiled grimly, tolerantly, sardonically, a little wearily.

Philip French in Edinburgh could seldom get away from Film Festival long enough for us to do more than walk around for a short space. I was always a pest in trying to lure him away, for he is one of the most fascinating talkers I know, and the myriad of different prospects of Edinburgh — the same which aroused the ribaldry of Dr Johnson with his famous remark as to the finest prospect being the road to England — took on additional magic for me with himself striding beside me as leading figure in their landscape. I recall one exit line from such a walk.

'I must go. I have to get into Derek Jarman's shorts.'

When I met him the following day I enquired how he had enjoyed being in Derek Jarman's shorts. He shook his head sadly.

'Derek Jarman's shorts didn't come off.'

We watched Derek Jarman's *Tempest* one year for *Critics' Forum*. Emphatically that did come off.

Critics' Forum from Edinburgh always reflected Philip French's anxiety that Edinburgh in Festival be Scotland's capital, centring new developments in Scottish cultural self-expression, not simply occasioning a report from a Festival-which-might-be-anywhere. If Festival fare brought Scotland to the forefront, so much the better, whether in theatre or in exhibition; if the Film Festival promised a good Scottish entry, we went for that.

In our programme's last year, 1989, we had a very full Scottish diet: Tron Theatre of Glasgow's production of Iain Heggie's *Clyde Nouveau*, satirically employing techniques of Glasgow music-hall to deflate the much-vaunted and mysteriously originating new prosperity of the larger city; an exhibition of Scottish Art since 1900; the film of Christopher Rush's *Venus Peter*, which under Ian Sellar's direction transposed the Fife-based prose narrative into an Orcadian childhood with Ray MacAnally giving of his best, and, as we sadly knew by then, also giving his last, work for the screen, as the austerely affectionate old seadog grandfather. As a child I thrilled to MacAnally as the hero of the Gaelic-language Abbey pantomime, and now I was watching his enchantment of a child at the age I had been then, and if the seafaring grandfather bore little resemblance to my memories of the dragon-capturing Prince Fernando, the enchantment was the same as ever, only more intimate and more multi-dimensional, and if forty years had blotted my own identity with the infant sitting enraptured in the Abbey stalls with one leg jammed under the other thigh, I had an excellent vehicle on screen into which to pour the ancient recollection. Dead or alive, old or young, MacAnally never blighted my idolisation. And we had two Scottish books, *Full Score*, an anthology of Fred Urquhart's short stories with many examples of his wizardry in so convincingly speaking through a female narrator, as fully an artist of many voices as any we might hear on stage, and *Coming to Light* by Elspeth Davie, a novel of Edinburgh juxtaposing its old and new intellectual traditions in a novel whose main character is the landscape itself. If all else failed, Philip French would assert the Scottish focus through our book for discussion, sometimes, as with Peter Whitebrook's *Staging Steinbeck* or Gordon DeMarco's *Murder at the Fringe*, choosing an item with specific Festival content (in both of which, once again, landscape assumed its own force of character). We educated ourselves in cultural evangelism under the gigantic and forcefully warts-and-all *Letters of Hugh MacDiarmid* edited by Alan

Bold; we gestated the invaluable *Macmillan Companion to Scottish Literature* edited by Trevor Royle and enjoyed our needle-in-haystack hunts for its very few omissions and errors; we happily double-bedded *The Lipstick Circus*, the staccato naturalistic new fiction of Brian McCabe, with his doom-laden, realist-romanticist brother-Scot James Hogg's *Tales of Love and Mystery* whose original individual appearances were made 150 years earlier; we saluted new Scottish poets in the persons of Kathleen Jamie and Ron Butlin; we diagnosed the Scottish varieties of International Brigade reminiscence in Ian MacDougall's devoted transcription of survivors' accounts, *Voices from the Spanish Civil War*. All of this had been a principle in full expression well before the Charlotte Square Book Festival: Philip French wanted his programme always to remain an Edinburgh as well as a Festival programme, and in the process he created his own Scottish book celebration. His insistence stemmed from no Scottish antecedents of which I know, but from a lifelong conviction that a country must be allowed to speak in its own terms, not simply in yours. Thus his Edinburgh programmes were never permitted to dispense with Scotland, as so many London reviewers and arts editors do in their Festival coverage, just as his Berlin, his Paris, his Dublin locations of *Critics' Forum* later on were made forcefully to reflect the cities whence they were presented. London parochialism is perpetually self-indulged; Philip French quietly but emphatically made it his programme's business to challenge it. His ear remained forever attuned in Edinburgh for what Scotland might have to say that was new, or to recall that was forgotten, and his listeners' ears were in due course brought to discover what their owners might most profitably pursue.

This might entail focus on Scottish publications from London, as with the MacDiarmid *Letters*, but he was deeply conscious of the revival in Scottish publishing as evidenced by Mainstream, Canongate and Polygon in particular. The break in programmes for a couple of weeks before Festival *Critics' Forum* gave a month's Scottish material on which to draw, but our hopes were from time to time dashed when some promising offering did not, after all, appear with Festival time. In 1981 we were put to the pins of our collars, or their more hygienic female equivalents, to get our hands on the long-promised latest volume of 'New Assessments', the Ramsay Head Press series: Ian Campbell's *The Kailyard*. The series is an excellent one, including miniature gems such as Allen Wright's *J. M. Barrie* and Allan Massie's *Muriel Spark*. But the publisher, the late Norman Wilson, father of *The Scotsman*'s musicologist Conrad (or Konrad), had his own ways of distribution, and while page-proofs were obtained, the final copies fell into our hands within hours of recording. They were well worth the blood-sweat, for Ian Campbell, bringing a wholly unrivalled knowledge of modern Scottish literature to his aid, re-evaluated the strengths of the Kailyard, hitherto a term of abuse as classification of comfortable unchallenging picturesque Scottish literary soap, but shown here to possess its own integrity.

From a Fringe play:

> *She (having discovered him in bed with her husband):* As for you —! I will never speak to you again as long as I live!!!
> *He:* But you and I are both appearing next week on *Critics' Forum*!

Festival BBC transmission for *Critics' Forum* began when the Queen Street station was abuzz with consciousness of its own glorious future, for in 1979 hopes of devolution were reflected in plans for the station's expansion. The dashing of those hopes into a long Thatcherite limbo ultimately cancelled the proposals, and settled a grey uncertainty on the station which in the fullness of time lost its news transmission to Glasgow. The Arts remained, partly maintained in their protected status by the efforts of John Arnott against all the insidious wiles of radio administration politics, but the station itself was then, in the late 1980s, closed for refurbishment. A studio was rigged up at the top of the Miller building, a converted office-block in the lane of Thistle Street, and here for BBC Scotland 'Festival View' on the dawn patrol Neville Garden would preside with invariable *sang-froid* while invisibly, and, thank God, inaudibly, to listeners at 8.30 a.m., his various reviewers would slide out at the conclusion of their reports during tiny intermissions for interpolated recordings of musical offerings in Festival, to leave chairs vacant for subsequent reporters, each briefed with hoped-for foolproof clarity as to who would follow whom. How John Arnott and his subordinate producers kept their sanity during these years would provide material for several alienists in quest of doctoral theses. *Critics' Forum* in 1988 was relocated to the Mountbatten building in the Grassmarket, normally the Heriot-Watt University's headquarters for media studies, but its ambience suggested nothing so much as an ante-room for Doomsday celebrations over which Heaven had thrown a boycott. We returned thankfully to the Miller building the next year, fortunate in that our deliberations would be uninterrupted by hidden exit and entry from the participants in the course of transmission. And through it all Christine Saunders, secretary to Philip French, maintained her smiling encouragement and invariable anticipation of virtually every possible crisis.

Christine was also an ideal colleague at exhibitions, quietly working out her own version of Philip French's constant search for neglected achievements in need of celebration. Her eyes went to the strength of the past, where so much comment fears to emancipate itself from the fashion of the present. So do those of Colin Affleck, another critic seeking to make the most of work of any kind which shows creative growth where wilderness once abounded. They pin-pointed for me much in Scottish Art in previous centuries which contemporary comment passes by with derisive remarks from short perspective. Exhibitions under Drummond became great events, especially during the Vienna 1900 celebration of 1983, and his own stamp was evident in many of his major exhibitions, particularly in that year. Frank Dunlop seems to have been less interested in exhibitions, and much of their success in his time depended on enthusiastic votaries whose work he was satisfied to accept: David Daiches and Peter and Anne Jones for 'The Scottish Enlightenment' Exhibition of 1986 designed by John L. Paterson; Duncan Macmillan's 'Painting in Scotland, The Golden Age' the same year; 'The Vigorous Imagination: New Scottish Art' in 1987 proposed and largely selected by the *Glasgow Herald*'s art critic Clare Henry; and exhibitions by the National Library of Scotland and the Scottish National Portrait Gallery celebrating Mary Queen of Scots in that year. But, from the first, Dunlop's régime coincided with greater abundance of Scottish-related exhibitions, sometimes singling out individual painters such as Wilkie, Peploe and MacTaggart.

Probably the most influential Scottish exhibition in Drummond's time had been 'Scotch Myths', devised by Murray and Barbara Grigor, shown in 1981 at the Lyceum Studio, temporarily dramatised into an exhibition site. Like Campbell's *The Kailyard*, it discussed Scottish self-salesmanship in the realm of *kitsch*. The Grigors, with extensive filmic knowledge, introduced symbolistics of high Scottish export romanticism inducing responses as Mendelssohn's with *Fingal's Cave*, here achieved by means of a grand piano spouting highly tourist-conscious water. The approaches were dominated by the figures of Sir Walter Scott and the enScotched George IV meeting at the famous 'King's jaunt' of 1822 whence so much Scottish socio-economic improvement was hoped and, in certain senses, was realised. A forest of picture-postcards gave all too much evidence of the forms in which Scottish images were transmitted to the world. As Milan Kundera would assert some years later in *The Unbearable Lightness of Being*, *kitsch* is an intervening stage between existence and oblivion. 'Scotch Myths' played a valuable part in confronting Scots with their own cultural self-destruction, and clearing the road for the cultural proclamation of a real Scotland.

Five years later the celebration of the Scottish Enlightenment revived the glories of the intellectual Scotland forgotten in the Tartanic explosion whose attendant horrors still gibber from the High Street tourist shops. The great medical figures of eighteenth- and nineteenth-century Scotland who prolonged the Enlightenment to its fullest chronological extent might have questioned whether the fullest precautions of self-inoculation against *kitsch* had been sufficiently observed in all respects. A National Museum of Scotland Exhibition on 'The Enterprising Scot' showed a distressing self-glorification with some lack of discrimination. But Paterson's design for the Enlightenment with its use of audio-visual material haunting a house of its own with the Royal Museum of Scotland gave a lift to the Enlightenment achievement with powerful and judiciously researched scholarly implementation.

The Scottish Enlightenment inevitably overlapped with Romanticism, which in any case considerably antedated its habitually assigned limits, and in dramatic form that was realised in 1986 by Frank Dunlop's presentation of two eighteenth-century Scottish plays, John Home's *Douglas* and Allan Ramsay's *The Gentle Shepherd*, both suggesting the Enlightenment drawing-room audience

113

by the inspired enlistment of the supremely elegant Signet Library as a theatre. The *Douglas* in particular put some strain on the audience's powers of time-machinery control in taste as well as in imagination, the diet of grand emotion and convoluted plot proving decidedly rich for some palates. The *Douglas* audience was forced to come to terms with its own inadequacy as an eighteenth-century assembly; an audience obliged to play so disconcerting a time-displacement inevitably felt inferior to its architectural surroundings. The actors, on their side, leaped the time-barrier with equally humiliating success.

But Romanticism made its conquests easily enough in the 'Painting in Scotland' Exhibition, for all of the daunting magnificence of the University's Upper Library Hall. This great long chamber customarily bestows as its greatest demands on the visitor, the neck-backwards reverence to its exquisite ceiling, and the tables at its extremity, one the work-table of Scott, the other the dream-table of Napoleon at St Helena (with indent from the burning cigar he absently left on it presumably in the mental refighting of some battle, possibly even a second thought for improvement of Waterloo). But Duncan Macmillan made them fight for their normal pre-eminence. Canvas-hanging for a specific exhibition in space normally bereft of paintings allows an imagination some freedom denied to exhibitors commandeering an existing gallery with appointed places, and Macmillan used it to chart a historical progress. The University's Raeburns were pressed into service; and the somewhat grim expression the artist preserved on Principal William Robertson looking across his new University Mace suggests its capture of the sitter's reminder to his immortaliser that it had been presented by the Town Council to replace the old Mace, lost by the burglary of Deacon William Brodie, a brother-Mason of Raeburn in Canongate Lodge Kilwinning. The Enlightenment seemed epitomised in the lively, eager, tranquil face of Adam Ferguson, successive tenant of the Edinburgh Chairs of Philosophy and Mathematics. A century later Sir William Quiller Orchardson's gifts for ironic and faintly sympathetic elicitation of mood and character from less intellectual subjects called on Macmillan particularly to make much of his rare but exceptionally fine use of contemporary themes. Among the earlier canvases was an impressive choice of the work of Raeburn's predecessor, the younger Allan Ramsay, whose aristocratic and eminent subjects reflected authority, sensuality, piety and mystery, in varying proportions, admirably counterpointing his eponymous father's *The Gentle Shepherd* staged in the comparably appointed Signet Library. Duncan Macmillan had brought to the Upper Library Hall and to adjoining David Talbot Rice Gallery not only the achievement of Scottish artists in the noon and the long waning of the Enlightenment but the successive dramas of the subjects they made speak so well.

It may be added that he had obtained its sponsorship by his own efforts, and then had to win it back once more when an idiotic sponsorship tout from the Festival in quest of the same patron flatly denied 'Painting in Scotland, the Golden Age' had any Festival connection at all. Naturally Dunlop had to endorse to the bewildered sponsors Macmillan's absolutely justified claim of Festival status: incredibly, the tout was not dismissed.

Mary Queen of Scots is all too frequently martyred once more in the cause of *kitsch*, as many horrible advertisements bear witness, and the quarter-centenary of her death (oftimes cold-bloodedly shorthanded as her 'centenary celebration') was happily distinguished by its absence. Admittedly the preceding year, 1986, brought a forerunner a little close to *kitsch* in the Maly Theatre of Leningrad's *Maria Stuart* by Sergei Slonimsky. It was not the company's main business, which lay in two Tchaikovsky operas, *Queen of Spades* and *Eugene Onegin*, but the Slonimsky concept of Scotland would at least offer an unusual means to see oorsel's as ithers see us, and to the King's Theatre I made my way, or at least BBC Scotland's way. It was no major triumph as an opera, but it was excellent family entertainment both in the recognisable and the alien. The Royal Mile was achieved by houses leaning intimately if perilously across the street, suggesting (possibly accurately) a city more narcissist than factionalised, and even when Rancour raised his sectarian voice, in the person of John Knox, the Reformation conflict was somewhat blunted by the Maly's efforts to remember what it could of Christian practice before the Russian Revolution — Knox's attentive Protestant audience made the sign of the cross to the last Protestant on the close of his every discourse. If anyone chose to read the lesson, it was a salutary reminder that from the perspective of Lenin, and possibly that of Rasputin (to whom this Knox bore a fearsome resemblance), one piece of Western

Christianity was very like another. Time also seemed to shrink in the post-Lenin perspective, as Mary, presented here as besotted with her rapist abductor James Hepburn, Earl of Bothwell, let out anguished cries of 'Boswell!' when, with no sense of the fineness of its prospect, she took the road to England. What Liz Lochhead, Fringe playwright of *Mary Queen of Scots Got Her Head Chopped Off*, describes as the second best-known fact about Mary (the first being contained in her own title), viz. that Mary and her cousin and ultimate executioner, Elizabeth of England, never met, was circumvented by shrewd use of lighting and blocking to separate Scottish royal victim from English royal conspirator while having both on stage simultaneously but obviously bilocationally.

I encountered less enthusiasm among the opera faithful when I pottered around at the interval, David Steel muttering dark things about critics whose poor taste led innocent punters to indifferent productions, present company emphatically not excluded.

'I remember last year,' he continued fastidiously, 'I read some rave *Scotsman* review of a Fringe show, I forget who by, Owen Dudley Edwards as like as not, and when I went on its recommendation, it turned out to be the greatest load of rubbish imaginable.'

I grinned carnivorously. If the eminent Liberal statesman wanted to play rough, who was I to let a Presbyterian minister's son leave combat without a mark, inspired as I naturally was by John Knox and the evocation of his historical consequences?

'Judy,' I said thoughtfully, 'has Ann Winder of BBC *Kaleidoscope* been in touch with you?'

'No,' replied Mrs David Steel with a smile quite as captivating as that of any performer of Mary.

'Ah. She was on the phone to me the other day to ask my advice about whom to approach for insights on the Scottish political situation, and I told her you were the most intelligent Liberal in Scotland.'

This was quite true; indeed all of it, I believe, was true. It rather divided the Steel family. Judy's smile broadened. A slight frown gathered in David's fine statesmanlike forehead.

'I fear we are detaining you, Owen,' he said solicitously, 'we are preventing you from getting to the bar.'

I departed with a civil leer. He has recovered since.

But Mary's year, 1987, produced work of a far higher order, notably

Liz Lochhead's play. Time is the playwright's enemy, or rather the absence of time. But in some circumstances that enemy may prove a friend. I have no proof that when the poet Liz Lochhead (whose renditions of her own work with supporting richly cut-and-thrust Glasgow feminist epigrammatic patter made her a Fringe performer never to be missed) agreed to write a play about Mary Queen of Scots for the Communicado Theatre Company in the four-hundredth year after Mary's execution, she ultimately found herself with far more material than anyone other than Eugene O'Neill or Bernard Shaw could have persuaded a director to stage. It is pure speculation, but the play was announced in the Fringe programme as *Mary Queen of Scots*, and God knows the Fringe programme is not mean in the length of production titles. The play itself covered the first half of Mary's reign in Scotland. It made wonderful usage of modern images and types to suggest the major protagonists. The whole thing proclaimed its sense of theatre from start to finish, with a strong implication of theatre as game. The actress playing Mary had her hair brushed by her maid, the maid then becoming Elizabeth whose hair was brushed by her maid, the actress otherwise playing Mary. Movement, encircle-ment, division, protagonists on a stand now and somewhere else the next, pace and the congealing of fun into horror were but a few of its strengths. Liz Lochhead showed an intense mastery of the diplomacy and intrigue in and out of Scotland, so that the cumulative effect with only half the story told was to leave the ongoing drama a do-it-yourself inevitability. Mary is doomed. There is one last tableau of children in a playground shouting 'Mary Queen of Scots got her head chopped off' and suddenly the tall actress playing Mary, portraying a six-footer, is surrounded with her neck encircled by the hands of the entire cast, her face hopeless, amazed. After nineteen years of imprisonment by her cousin Elizabeth, the real Mary can hardly have been amazed, but the tableau brilliantly encapsulates Mary's amazement as Queen in growing realisation, and desperate efforts to deny, that her situation was fatal to her rule, her liberty, and her life. And the final game, based on the children's old skipping-rope ditty, reflected back on all that preceded it to show Mary's doom accomplished almost with the rule-book simplicity of a series of children's games, with their counterparts, their up-one-minute-and-down-the-next, their inexor-able and sometimes cruel logic, their love of performance, their low tolerance of anything going on too long. A remote drama of politic rulers, ambitious nobles and relentless demagogues became a theme for all time by showing how much it reflected the games of endless successions of children down the range of time. No finer use could have been made of the late, lamented Lyceum Studio than to have its intimate space shroud two courts which suddenly prove vantage-points on a playground. But at what point in the writing did Liz Lochhead decide to call it *Mary Queen of Scots Got Her Head Chopped Off*?

Frank Dunlop's production of Schiller's *Mary Stuart* at the Assembly Hall met with much criticism. For *Critics' Forum* I had the advantage of seeing if half-way through the run. Many production difficulties arousing the wrath of first-night critics had by now been ironed out, notably in the improvement of enunciation in Jill Bennett's Elizabeth. I was fascinated by the force of the encounter-that-was-not when in stark defiance of historical reality the ladies confronted one another, Hannah Gordon as Mary moving from suppliant to seething virago, hurling the shame of Anne Boleyn at her offspring with venom enough to corrode Fotheringay Castle to its foundations. The two figures on the huge stage overrode Schiller's grand impossibility by symbolising the separate worlds they inhabited, divided — in the play at least — by integrity (and the lack of it) as fully as they were actually divided by geography. And it was a fascinating revelation of early nineteenth-century Romanticism. It might be tempting to write Schiller off as *kitsch,* if you are reducing Mendelssohn to *kitsch,* on Scottish themes, but there was deadly logic at the heart of his high emotion. His most obvious chief source, William Robertson, was famous for a coolly unemotional style, although its quiet tones could unleash Romantic floods in the next generation — his passages on Cortes's first sight of Mexico City and Balboa's discovery of the Pacific Ocean had induced Keats's famous conflationary simile in the sonnet *On Chapman's Homer*. But Schiller had previously written the histories of the Dutch revolt from Spain and of its sequel, the Thirty Years War, and judged the outbreak of the latter, so utterly divisive and destructive to his beloved Germany, to have followed from the failure of the Dutch to consolidate their defeat of the Spaniards for want of sufficient support from their ally Elizabeth (whom they aided so well by tying up the land armies intended for the Armada). Schiller's whole cultural being was caught up in the cause of awakening German nationalism, whose apparent hopelessness in 1800, the year of *Mary Stuart*, he saw as perpetuated by that fragmentation unsurmountable for the previous 150 years. So *Mary Stuart* was his vengeance on Elizabeth, and Hannah Gordon showed herself his instrument. In seeking to commemorate one historical event, the production eloquently testified to another. It symbolised the strange meaning Scotland had historically possessed for Europe, as usual in the form of a means to punish England. The tradition may not be forgotten. I thought that the production's sense of dawn for German Romanticism and nationalism was a valuable intellectual service. The initial difficulties arose because Festival pressures on Dunlop prevented his putting a sufficiently rehearsed piece of work on stage. It was a pity, although the attempt to combine theatre and Festival direction was an impossible one: but the truth was, he was a theatre man who could not bear to tear himself away from production work. Hannah Gordon's strength at least testified to his directorial capacities. And inability to forswear theatre production seems a much lesser sin in a Festival Director than playing duenna to the same prima donna every Festival night she chose to perform.

As for the exhibitions, the National Portrait Gallery's 'The Queen's Image' and 'The Queen's World' gave illusory glimpses of artistic conceptions of Mary and her environment, behind which her enigma held its fastness. They were charming, but essentially conventional in form, and while the first was comprehensive in selection of images, the second was rather slight in trying to capture so great a theme. The major honours went to the National Library of Scotland, whose exhibition space is small, but has never disappointed me. Alastair Cherry placed Mary firmly in the chain of her Stuart ancestor-predecessors and her male descendants, with imaginative use of music of her time (making this the only exhibition at which I have ever wept). As a result Mary's was brought into perspective as an episode, however dramatic, in the centuries-old struggle of the Stuart house for consolidation of its kingdom and assertion of its place in Europe above all in relation to its formidable southern neighbour. Particular gems included Mary's last letter to her brother-in-law King Henri III of France, as well as memorabilia of her possessions for religious consolation in the years after her imprisonment. Cherry made the controversies on her character his ally rather than his pitfall, by throwing up marble-epitaph-like recitals of adverse and favourable judgments from such eminent commentators as Knox, Buchanan, Carlyle, Froude, Hume and Robertson. His scholarly artistry is in part preserved by a remarkable catalogue, *Princes, Poets and Patrons*, but the exhibition itself was entitled 'It Cam' Wi' a Lass: the Stuarts in literature, legend and the arts'. The quotation is from Mary's father James V, dying in the knowledge that his only successor was his infant daughter, whence he gloomily ruminated that Stuarts had won the kingdom from marriage to a Bruce daughter, and he prophesied it would now 'gang wi' a lass'. In theory, of course, it did not: Mary's descendant is still on the Scottish as well as the English throne. But in another sense the dying King was right: Mary's reign ensured that the destinies of Scotland in future would lie irrevocably with England.

Chapter Five

Whose Shakespeare is He Anyway?

fringe '85

EDINBURGH FESTIVAL FRINGE   AUGUST 9-31 1985

Opening of *Teague, Shenkin and Sawney, Being an Historical Study of the Earliest Irish, Welsh and Scottish Characters in English Plays* by J. O. Bartley, MA, DLit (Belfast), Lecturer in English, University College of Swansea (Cork, 1954):

Most Irishmen, most Welshmen, and most Scots are, I suppose, agreed among themselves that English generalisations about their particular nationality are false and libellous, although something (each will admit) may be said for the generalisations about the other two; this in spite of the not inconsiderable number of individuals who, perhaps not always consciously, live up to and indeed exploit the notions of national peculiarities current among the English. 'In a time of war,' Dr Johnson observed, 'the nation is always of one mind, eager to hear something good of themselves and ill of the enemy' — and there is just enough hostility between the nations crammed into Europe's western islands to make the dictum permanently, if only partially, true of them.

The generalisations are indeed false and libellous in many ways, but patriotic sentiment also has little to learn from Procrustes. Discussion of these matters usually generates more heat and smoke than light: the question that nearly always escapes being asked in the confusion of charge and countercharge is how in fact the generalised notions came into existence, upon what foundation they were able to establish themselves at all. The broadest generalisations are found in the limited field of the drama, because the stage provides the most fruitful soil for the growth of stock characters. To raise the question within this field is to throw light on similar problems over a wider area. . . .

The very nature of drama forces a high degree of convention upon it. The playwright, who must consider the stage, the actors, and the acceptable length of performance, is confined by physical restraints which do not affect the novelist. Even a best-seller is read privately, and the reader can stop, refresh his memory, pause to consider, or lay the volume aside; but the audience in a theatre can do none of these. If an audience's following of the play is to be effortless enough not to impede the 'willing suspension of disbelief', they have to accept, readily and almost unconsciously, a set of physical and mental conventions; and hence drama uses and clings to convention more than other branches of literature, especially as the audience, being a social congregation, as a whole tends to be less critical in judgment than the individual members.

Theatrical convention varies with physical conditions of performance such as the size and design of stage and auditorium, with fashion, with the balance of the continual struggle between tradition and innovation, with the purpose of the actors and the attitude of the audience, but at all times its essential function is to increase the efficiency of the performance, making for fuller penetration of the audience by the play. By what may be called the ritualistic quality of its emotional effect it can do something towards bringing into being appropriate moods, expressive on the part of the actors and receptive on the part of the audience, and so help to create a condition of rapport *between them. But there is also a less transcendental aspect of its function. Convention is labour-saving. It provides short-cuts — which are the more necessary because of the time-limits imposed by dramatic conditions — for writer and actor in presenting and for audience in paying attention to and understanding the play. . . .*

For strictly dramatic purposes it may not be necessary that the aged parent, the sinister villain, or the comic servant should do more than stir up the audience to provide their own generalised image of the type, and if a few broad conventional strokes will do this, well and good. But if writer and actor can touch the stock character with individual life, so much the better from every other point of view, provided there is no failure to preserve that economy which the exigencies of the stage so imperatively demand.

But I do not think that any of the greatest parts can be described as stock characters. A stock character is typical but not universal. There seem to be two ways in which a dramatist may set about characterisation: he may start with an individual — Shakespeare's usual way — or with a type — Jonson's usual way. . . .

IF THERE IS ANY ONE PEOPLE WHOM THE EDINBURGH FESTIVAL affords the opportunity to study in depth from their portrayal on the stage, it is the English. The English themselves are by now a little cautious about portraying Scots, Welsh or Irish, unless they can rely upon script-writers from the nations in question. This sensibility to ethnic subtlety either as subject or as audience is of recent vintage: even so vigorous an innovator as Joe Orton fell back on the stage-Irishman for *The Erpingham Camp* (originally the 'Pride' play for the 'Seven Deadly Sins' series). Admittedly the protagonist in that play is a stage-Englishman, and the work itself is far weaker than Orton's genius would normally permit. (It is much weaker than several other plays by other hands in the series — notably 'Wrath', 'Avarice' and 'Lust' — and whatever happened to them and to their authors?) Sixty years have been needed to take hold of the lesson of English intellectual self-emasculation, induced by self-hypnosis on the stage-Irishman, a lesson punched home so abrasively and so amusingly in Shaw's first act of *John Bull's Other Island*. But eventually it seems to have been learned. Stand-up comedy, sometimes the sad remnant of drama, sometimes its progenitor, took longer to profit by it, but with the arrival of a much more naturalistic style of Irish forcefully and most influentially (to judge by its many imitators) brought to the Festival Fringe by Ian Macpherson, the wiser English comedians sheered away from the Serbonian bog in which so many of their predecessors in many forms of theatre, chiefly politics, had met their doom.

The stage-Scot was less easily shaken off. Wodehouse, normally assumed by most commentators to be a traditionalist, was very clear by 1949 that the stage-Irishman would no longer do, and made Gussie Fink-Nottle, of all people, remonstrate against the survival of the stage-Irish usage in music-hall, a characteristic Wodehouseian revenge against his own critics' obvious argument that he was prolonging the life of the music-hall far beyond its actual time. Gussie, in *The Mating Season*, is complaining about a script from Catsmeat Potter-Pirbright: 'Pat . . . prefaces his remarks at several points with the expressions "Begorrah" and "faith and begob". Irishmen don't talk like that. Have you read Synge's *Riders to the Sea*? Well, get hold of it and study it, and if you can show me a single character in it who says "Faith and begob", I'll give you a shilling. Irishmen are poets. They talk about their souls and mist and so on. They say things like "An evening like this, it makes me wish I was back in County Clare, watchin' the cows in the tall grass".'

Wodehouse is delicately pointing out that Synge had created his own brand of stage-Irishman, whose immediate local applicability gave no guarantee for any generalised authenticity, but at least it started somewhere. And he was also indicating that, be the staginess of Synge's types what it might, they would not take purloining by English hands. Characteristically he did so in the one context where an Englishman could bend the Synge bow, but it demanded certain prerequisites, the chief being that the Englishman was Wodehouse. Twentieth-century Scots had also produced their own authenticity on the English stage, but it was closer to the traditional stage-Scots, coyly substituting caution for parsimony and making other comparable exercises in euphemism, and its enemies called it the Kailyard. J. M. Barrie and James Bridie played with it a great deal, and gave their English public what it expected combined with much more vigorous authenticity. This prolonged the life of the stage-Scotsman, who had in any case survived in his own music-halls quite apart from their rather different brethren of the south. But inevitably the work was daunting to English imitators, and its strength and its hostages to naturalism had the effect of warning English scribes off.

Welsh stereotypes had become very weak among English playwrights by the twentieth century, partly because of the force of the Welsh language in playwrights such as Emlyn Williams, and of its imprint on the English spoken by the characters of others like Rhys Davies and even Dylan Thomas. Once 'look you' had been placed beyond all possible 'Pales', it was difficult to summon up stock audience reactions to a Welsh character. The English were thrown much more thoroughly back on themselves.

The difficulty here was that the traditional English reach for stock characters made an English metropolitan desire to summon up amusement at provincial types a potentially damaging dilemma for the provincial playwright caught up now by his search for success, now by his desire for authenticity and perhaps to consider his personal loyalties. Shakespeare guying rusticity in his rising career with *As You Like It* and venerating it in his last days in London with *The Winter's Tale* made himself a type of what would follow down the centuries: even the name of *As You Like It* has an important element of auctorial disengagement for his petty treacheries. The London audience was probably no greater in its enthusiasm for provincial naturalism at most times than was Synge's Dublin audience, though it expressed its preferences in the matter rather less violently. What London seemed to want, or at all events accepted, was a general condition of provinciality moving the mirth of sophisticates without problems of immediate authenticity. The convention in its dialect form became known in acting circles as 'Mummerset'.

What the Edinburgh Fringe offered the theatre of the English provinces was the opportunity to be themselves and display their own roots. It is not clear how many of them made the connection, but the drive to reveal Leicestershire for Leicestershire's sake had every basis for self-confidence in a city whose indigenous theatre was wrestling with the question of Scottish theatre for Scotland's sake. As a result, many Edinburgh reporters found themselves becoming very much attached to certain English shires of which they might have no personal knowledge other than the theatre exported thence to Edinburgh. Thus in 1990 a Leicestershire version of Euripides's *The Trojan Women* deliberately making the most of local coal-towns' culture and intonation to suggest an ancient Troy contrasting with the Greek sophistication, added a strength and force of its own to the production. Cockneyism, for all of its place in the metropolis, was similarly the victim of sophisticated condescension, and here again a fine example of what it could bring to the Greek classics was shown in a Westfield College production of Euripides's *Alcestis*, in which one performer, Charlie Snow, gave a posh rendition of Apollo, and then dropped with swinging freedom into a drunken Cockney wide boy, secure in his certainty of his welcome in the stately home whither he has blundered, to make Heracles accessible to a modern audience in the terms Euripides wanted to convey. The unnatural rigidity of the first rôle, highly appropriate in context, followed by the readiness of the intoxicated strongman to take on Death as his adversary, showed a splendid range in Snow's capacities, and yet it seemed to be done by allowing his own cultural roots, or roots with which he was personally very familiar, to give him his purchase on the major rôle.

Even such a public relations device as that of Nottinghamshire in travelling with a posse of local councillors added its own means of under-scoring the stress on Nottinghamshire's voice being heard on the Edinburgh stage. The experience of being escorted to one's seat by an enthusiastic local Solon, ecstatically hoping that one would give a good hand, in applause and/or in review, to the local kids who have put so much into bringing you this little entertainment, had precisely the needful effect of saturation in the aspirations of Nottinghamshire culture. A smoother-spoken public relations person showing the same concern is at best a figure to be lost as quickly as possible, at worst an irritating interposition between the audience and what it has come to see. But when the wonderfully fast-moving Nottinghamshire Hiawatha and Mudjekeewis produced their indigenous accents in portraying a Harvard professor's notions of Indians talking in a Finnish metrical scheme with whatever cosmopolitan folk-myths he chose to supply, the omnipresence of the elderly supporters had already done their work in making it seem wholly appropriate for the dramatised poem to take this form of authenticity.

As matters worked themselves out, the English shire with which I became most deeply engaged by the study of its theatre presented in Edinburgh was Staffordshire, or, more specifically, the town of Stoke-on-Trent.

When I first saw Stoke Original Theatre, I did not know Stoke, though I thought kindly of the town in the light of my mother's enthusiasm for Arnold Bennett, a regard greatly shared by a colleague on the student publications board, Graham Richardson. In the late 1970s we began to spend our family holidays in south Staffordshire (in a Dominican priory), frivolously describing the location as a foreign country but in fact finding it so. The general kindliness of the inhabitants, and their readiness to put themselves out to help strangers in difficulties, made it especially appealing. Mother's own love of Bennett had much to do with finding many common reactions in his record of the potteries with her own rural Cork and the Kerry of her education, as well as many fascinating individual characteristics. So I went to Stoke with no greater expectations than those of finding people I might well like, reflecting a culture I had every reason for wanting to treat with respect.

What I found was Ray Johnson, an actor-manager of remarkable character and attainments. He was not himself a Staffordshire man, but had accepted his civic post with a firm desire to draw on the local strengths in acting talent, scripting creativity and source-material within the area. In this he showed comparable preoccupations to those of another Englishman, Chris Parr, then proving so great a stimulus for Scottish potentialities in the same lines, in his work at the Traverse. Like Parr, Johnson had experience as a drama teacher which he put to excellent use, although both of them must have been very good teachers since neither sounded like a teacher. They held the high respect of their associates for what they were and knew and could instil, not for what position of authority they might occupy. I came to know Johnson, his wife Fran who was on his acting team, and several of his other actors, fairly well over the years, chiefly by meeting at the Fringe Club at the end of an evening, so this is not simply a verdict from the stalls and a few judicious conversations in the front of house.

Johnson usually had several Fringe offerings which he balanced

128

with a sure hand, much as many wise Fringe company directors do. The pattern is to combine a new play, a late-night revue, a Shakespeare, and a kids' show. The new play as a rule is a passenger. If the kids' show is fortunate it may make money, but probably not much. The Shakespeare, especially if reviewed favourably, may make a profit. Here questions about the effectiveness of reviews for box-office results are easier to determine. A punter looking for material may remember little enough from huge swathes of reviews in *The Scotsman*, the *Festival Times,* the *Glasgow Herald*, or elsewhere. (As the huge bulk of ticket sales are to Scottish residents, it is these publications and not their more exotic London counterparts which are likely to exert appreciable effect on the immediate profits making the difference between financial success or failure, though good London notices will be made much of by companies in the hope of future life for their productions.) But the many readers who want a little Shakespeare will pick out notices of his plays and set their reports one against another. The experienced Fringegoer may recall critics' names which served their interests in the past, but in general a review must be logical enough, however expressed, to compel respect for the argument that this production is worth seeing, or that that, on the whole, is not. It may well be that a reviewer, waxing lyrical on the dislike s/he feels for what s/he has received, may inspire Fringegoers to attend to see if it is as bad as s/he says, or to confirm their view that s/he is an empty, conceited fathead.

The revue is expected to make money, and here, also, punters probably study form. Reviews of revues are easily singled out to be balanced against one another, and an investment in a taxi or a wait for a late-night bus must be considered; this will sharply focus the weighing of critics' selection of pros and cons. A hostile notice may drive away the revue audience where the Shakespeare punter may be ready to take the best that offers, knowing that Fringe Shakespeare is unlikely to be as good, or indeed as disappointing, as what will be found from Shakespeare on the main Festival. Shakespeare at least offers assurance of a good script. Even the Oxford and Cambridge revues have seen their expected audiences dramatically slashed by a reviewer who really puts his or her heart into demolition work. And not much is needed. With such ferocious competition for early notices in *The Scotsman* pages, Allen Wright is more anxious to see a good show getting its merited support than to give pride of place to saturation bombing, however justified. He once reduced my review of the Cambridge Footlights from the permitted 200 words to fifty, and the adverse verdict was quite sufficiently conveyed to discourage the innocent. On BBC Scotland I once arranged with Neville Garden, the presenter, moments before our early-morning live transmission, that my report on the Oxford Revue would run as follows:

*Self (after discussing two other shows):*I suppose there is no time to
       report on the Oxford Revue?
Neville: No.
Self: Thank God.

Children's shows are probably the most judiciously studied in their notices. A parent or relative with children to satisfy, and to keep from noisy attention-wandering, will look very closely indeed at the alternatives. For this reason, and from the personal pleasure of their company, I always take a child to review a children's show, if I can persuade one. It is all too easy for adults to wallow in nostalgia by reason of some adult manipulation of their emotions from the stage. Children are much better at seeing and judging exactly what appears before them with no messing around as to what one wants to tell oneself is happening when it is not, or how far the production fails to come up to some cherished and perhaps overvalued adult memory of an earlier treatment of the theme. Sometimes, admittedly, the quality shows clearly enough to reach even adult comprehension. I recall one Oxford show for children which began with three clowns coming out and standing on stage in attendance for the next entry. A child in the audience began to cry. One clown took a flying leap from the stage, shot over to the child, produced a lollipop from its pocket, gave it to the child with a brief, reassuring, but nonetheless magical touch of ceremony. The child stopped crying and began to laugh. The clown resumed its position. The play got underway. And so far as I could judge every member of the audience shared my view and that of my infant fellow-critic that we were in excellent hands, an assumption subsequent events did nothing to belie.

Ray Johnson and Stoke Original Theatre varied the formula to the extent that his Shakespeare in 1978 was *Macbeth-7*, a truncation of the original tailored to cast limitation by the reduction of its actors to that symbolic number. And instead of having a kids' show, he offered a family entertainment of his own composition, *Jellies, Jam and*

Jubilation, the ticket price covering refreshments and raffle. I was instructed by *The Scotsman* to review the family show and the new play, and I also saw the *Macbeth* later. *Macbeth-7* was as close to classical form as the deletions and cut parts would permit, running to seventy-five minutes. Johnson had no intention of allowing the work to lose dramatic intensity, to raise laughs by cute cutting and doubling/trebling/quadrupling, or to invite derision. Other Fringe truncations have been much less austere. *Macbeth* is an unusually short Shakespeare tragedy, and offers no major opportunity to lose lines and characters by deletion of an obvious subplot, as is the case with the Gloucester material in *King Lear*. (In 1990 I saw the Welsh College of Music and Drama make an excellent point by the excision of Gloucester and his sons, while retaining Mad Tom as a real and not an assumed character. Mad Tom is vital, as the Gloucesters are not, in that Lear's madness in part derives from the contagion of Mad Tom, and it was possible to glimpse in this production what the play may have resembled as Shakespeare originally conceived it. Reconsidered in this light, the full play now raises the question of Edgar, however unintentionally, being the agent of his king's madness and his father's death — which invites more attention to the direction and interpretation of Edgar than he usually gets.) But *Macbeth* has little to lose to its advantage, even for purposes of greater elucidation of its draft possibilities. Yet Johnson and his cast made it work well, Johnson's own menacing inscrutability adding an element of psychological mystery contrasting impressively with the habitual Macbeths telegraphing the vicissitudes of their part in advance.

Stoke's new play, *Manoeuvres* by Bob Wilson, was a neatly orchestrated black comedy of two men locked in mutual rivalry in small space. But it was the family show which proved a knockout. This was because behind the superficial appearances of a 1951 Staffordshire Festival of Britain entertainment, there was an intricate and sensitive play turning on the characters of the performers and their supporters, in which battles of integrity and self-realisation made their way into the production within a production. It engaged the intellect as thoroughly as the risible emotions, and flirted dexterously with petty tragedy while keeping the punters for family fun happy. Celtic Lodge on the Lawnmarket is a friendly venue, all the more with a well-managed adjoining tearoom, but the auditorium looks from many rows straight down to a stage area usually sealing off performers from

131

viewers. The method of family entertainment, and the inspired use of an exit midway on the aisle alongside the audience, gave a much greater involvement of the entire theatre with the imaginary planned festivities, and their less imaginary products for gastric consumption, ensuring all the more strength to the discovery that matters were far from well in the reality of lives of the supposed actors which swirled into various forms of resolution dictated by their transient rôles. The Fringe is particularly well suited for the play-within-a-play, when one considers all it involves, but few companies rise so effectively to the potentialities of the Fringe as Ray Johnson's Stoke. The Edinburgh audience felt itself admitted to Staffordshire characters and characteristics in the classic forms of stock deployment, and if we did not know much of Staffordshire, it was an easy transposition to respond as one does to other stock ethnic types. And then it became judiciously plainer and clearer that what we had accepted on trust as Staffordshire character was in fact a theatrical illusion, that stage Staffordians were as unreal as stage Scotpersons, that stage Staffs was a local variant of Mummerset, as the real Staffordshire broke through in the scenes behind the scenes. It was the use of convention first to ensnare and then to disillusion the audience in Bartley's sense, with the effects Shaw had made work so well. That Johnson was daringly doing it within the perennial economic place of the family-pleasing slot, and holding his audience with their traditionalist expectations, said all the more for it. And the hold on the audience was vital to the dynamics, as everybody became enthralled by the village moron's battle to break free from his imprisoning rôle as the village moron; his catharsis occurs when the spiv tells him his dead father *wasn't* a World War II hero. The heroic exemplar has been the bane of the boy's life.

The result was a Fringe First, to the company's considerable surprise. They knew they were doing something good, and had put their hearts into it. But they were themselves sufficiently the prisoners of Fringe convention to assume that any hopes of the award must be entrusted to the 'new play'. The successive *Scotsman* adjudicators had no doubts, however. Above all else, the Fringe must honour successful revolution in conventions. Children are fascinated by the impact of realism on the world of make-believe, provided that they are not insulted in the process. An entertainment for children in which they are told they are morons for wanting tradition, they ferociously denounce as patronising, an admirable word which children are

132

increasingly learning to use as early as possible. But to invite children to enlist in protest against anyone being told s/he is a moron makes excellent, and rewarding, sense.

Each year Ray Johnson continued to show virtuosity in his choice of material, and also to make the most of dramatic possibilities provided by traditions and folk-memories in Stoke and its hinterland. In 1982 Stoke produced a splendid realisation of Staffordshire soldiers' experience in the Napoleonic wars, *Going for a Soldier*. It was an eloquent mingling of historical reconstruction with an underlying remorseless assertion of the waste of humanity perpetrated by war. Class implications were asserted convincingly rather than incessantly. My son Mickey became involved in a Fringe Marathon for the children's pages of the *Festival Times,* cycling frenziedly from venue to venue to see the maximum possible within twenty-four hours. He knew nothing of my interest in Stoke, so it was very pleasing for me to read in his published report that of all the shows he saw, the one that he liked best was *Going for a Soldier.* A child's unpromoted support for parental enthusiasm is a greater happiness to receive than that from any other source, however eminent the authority.

But that, I think, was the last year of Stoke Original Theatre at Edinburgh. The Fringe had become increasingly exhausting for the Johnsons to carry, on top of their normal responsibilities for the theatre throughout the year. Fran was expecting a child when they made the last visit, a very natural point for them to decide on summers of greater domesticity for the future. I have never seen them since, but hope they and their company received the happiness they had brought to so many of their Edinburgh followers. I had at one point coined the term 'No Stoke without Fire' in a review, but as the years went on without an entry under their company I sometimes found myself muttering 'No Fire without Stoke'.

From P. G. Wodehouse, *Uncle Dynamite* (1948),
Part Three, Chapter IX:

> In the literature and drama which have come down to us through the ages there have been a number of powerful descriptions of men reacting to unpleasant surprises. That of King Claudius watching the unfolding of the play of 'The Mouse Trap' is one of these, and writers of a later

133

date than Shakespeare have treated vividly of the husband who discovers in an inner pocket the letter given to him by his wife to slip in the mail two weeks previously.

Of all the protagonists in these moving scenes it is perhaps to Macbeth seeing the ghost of Banquo that one may most aptly compare Pongo Twistleton as he heard this voice in the night. He stiffened from the ankles up, his eyes rolling, his hair stirring as if beneath a sudden breeze, his very collar seeming to wilt, and from his ashen lips there came a soft, wordless cry. . . . That intelligent Scottish nobleman, Ross, whom very little escaped, said, as he looked at Macbeth, 'His highness is not well', and he would have said the same if he had been looking at Pongo.

Shakespeare is our common second language. Even in a university, the specialisations of whose faculties are necessarily their curse as well as their blessings, it still prevails. Thus at Edinburgh University some years ago Professor W. W. Robson, from whom I have learned so much, could choose as the title of his inaugural lecture *Did the King See the Dumb-Show?* as a problem which might well have crossed the minds of many students and staff far from the confines of his own Department of English Literature. I seem to hear in my ears the roar of the crowd as Robson pointed out that aurists tell us poison cannot be administered through the ear unless the tympanum has been fractured and perhaps King Hamlet had fractured his tympanum by all the roaring of cannon and banging of drums he was so fond of, and then, without so much as a glance at his rocking audience, 'But this is to be frivolous'. I recall the masterly essay of my own colleague in History, Professor V. G. Kiernan, on European mercenaries in the seventh century, remarking that King Claudius was far from being the only European ruler who, in facing a crisis with his rebellious subjects, called upon his Swiss mercenaries to bar the door.

Hamlet has been a Fringe favourite, but if the shires have generally presented it without much assertion of their own local antecedents, what fascinating alternatives they have offered! I think no review I ever wrote for Allen Wright gave him as much pleasure as that of the Leicestershire *Hamlet* which I commenced: 'Rosencrantz and Guildenstern are alive and well and Lesbian feminists.' Leicestershire Youth Theatre was in those days under the profound influence of a director compared to whose work the Glasgow Citizens' Theatre seemed as square as a barrack yard. We began with the funeral of King

Hamlet and his encasement in the tomb on which Claudius and Gertrude then writhed in ably simulated (*instruction to printer:* no 't', repeat no 't', between 's' and 'i') fornication while Prince Hamlet declaimed, 'O that this too, too solid flesh would melt,/Thaw, and resolve itself into a dew!' etc., thus opening up an instructive ambiguity in the text as to whose flesh he was referring. Rosencrantz appeared to have had an affair with Hamlet from which Guildenstern had clearly emancipated her. Osric seemed to be a brothel madam, which certainly had ample textual corroboration from Hamlet's views both on her and on the court where she mistressed the ceremonies. It was all splendid fun, and heartily to be recommended for lovers of the play in need of some challenge to their fixed assumptions, and most unlike a hideously depressing burlesque of *Hamlet* unleashed in the same year, 1982, by alleged humorists from Cambridge. But it had less success in rivalling the strengths of Warwickshire's version, where the local boy certainly made good.

Theatre Warwickshire's most startling achievement was Polonius, who made infinitely better sense than any Polonius I have seen. In public life he was a smoothly efficient Tudor civil servant with all the customary Court disinclination to trust anyone, preference for eaves-dropping, and fundamental insistence that the stability of the state must be preserved come what may. He was, in fact, a natural colleague for Walsingham or Burleigh. In private life he was a father incapable of concealing the depth of rich love for his children, and was loved by them in return, his sermons something of a family joke but also a family game. In the text, Polonius clearly means so much to his children that when they learn of his death, one goes mad and the other commits high treason. Warwickshire came to terms with this in 1982: how many others, however eminent, have done so? Claudius was also remarkably conceived, as having one serious ambition, his love for Gertrude. All else was incidental to that, King Hamlet's life, Prince Hamlet's inheritance, Prince Fortinbras's threats. Claudius was in fact shown as a good man who had loved not wisely but too well and had committed one great crime for its fulfilment. The result was that all of his anxieties for Hamlet were decent solicitude for the son of his beloved but not very bright wife; Hamlet was a youth whom he did not love but was ready to try to love, keep around the Court to please her and so on. So Claudius's speech of apparent repentance really was repentant, until his voice broke on what he could not renounce — his

Crown and ambition he might sacrifice, but never his Queen. And then, confronted with Hamlet's murder of the invaluable and obviously exemplary Polonius, he realised that it was either his nephew or him and resolved on murder with all of the implacability of a naturally kindly man wishing to get unpleasantness over as quickly as possible. Inevitably one became too sympathetic to the 'tragedies' of Polonius, Claudius, Laertes, Ophelia, and Gertrude to leave much over to waste on the rather posturing Prince.

Many years later I saw an Oxford *Hamlet* where the eponymous Prince was portrayed by Richard Leggatt, a student who told me when we met at the end of his Festival that he had never seen nor read the play before taking on the part. This was a set-down for my thesis of the universal acquaintance with its plot, in university circles, and never was ignorance more blissful for its audience, for Leggatt did wonders with the most straightforward interpretation of his rôle I have ever witnessed. This time general sympathy ranged itself on Hamlet's side, since he performed it as a thoroughly decent, straightforward young man, anxious to do his duty yet disliking its ugly nature and insisting he must have proof positive. Of indecision he gave no sign. Horatio was presented as a hippie, which naturally explained his lack of enthusiasm for frequenting Court circles and thus at a stroke disposed of the problem of his long delay in renewing his friendship with Prince Hamlet despite having come to King Hamlet's funeral: he was clearly filling in time until they might bump into one another, by having a long freak-out in which he had ultimately picked up Marcellus and Bernardo. It was hardly Director's Theatre: it was more a matter of directorial acquiescence in actors' choices. Guildenstern was once again a woman, but this time played as a rather bemused games mistress, or vicar's schoolteacher sister, or something. Gertrude was voluptuous beyond all description, but Hamlet had no disposition to play Oedipus. Hamlet's integrity in cleaving to his purpose won all the more admiration despite the obvious perils of cross-examining Guildenstern (who for two pins would have sent straight for the police) and his mother (who for two pins would have sent straight for the police or any other man she could get her hands on). In fact, Richard Leggatt is a very fine actor, with a strange ability to walk through any crowd in solitude. I have seen him in two subsequent plays, both new, both times with something of the same haunted integrity, and the same heartwarming remoteness.

Playing Shakespeare by the book can be the greatest Fringe revolution of them all, though it helps if the rest of the cast follow suit.

Hamlet may be a Renaissance Man caught up in a Revenge Tragedy of depressing antiquity (and I look forward to seeing someone play it like that before I die) and, as such, a fascinating figure for Everyperson to contemplate in our eternal war of present against past, but *Macbeth* poses more immediate problems for a contemporary Scottish audience. It is all very well to say that Macbeth had been dead for over half a millennium when Shakespeare got at him. Half a millennium later still, or nearly, *Macbeth* is fairly combustible stuff for Scotland. Quite apart from its atrocious libels on a fine man whose greatest excess was his profuseness in alms, who owed no fealty to the youthful usurper Duncan and killed him in fair fight, and who was the last King of Scotland to visit the Pope (conceivably libelled too, with his tiara, as the three witches), there is its malicious reminder in the final conjuration of thanes into earls that if King James of Scotland has become King James of England, he will Anglify his Scots magnates beyond all recognition and consolidate his Anglifying power by English troops. Shakespeare knew all about the symbolism of having one's country conquered by a foreign army however liberating its official intent: it may happen in Denmark, it must happen in Scotland, it cannot happen in England. (It does of course happen in *Richard III*, but there the foreign army is made English.)

Of these things the Fringe has shown itself well aware, most notably in a 1982 Fringe First winner, Stuart Delves's *The Real Lady Macbeth*, which dealt with the problems of Shakespearean myth, historical reality, and the politics of King Jamie. That production also addressed itself, with a malice equal to Shakespeare's own, to the question of *Macbeth*'s hoodoo whose impact on the stage still leads some theatre persons known for their sanity in every other respect to refer to it timorously as 'the Scottish play'. From this hoodoo, Edinburgh's Royal Lyceum Theatre has by no means shown itself exempt. Three successive artistic directorships, two of them good, have reached rock bottom with their *Macbeth*s. One exhibited Siward's army crawling on its belly around the back of the stage in order to defoliate Birnam Wood in seeming sufficiency; the gods, as their ironical cheers proved, were athirst. One, after innumerable antecedent disasters, culminated in Macbeth's apparently vanquishing Young Siward, but postponing his despatch of his victim until he had first turned round and presented his opponent with his buttocks 'as though inviting him', complained that otherwise habitually benevolent critic Alistair Moffat (broadcasting, but not in his Fringe Administrator capacity), 'to give him six of the best'. And another production, for reasons best known to itself, had the Macbeths constantly maddened by a dripping roof, while Lady Macduff emptied water into a crack in the floor, thus ensuring that all present realised Shakespeare had anticipated O'Casey's discovery of a slum tenement brawling as theatre fodder by several centuries.

Frank Dunlop may justly claim to have smashed the hoodoo in the Lyceum for good and all, whatever abominations of desolation may yet seat themselves in that holy place, when he had the Toho Company of Japan (now the Ninagawa Company) stage their magnificent Samurai *Macbeth* within its walls. Everything worked, including the raven's croak at Duncan's arrival at Macbeth's castle, the owl screaming and the cricket crying on his departure. The audience seemed perfectly satisfied with beautifully sharp renditions which left everyone clear where they were, although not one word was in English, bar proper names. It asserted itself magnificently as a play of ambition, magic and terror. How far it did so as a tragedy is a nice point. My own definition is that if the audience lacks a sense of unfairness when Malcolm makes his closing remarks on 'this dead butcher and his fiend-like queen', we have not seen a tragedy.

But *Macbeth* on the Fringe, under infinitely more modest auspices, could still be a tragedy. The very next year, 1986, it was realised as such — across the road from the Lyceum in the Heriot-Watt Theatres, under the banner of Compass Theatre. Nick Chadwin as Macbeth was young, Geordie, diminutive, and a fanatical follower of Newcastle United. He possessed the aura of a football hero eminently decent within himself but hopelessly outclassed by the sophisticates around him, whether of the ancient wisdom of the witches, or of the modern, expressed by his upper-class snobbish wife. And he made such fine work of 'If 'twere done — when 'tis done — then 'twere well it were done quickly' that the full pathos of what lay in store for his mind and soul proved heartrending, and he got my annual weep, more or less on the basis of Dorothy Parker's lament for F. Scott Fitzgerald, 'the poor Goddam son of a bitch!'

Perhaps *Macbeth* in English improves when responsibility is thrown to individual actors, provided they know what to do with it. The porter, given his head, is very apt to lose it and, in the case of my former student Hamish Clark (not in a Fringe production, although otherwise a versatile and sometimes powerful, often hilarious Fringe performer), the porter also deliberately lost his most recent meal with the effect of almost inducing several members of the audience to follow suit. Kingdom, of Fife, gave me the pleasure in 1979 of seeing what could be done with Banquo, on the actor's own initiative, as I later learned. The text leaves Banquo's vulnerability to the witches' temptation a little ambiguous: he is certainly no longer an innocent man in his heart by the time he is killed. The Kingdom production removed any ambiguity about him. It became chillingly evident that if Macbeth did not get Duncan, Banquo might, and even more that if Macbeth did not get Banquo first, Banquo would get him, and not for the benefit of Malcolm and Donalbain either. Banquo was played by a Lecturer in Geography at Dundee. I should have liked to see him play Iago, but he would probably have been a little over-sinister in the genial scenes. Macbeth was played by the company actor-manager, who, no doubt with ample precedent, never fully lost his enthusiasm for managing in his acting. But Banquo was much deadlier, and much more of a Renaissance villain. I can still feel the cold wind of his reply to Macbeth's openly untrustworthy 'Good repose the while' — 'Thanks, sir: the like to you!' If heredity counted for anything, Macbeth was only one person with reason to deplore Fleance's escape. I have found most subsequent Banquos a little insipid. I doubt if Shakespeare intended insipidity as a predominant feature in his second general.

For horrific contrivances I should have taken it that Toho had put themselves comfortably beyond all rivals, what with the bloody child proving an enormous foetus, and comparable attractions, but in 1990 Polkatz easily transcended these limits, operating — and it is the right word — in the Roxy (formerly the Roxburgh Rooms, but nothing so archaic would have befitted Polkatz). The murder of Duncan behind corrugated iron declared itself in an enormous bloodfall which the witches hygienically caught in a tin bath. This they brought into prominent use during their entertainment of Macbeth, requiring him to duck, for what proved the armed head etc., within its ruby depths. What was undeniable was that, however ferociously, the production eloquently expressed the omnipresence of pagan ritual in Hallowe'en games which are familiar to you all, and thereby asserted the mingling of blood-guilt, paganism and domesticity. The totality would have sent Margaret Mead into nightmares, and Margaret Murray with her.

One of the most startling discoveries in a Fringe show can be that of pure gold concealed in the most obscure places. Festival productions may aim at it, but if the company is playing its ace far down in the hand, there will be few to miss its hype in advance. Kenneth Branagh in 1990 played Peter Quince in *A Midsummer Night's Dream* and Edgar in *King Lear*, but this simply ensured that before they wrote a line the critics had every intention of giving much more than their accustomed space to Quince and Edgar. But who in 1978 could have predicted star performances in the Royal Scottish Academy of Music and Drama's *Two Gentlemen of Verona* to be Launce from Alexander Bartlette, and Panthino (servant to Proteus's father), the first outlaw, and Sir Eglamour (the self-serving nimble-footed agent in Silvia's escape) all from Grant Cathro? I suppose I might have kept an eye out for them from the first, as Bartlette directed, and Cathro designed, the Canongate Lodge production. But, after all, I had used that device myself in *An Ideal Husband*, and nobody was likely to find any great quality in my butler, apart from some relief, when, as Fletcher Collins dispassionately remarked in rehearsals, I would finally realise where the audience was. A good Launce one may hope for; but this Launce was a marvel. As for Cathro, he seemed born to bring flesh and blood to any line Shakespeare ever wrote. Fortunately the rest of the company was good, if not quite up to their standards.

Oxford prompted some of the same reactions in 1982 with a Marlowe *Edward II* in the round, all members playing several parts save for Edward himself. Their uniform dress of white shirts and black leggings made them a trifle indistinguishable, but I became enthusiastic about the vigorous dedication of Chris Jones, whom I saw two years later doing sterling work in holding together a monstrous play, *The Oddity*, which had managed to lose its eponymous character and original plot between deadline for the Fringe programme and performance; and the result, largely thanks to Chris's professionalism, was a vastly engaging piece of neo-mythologised lunacy. But the high point of *Edward II* was a tremendous performance of Lightborn, the regicide, from Humphrey Bower, now sparkling almost to Heaven, now exulting in the uttermost depths of Hell. I raved about this to a sceptical John Drummond (Drummond complained that he did not see anything like enough Fringe productions and was vigorously ready to engage in discussions about one's enthusiasms when it was possible to catch him, as it so frequently was). The Festival Director was sympathetic to support for new talent, but pooh-poohed this one. 'Lightborn! Anyone can play Lightborn well! Why, even I have played it well!' I have seldom heard a worse argument. He genuinely had no notion that he had proved my case, for I could not imagine a more appropriate antecedent for Bower than the Mercurian celerity, and the mercurial temperament, of John Drummond.

Curiously enough, both of them had Australian mothers. Humphrey Bower's father was an Austrian Jew who had managed to escape before the holocaust. I saw him next year in a breakaway Oxford *Lear*, playing Gloucester, into which he threw the same versatility, now a self-assured English nobleman at the heart of court politics, now a writhing victim in mortal agony, now a bewildered yet deeply dignified blind fugitive. If Hitler had had his utmost wishes, that rich gold in performance would never have existed. That production, taking the perilous path of modern dress, reached another great height in Martin Moriarty's Fool, amply justifying the modernity by his realisation of a mad civil servant. He completely conquered the heart of my fourteen-year-old daughter Sara, who had *her* annual weep when he punctiliously closed and locked his briefcase on 'And I'll go to bed at noon', and walked out with no further purpose, mad or sane, to keep him alive. He had created his own storm-torn heath in his own mind, and made us its spectators.

I was less impressed by Stafan Bednarczyk, playing Gaveston, and young Prince Edward in *Edward II* — not his true environment. A few years later I saw what was, when he came to the Assembly Rooms with a succession of his own mordantly satirical and elegantly fantastic lyrics, so much so that we included his version of the social problems of an unexpectedly surviving dinosaur in an *Apocalypse* BBC radio compilation I scripted for Jonathan Wills's production. It was a curious contrast: what had seemed a dutiful and unimaginative performer in *Edward* radiated extraordinary talent from his fingers' ends whether on the piano, in his intricately plotted and gloriously declaimed songs, or his sardonically bewitching stage presence.

I am disinclined to give much credit to the Thatcher Administration in prompting cultural development, or indeed any other positive accomplishment. But it had powerful negative effects, as in the deepening and hardening of Scottish nationalism. The upsurge of enthusiasm for *King Lear* in the Thatcher years may also possess more than a chronological coincidence. For decades it was regarded as unplayable, and this by commentators who thought it the greatest work Shakespeare ever wrote. Shaw revered it, and has no review of it. In our century a few notable Lears surfaced before the 1980s, such as Gielgud's and Wolfit's, but most Shakespearean actors did not care to attempt it. Television Lear seemed to bear out the warning with Michael Hordern's apparent desire to have his audience as unmoved by love for him as his elder daughters, while Laurence Olivier's insistence on apocryphal solitary scenes culminated in washing his underpants and eating smoked salmon out of a dead rabbit. Maybe such disasters in high places before a mass audience emboldened the hardier spirits on the Fringe, and eminent persons have followed their brave lead. Sometimes the brave leaders have become the eminent persons.

The most notable rise to stardom from a Fringe *Lear* was the director Deborah Warner. Her Kick Theatre Company had won many Fringegoing friends, with its brilliant mix of the experimental and the classical. She turned the space in St Cuthbert's Church Hall in King's Stables Road, near the Lyceum but far below it in height (at least topographically), into a splendid double stage with the main floor for much of the work while the actual stage was employed for special purposes. Her *Tempest* discovered Ferdinand and Miranda playing their chess-game on that stage, and Miranda, suddenly alerted to the brave new world that had such mortals in it, took a flying leap down to the main concourse and shot diagonally across it to confront as the chosen example of her occasion for starry-eyed wonder, the person of Antonio, her father's and her own attempted murderer. Deborah Warner's *Lear* went much farther. Lear, a Surrey stockbroker of military affectation, so far as appearances permitted judgment, made his own storm sitting on top of a ladder and hurling buckets of water. The Fool was a legless wizened changeling pushed around in a cart. Something of the old incest-theme in the *Ur*-Lear myth asserted itself in Lear's obscene capering bereft of his nether garments. The overwhelming effect on the audience was that of being engulfed in man-created chaos, Lear's insanity reflecting the world's, and now

142

ours also. It subordinated individual acting achievement to the grand design, but her National Theatre *King Lear* some years later showed how well she could harmonise her strategy with the isolated power of Ian McKellen's Kent and the Scottish civility stripped away into primeval Ishmael in Brian Cox's Lear. Her miracle of modernistic lighting to produce an archetypally supernaturally charged storm was wonderful to behold, though actually less frightening than her old Lear and bucket.

Deborah Warner's work was primarily intellectual, while its assault on the emotions was strongest in calling up irrational response. The *Lear* which above all others made straightforward conquest of my soul was a much more traditional affair, although its moving genius insisted it was in tune with the latest big thinking on direction.

Richard Demarco, of the Demarco Gallery, had for some years been extending the heterogeneous body of companies performing under his auspices. He preached their merits, as he preached everything else, with a combination of the talents of an Old Testament minor prophet, an Italian *gamin*, a revolutionary medieval Scottish mystic, Vladimir Stroganoff of the Brahms and Simon chronicles of the ballet, and an unexpected use of his own form of Shavian epigram usually uttered in a Beardsleyesque aura. His casual introductions were fabulous: I recall having my hand thrust into that of a terrified teenage Italian viscount with the words, 'This is the son of the only private collector of modern art for whom I do not feel the utmost contempt!' I found it impossible to make anything of Demarco in our early meetings, and then in 1978 I was a witness of a session at a Toronto conference on Celticism in which, enraged by being let down by two previous speakers of whom his generous expectations had clearly been excessive, he opened a carefully prepared typescript, snarled at it, denounced all prepared lectures, tore it up, jumped on it, and spoke for two hours to the rapture of all present. He bestrode the universe, vanished into the infinite, and fought his way into and out of theories of human experience and their Celtic implications with sufficient energy and electricity to fire seven Renaissances into orbit. Thereafter I liked him greatly, thought him one of the most exciting signs of cultural vitality in Edinburgh, and otherwise guided myself by the conclusion that to him his geese must always be not merely swans, but soaring eagles. And some of them were.

In 1982 he was streaming fire about what he called his Etonians. To the uninitiated in Demarcese, this might seem simple snobbery, given the place King Henry VI's foundation for poor boys has obtained in the English class structure, public life rat race, etc. But it was clear enough to the working student of Demarcism that he extolled the Etonian glories with all the force he had brought to yesterday's invasion of Polish drama or would bring to tomorrow's convoy of Martians. His Etonians, it turned out, called themselves 'Free Shakespeare', and I dizzily wondered whether Ricky was liable to demand that I take the matter up with Amnesty International. They explained earnestly to anyone who would listen that they believed in undirected Shakespeare, according to the principles enunciated by some guru whose motto appeared to be 'If Nunn, write None'. To all of this Ricky, his customary Scots proceeding at its usual Italianate profusion, responded with rapturous panegyrics beneath which no enthusiasm for directorless theatre showed any visible existence. And he was dead right. Free Shakespeare may have thought, doubtless did think, that it was doing what it claimed, but it was in fact classic actor-manager work. The moving spirit was Jonathan Rigby, a highly autocratic figure, who knew what he wanted in direction and intended to get it. He himself was directed by James Brown, who played Albany. Brown didn't do much with Albany, but he made a perfect conductor and reflecter of directorial electricity to play back on Rigby. Rigby was of course Lear, and he played Lear with all of the genius of youth for the impersonation of age, save perhaps for an undue firmness of step. This was a Lear who was feeling his years, but who had been a warrior king, and a powerful force in council if not in diplomacy. He also conveyed with fine economy that he liked and understood children, but he was bewildered by their growing up. The great expression of this was when the Fool made his entrance by tumbling down a staircase — the Fool was considerably junior to most of the schoolboy cast — and stood on his hands whereupon Lear grasped him by the ankles, delighted to find someone still playing the games he knew and understood. The Fool became the proof of Lear's hunger to show himself a father. Lear's death provided my annual weep. Sara said afterwards that she didn't cry but thought it very right that I should. On that, she summed up the greatest strength of the production: it was fathers' Lear.

Free Shakespeare produced *Othello* the next year, again with a stunning performance in the title-rôle. Once more it was the autocrat with rare gifts of expression of love. Rigby's considerable height gave him fine powers of intimidation, and in both plays he faced his doom in the realisation that his real unconquered adversary was himself. His voice could do great things in its movement from strength to softness, almost reflecting surprise in the discovery of his own tenderness. He himself went on to university, and brought his company back with variations to play Anouilh well, but not so as to convince anyone that it was an appropriate alternative to Shakespeare. He undertook Angelo in *Measure for Measure*, and contrived to suggest an Angelo happily at peace in the conclusion by his discovery of the larger designs of the Duke. He even took on Parolles, in *All's Well That Ends Well*, luxuriated in his own antithesis of the martial and chivalric virtues, and eloquently conveyed the meanness contrasting with Falstaff in such comparable situations. He is a professional actor now, and one awaiting recognition. I saw him a few weeks ago as Mr Rochester in *Jane Eyre*. He retains and has somewhat enlarged his capacity for making his rôle eminently credible within its conventions, and for subtle indication of what the person of that rôle must have been like in earlier passages of his life. He is an eagle, and I hope will gain his chance to soar. In a very different sense from his initial meaning, he sets Shakespeare free.

Who sees them, these Rigbys and Bowers and Cathros? Audiences may come, and critics may smile, but what talent scouts are at work from the professional theatres? In all my footslogging around the Fringe, I have seen only one Artistic Director in quest of potential recruits. I sat on a panel in 1981 with Michael Holroyd and Melvyn Bragg, in which Holroyd and I heartily cursed the Television Festival, a lamentable congregation of envenomed introverts: we were performing at a Drummond-created symposium not entirely destitute of the sense that here in the actual Festival the symposiasts were serving the public as the Television Festival should be doing and was not. But what infuriated Holroyd and me was the thought that the television brethren should employ their time at Edinburgh with their own obsessions, instead of scouring the Fringe. Bragg weakly expressed the belief that television scouts were out and about, and later confessed that he doubted if they were. The whole situation gets progressively worse with the Fringe now at enormous numbers — 'the Largest Show on Earth' as Allen Wright has named it — where less than fifteen years ago the entire Fringe programme was listed on a single sheet. But, as its numbers rise, professional theatre directors seem more imprisoned in their offices, more dependent on the whimsical preferences of their executive secretaries, more hypnotised by the sight of forms and CVs. The one significant exception I know of is Giles Havergal, of the Glasgow Citizens' Theatre, whose lean, sardonic form habitually makes its way through the Fringe, elegantly festooning critics with charmingly rude remarks as he wings them on his progress. I doubt if there is a more delightfully deflationary companion. His balance of exquisite courtesy and a high, theocratic, wickedly hilarious dismissal of any judgments rashly made in his hearing (by those who presume to know theatre from seats in the auditorium and nests in the newspapers), ensures as improving and as exhilarating a tonic as any critic could ask. God help the innocent who compliments him on his public and professional spirit in his pilgrimages. Of course he is not being public-spirited! He is simply going to look at something out of idle curiosity, or because he has a moment, or in the light of some friend's probably idiotic recommendation, or anything other than the great work he takes so seriously and denies so mischievously. He will kid the daylights out of me for this passage, should he ever see it.

But where are the rest of them?

Chapter Six

Enter Rumour, Painted Full of Tongues

From Jerome Hynes comp., *Druid: The First Ten Years* (Galway, 1985), chapter 6, 'Giants on the Fringe' by O. D. E.:

> . . . *Druid had to plan their 1980 campaign, and while its success in the end was due to the company's excellence, its initial victories were the work of the most extraordinary public relations assault the Fringe may ever have known. It began, for those of us in Edinburgh, with a modest little letter from Jerome Hynes, arriving some time in May. As though to stress their alien character, Druid's method appeared to be that of the traditional Chinese self-abnegation whose superlative humility symbolises a pride without peer. Mr Hynes seemed to apologise for everything: for existing, for troubling the invaluable intellectualism of his recipient by the trespass of time caused by the mere opening of his envelope, for the impudence of venturing to address the recipient, for the audacity of implying that the offerings of the company could be mentioned using the same postal service that brought news of the illustrious work that normally preoccupied the critic, and so on. But Druid would be coming to the Fringe, on the last week of the Festival, at the Bedlam Theatre on Forrest Road, would be putting on certain plays, and would repeat the present unspeakable breach of the decencies by writing again nearer August.*
>
> *The critic could note that the venue was a very good one, using a well-known Edinburgh student theatre which commanded the fashionable George IV Bridge and was within minutes of Festival and Fringe Clubs. The critic would be struck by the extraordinary courtesy of the letter: almost all Fringe companies seem to compete in brashness, noisiness, crescendo of superlatives. Yet the letter, underneath all its apologies, did not apologise for one thing: there was no hint that an audience would have to make allowance for inadequacy of production. The Chinese diplomacy was convinced that it had something to sell.*
>
> *The first strike had been early: in those days few companies wrote so early to the critics, although since then a few others have learned the trick if not the tone. The second letter had much competition. Its tone was unaltered. The writer knew that his pre-eminent recipients had matters far too momentous ever to remember his earlier, doubtless contemptibly egregious epistle. He therefore would so far forget himself as to repeat contents, give a few more details of the plays, say a word about Irish successes, and again beg the recipient that if by the*

smallest possible chance the far more illustrious claims on the recipient's time permitted a visit to the Druid venue, would it be beyond the remotest reasonable limits of possibility that such a visit might be made? The company would venture to ask the critic to do it the honour of attending a reception, at which the generosity of Bailey's Irish Cream would enable some small return in liquid form to the critic for deigning to notice the existence of the utterly despicable communications of the public relations officer.

The press was not blind or deaf to the hospitality of Bailey's Irish Cream. As the English would say, the press didn't mind if it did.

So far, few critics were fooled by the self-denigration of Mr Jerome Hynes into thinking him other than the very shrewd manipulator of audience-attraction that he clearly was. But if any doubts remained about the wisdom of the serpent behind the seeming innocence of this particular dove, they dissolved with the next strike. Although the noise of Festival and blandishments of Fringe were by now reaching Niagara-like volume and force, the third letter made its way, and it carried that which ensured it pride of place in any postbag.

. . . Mr Jerome Hynes, prefacing himself with renewed and even more profound regret that yet once more o ye laurels and once more ye myrtles brown with ivy never sere he came to pluck their berries harsh and crude and with forced fingers rude shatter their leaves . . . or words to that effect, anyhow, begged to remind his utterly sublime auditors that the Druid Theatre, and its theatrical offerings thus and such, and its Bailey's Irish Cream reception, would also feature the delivery of the greetings of Her Ladyship the Mayor of Galway to His Lordship the Provost of Edinburgh! On reading which, the present writer collapsed in helpless laughter on the nearest chair. It was the neatest coup *in public relations seen at a Fringe in living memory.*

For what Mr Hynes and his associates had done was to grasp the essential point about both Festival and Fringe: they are a civic occasion. Hence what the Provost does is the big news of the Festival. . . . News editors mark his progress, as that of no other single person. Cameramen follow his daily rounds, local government journalists — quite distinct from arts reporters — will con his schedule and report his every utterance, the official Festival dogs his footsteps, the Fringe languishes for a civil leer from him. And he absolutely had to accept the greetings of his sister potentate. Edinburgh could not ignore the illustrious distinguished representation of Galway: nothing short of a one-man show in the White House War Room could stop the civic protocol from receiving the distinguished sentiments of peace and friendship.

The matter was certainly improved by the good relations now obtaining between Festival and Fringe, and by the fact that for once the Tories had produced, in Mr Tom Morgan, a Lord Provost of charm, civility and good nature with no particular anxiety to make much of his own importance. Mr Morgan did not arrive at the Bedlam under protest: he was glad to receive the embassy from Galway, and captivated by its eager and equally unpretentious members. Since the Fringe is unofficial, he had not much opportunity of making goodwill to it evident via a state visit but thanks to his Galwegian sister he might now do so, and how better than in the hands of these gentle and charming people, who seemed to make so little of themselves. The press on its side took many photographs, and decided it seemed only logical to bend its footsteps into the auditorium, having bent its elbow in the anteroom. It was in a mood to be benevolent and indulgent to the entertainment these little people were going to present before it.

But once in the theatre, a very different mood swept the audience. All of the brilliant public relations, and the discreetly invisible humour which had charged them, were set aside. We had left the world of the diplomat and entered that of the director. What was presented was theatre at once shining with simple verities, rooted in western Ireland, fiercely filio-pietistic, deeply conscious of antiquity behind its ritual as old as the druids, yet utterly modern in the perfectionism to which the director evidently aspired. Garry Hynes quite clearly believed in actors trained to a hair, in blocking and timing as precisely executed as Euclid might demand in a geometrical proposition, and in a spirit of conviction which saw theatrical performance in sacramental terms. Whatever Galway had meant to its Edinburgh audiences before they took their seats at the Bedlam, Druid had ensured that for the future it would mean professionalism.

It is an odd name, albeit, by ancestry, an Irish one to mention in the context, but Garry Hynes's direction suggests Henry James without fuss and clutter. Exactitude, nuance, scruple, subtlety, the hint of fleeting motive and mood behind the obvious convictions and actions of protagonists — these are the common ground between them. But the clarity of overriding purpose and goal distinguishes her Napoleon-like attention to detail from his labyrinthine preoccupations and occasional drowning in the minute. Her eye for the microscopic is unrivalled, but it never seems to get in the way of her sense of the totality. It was unanswerable that her work was great in 1980, and when in 1982 the company returned with Synge (the 1980 offerings were present-day work) its place on Parnassus was firm. Synge, it was argued by Lindsay Anderson, when he brought his production of The Playboy of the Western World to the Fringe in 1984, had been in danger of ossification in Dublin; but he was told plainly in his press conference that while he

151

might rival and even vanquish Dublin, the challenge before him was to reach the heights of Galway. It is no shame to him that he never came near them. I have yet to meet anyone who saw the Druid Playboy *not agreeing that, as Macaulay said of Boswell's* Johnson, Eclipse *is first and the rest nowhere. . . .*

Self on long-distance telephone to Galway, 1985: I hope you're printing the lot?
Jerome Hynes, compiler: Well, I — I wanted to cut out the bit about me but *they* wouldn't let me.

T HE SEARCH FOR PUBLICITY ON THE FRINGE HAS TAKEN MANY forms in its time, and we must think of the heartbreak and despair its lack fastens on so many decent, dedicated company members, of the productions meriting recognition yet sent homeward without notices, without audiences and without a cent. Allen Wright does what he can, the *Festival Times* despite the vagaries of its priorities under successive régimes does what it can. *The List*, begun in the mid-1980s under former *Festival Times* editors, goes far afield; now that the London *Independent* reporters have given up going to all the same productions at once they get some distance around; *The Guardian* extends its coverage as well as its generous heart will permit; and those of the London press capable of going beyond the Traverse Theatre, the Assembly Rooms and the Oxbridge Universities sometimes find rare nuggets. BBC Radio covers a great deal, local radio has rather dried up after promising saturation in the mid-1980s, TV makes a great nuisance of itself to singularly little comprehensive effect; but we all know we should have seen the ones that got away. Nobody has obtained more thorough coverage of the Fringe than Allen Wright, and he remains the most bitterly conscious of all arts editors and reporters of the number of shows which elude his resources. One of the few times I have seen him blazing with rage was when some idiot (whose name I think was Pile) informed the readers of *The Sunday Times* one week into the Festival that he had seen every show on the Fringe. It was only a joke, and its principal message to me was that the standards of humour fashionable in Mr Murdoch's prints are on the same level as their standards of integrity, but if ever a god cursed a dunghill fly, Allen Wright was that god. And what lent wings to his fury was the thought of those unfortunates whose work *The Scotsman*, for all its desperate efforts, would never see.

In the mid-1970s, before the breakdown of marital ties and family structures had become an accepted social norm, there was the possibility of public denunciation on grounds of filth and/or impertinence to the Royal Family. Certain local councillors of this period made themselves conspicuous by what they took to be vote-catching Philippics. Of these the most famed was Councillor John Kidd, whose unrelenting war against filth made him something of a local tourist object. I was not in the country when he was said to have denounced Christopher Marlowe's *Edward II*, then in production — in the Diamand régime, to its honour — with Ian McKellen in the title-rôle, as more of this filth churned out by present-day London pornographers, but I certainly recall how a Fringe show bereft of houses tearfully confided its plight to a kindly *Evening News* reporter who promptly phoned the councillor, demanded and got a denunciation, subsequently answered the councillor's query (before putting down the phone) as to what it was he had condemned, and justly received the grateful thanks of the company whose ticket-sales rocketed.

The Right Hon. Sir Nicholas Fairbairn, MP, then still in quest of the titles he subsequently obtained, made a gallant attempt to usurp a patriot's all-atoning name — and no doubt he had his reasons as to his urgent necessity for atonement — by denouncing in 1977 a Fringe show of Medway origin, *The Tragedy of King Charles III*, alleging it intended to make a vicious attack on the Royal Family (powerless to protect themselves against the insidious and evil personal calumny since the play, in pseudo-Shakespearean verse, treated of Elizabethan abdication, Caroline *mésalliance* and familial reactions). The company sold every ticket and then issued a press release consisting of a letter which thanked them for the courtesy in sending the signatory a copy of their script, said that he had read it with enormous enjoyment, hoped that they would have a most successful run for their production, and remained theirs sincerely Charles, Prince of Wales. How Sir Nicholas later brought himself to accept a place in government alongside Mr Douglas Hurd, part-author of a romance in which King Charles III is kidnapped and manhandled, is as yet unknown.

Faynia Williams, a considerable authority on modern Russian literature and drama, inspired her husband Richard Crane to adapt for the stage Mikhail Bulgakov's *The Master and Margarita* under the name *Satan's Ball* which Faynia then directed in the Bedlam, throwing up three levels of stage with a nude crucified Christ at the far back top, stage right. The production showed the theatre possibilities of the Bedlam which thereafter ceased to be a mere venue for teach-in meetings and staged readings. Richard Crane, son of a charming High Anglican priest, worked with constructive artistry on Bulgakov's powerful religious themes, including questions as to the accuracy of St Matthew as evangelist, while the Devil, with his attendant cat, proved the — well, it is the only word — catalyst of the proceedings. But the then Moderator of the General Assembly of the Church of Scotland denounced *Satan's Ball* without, of course, having seen it. This too sold every ticket. Faynia, I recall, was annoyed by the business, having no need for this sort of assistance what with the Cranes' by now unmatched reputation as Fringe stars, the unquestionable box-office attraction of the play's name, the excellence of the location and the voracity of the press to cover it. What she had done was to produce a celebration of Soviet literature together with a denunciation of the stifling banality of Soviet bureaucracy, and she had every right to want the discussion focused on the several themes. Inevitably the necessary seminal reflections for which she had hoped were subordinated to the controversy, and here am I now dragging the matter in under this head. Regardless of the Moderator or myself, it was one of the finest, most innovative, most thought-provoking and most resourceful productions the Fringe has known.

Sometimes these attacks were nauseous enough to outweigh box-office advantages that might accrue from them. In the late 1970s Morgan's predecessor as Tory Lord Provost launched a violent attack on the theatre company Gay Sweatshop, who were then performing in the Heriot-Watt Theatres opposite the Royal Lyceum in Grindlay Street. He announced to a reception of his Festival guests that the production would merely act as a pick-up joint for maurauding homosexuals. Ian Dunn, the Edinburgh Gay Liberation leader, sent a letter to the *Festival Times* denouncing this attack — in fact it was an appalling insult to at least two of the guests at the reception, Ian McKellen and Derek Jacobi, who were supporters of Gay Sweatshop — and pointing out, perfectly correctly, that Gay Sweatshop under its leading writer Drew Griffiths (whose *As Time Goes By* performed a great cultural service in illuminating a deliberately obscured European past as to the experience, extent and destruction of the gay community) was deeply hostile to promiscuity in its creed, but that if the Lord Provost wanted to know what was the leading upmarket pick-up joint in the Festival for gays in quest of something more than an ordinary friendship, the answer was the Festival Club, then in the Assembly Rooms, patron the Lord Provost.

The following year *Festival Times*, in want of some satirical squib, besought me for copy and I wrote them a piece of genial tripe to the effect that Gay Sweatshop were scheduled to bring up a play about a man who openly admits himself to be a Lord Provost, that it was predicted this would lead to widespread demands to close down the Fringe, that Fringe Administrator Aristotle Muppet (i.e. Alistair Moffat, Milligan's successor) had said that while he had never knowingly met a Lord Provost we had to face it that there were Lord Provosts and people were entitled to be Lord Provosts if they wanted to be and, let's face it, Lord Provosts were here to stay, but 'the Moderator of the Generous Assembly of the Church of Scotland was outraged, although it is not yet known by whom'. Unfortunately *Festival Times* in one of its more catastrophically cloth-headed moments printed the item on its front (news) page, and Gay Sweatshop, naturally sensitive to lies at its expense in every quarter, denounced the story as a fabrication, insisting that it had no plans whatsoever to produce on the Fringe a play about a self-confessed Lord Provost. I think we failed to retract.

Pope Pius IX, asked to assist a struggling Catholic author, is said to have offered to place his works on the *Index Librorum Prohibitorum* on the ground that this would make him a best-seller.

But however far this may have inadvertently imposed on an innocent public, it was as moonlight unto sunlight, as water unto wine, when compared to the career of Anton Krashny. I apologise to old sweats, gay or otherwise, to whom the story is also old — and whose vigilance will I trust pardon any omissions of substance — but it has become painfully clear to me that Krashny has returned to the obscurity from which he never actually emerged. If I had any decency, I would shut up about it.

The story begins at a Scottish Television Festival party . . .

Mathematical problem, for pupils of aptitude but as yet wanting discretion:

> If all the money expended on Festival parties were to be put to the subvention of Fringe productions, how many Fringe shows would balance their books?
> *(The Invigilator will provide an accountant on request.)*

The 'Authorised' Version:

And it came to pass that the Caledonian Clark Tait, he that is now gathered to his fathers but was marvelled at by mankind for that he did produce and present for the Scotch nation images of divers persons of cult, of culture, of horticulture, and of exhorticulture, held converse with the wise woman of the South, who calleth herself Joan Bakewell, and hath a smile of dark wizardry holding the multitudes in thrall, both the men and even also the women, and into their midst there came a young man who is now perched in the seats of the scornful but whose name is haply hid from the mind of man, and whatsoever they might say they had seen, the young man had seen it, and whatsoever they might say they had heard, the young man also had heard it, and whatsoever they might say they had done, yea the young man saith that he doeth it also.

And the tempter troubled Clark Tait in his heart, and the knees of Clark Tait were loosened, and he gave his consent, and spake to the woman, and said he wept him sorely that men looked not upon the exhibition of Krashny.

And he closed upon himself his left eye that its closing might be looked upon by Joan Bakewell, whose eye seeth all things. But the young man saw it not.

And Joan Bakewell looked into her heart, and poured forth in praise of Krashny, and the signs and wonders he had given that a new mystery was at hand.

And Clark Tait made oath, and swore that he would that all exhibitions on which the city looked might be placed in one scale, and the prophecies of Krashny given in paint and in pencil within the other, and the scale of Krashny would prevail and go down, even unto the limits of the scale, whereof it might break, so great was the weight of the work of Krashny.

156

And Joan Bakewell sighed that it was even so, and that a judgment would yet fall upon the city and all who made their pilgrimage within its walls, for that they had used Krashny contumeliously, paying no heed to his epiphany among them.

And the young man burst forth, fearing lest his bowels would break within him, and cried that he also had seen the marvels of Krashny, and had bowed down and adored them, saving only that he misgave him at Krashny's rashness in wantonly giving voice to the accursed pestilence of neo-reductionalist post-impossibilism.

And Clark Tait and Joan Bakewell bowed their heads and went their ways, and their hearts were light within them, for that the young man had shown himself to their gaze in the whiteness of his sepulchritude.

And encountering divers of their acquaintance they spoke of Krashny and that he held his being neither above the earth, nor on earth, nor under the earth, save only now in the mind of the young man in his lusting for honour by his fidelity to any fair wind that bloweth itself.

And they sought the young man's likeness in Gath and in every citadel of the Philistines, and found none calling himself Philistine who in emptiness and fraud waxed with eloquence sufficient to be his fellow. And they laughed him to scorn.

And the young man rose into oblivion. And his name no man knoweth, save perchance himself, for the beloved eyes of Clark Tait are closed in death. And Joan Bakewell will disclose it in no wise.

And when the faithful gathered once more to make Festival, they made secure search for the Philistines among them by wicked speech tempting them to learned discourse of Krashny.

And Richard of the Italian children of Mark had voyaged among the Poles whereof Krashny was named as a son (but of the blood of the children of the holy Stephen of Hungary), and spake of his encounter with Krashny in the valley of the Vistula. And Michael, that was the son of the poet Hugh of the tribe of Diarmaid, whom men call Christopher the Grieve, spake of Krashny also, and of his voyage to the house of the poet, and of his knowledge of a maidservant within that house, and of the child she bore him. Or if they spake not these things, yet others deposed that they spake them.

And in the fullness of time the faithful grew sated with Krashny, even unto the backs of their teeth. For they had other whips and scorpions in wait for the Philistines.

157

And the Beautiful, Beautiful People visited the name of Krashny and all who had called upon his name, with sore stripes. For lo! they who had given accord to their witness of Krashny, when the scales fell from their eyes were fain to cry aloud to all the world that Krashny was a jest, yea such as the Philistines make, and this they had known even within their mothers' womb, those of the Beautiful, Beautiful People who confessed themselves to be of woman born. And further they said, and spake truly, that Peter Diamand cared for none of these things.

And for a space Krashny was silent.

The Hemingway Version

'What's the news?' he said.

'I don't know,' one of the men said. 'What's the news, Rod?'

'I don't know any news,' said Rod.

'Come on,' he said. 'You know me.'

'What kind of news?' said Rod.

'The Poles are rising,' said the first man.

'Oh, to hell with the Poles,' he said. 'Everything I want's the Festival. Who's gotten egg on his face? Who's done something he wouldn't want our readers to know?'

'So you can tell them,' said Rod.

'That's right,' he said. 'So I can tell them.'

'Nothing except the Poles,' said the first man.

'Who cares about the Poles?' he said. 'I bet you don't know any Poles.'

'I know Krashny,' Rod said.

'We all know Krashny,' said the first man.

'I don't know Krashny,' he said. 'Is he a Festival visitor?'

'You don't know Krashny?' said the first man.

'I don't know Krashny,' he said.

'He doesn't know Krashny,' said Rod. 'You new to the Festival?'

'I'm not new to the Festival,' he said. 'I know the Festival. I know this town. This is a hot town.'

'He knows this town,' said Rod.

'Then why doesn't he know Krashny?' said the first man.

'Krashny isn't here,' said Rod.

'Is he coming here?' he asked. 'To the Festival?'

'I guess he's coming here, at that,' said the first man. 'I guess he's got to come here. The Poles are revolting. He's got to come here.'

'Is Krashny revolting?' he asked.

'Krashny's always been revolting,' said Rod. 'As long as I've known him Krashny has been revolting.'

'He's coming here to the Festival?' he asked.

'I guess so,' said the first man.

'Where else?' said Rod.

'Who does he know?' he asked. 'He's got to know someone or else he wouldn't come.'

'They say he stayed with Chris Grieve when he was here before,' Rod said.

'But Chris Grieve is dead,' he said. 'He died two years ago.'

'That's right,' said the first man. 'Chris Grieve is dead.'

'He can't come to the Festival unless he's invited,' he said. 'If it's the official Festival he's coming to. Unless it was Demarco who invited him. But if Demarco invited him, it should be in the Fringe programme.'

'Maybe there wasn't time for Demarco to put it in the Fringe programme,' Rod said.

'That's right,' said the first man. 'The Poles weren't revolting when they made the Fringe programme.'

'Except Krashny,' said Rod.

'But nobody knew that then,' he said. 'I didn't know it then.'

'Bright boy,' said the first man. 'So it can't be Demarco.'

'Is it Drummond,' he said, 'is it John Drummond?'

'If Krashny is flying here as the representative of revolting Poland at the Edinburgh International Festival,' said Rod, 'I guess Drummond would need to be the one to ask him. Diamand left two years ago.'

'So where will he stay?' he said. 'With Drummond?'

'Maybe not with Drummond,' Rod said. 'Drummond has a lot of visitors as it is.'

'Krashny isn't too easy to have in the house,' said the first man. 'They say when he stayed with Chris Grieve he got the maid pregnant.'

'Drummond wouldn't want him to do that,' he said.

'No,' Rod said. 'I guess he wouldn't.'

'Maybe he's going to stay with his illegitimate child,' he said. 'People don't have maids nowadays so it must have happened a long time ago. The kid must be grown up now. Is it a girl or a boy?'

'Mike didn't say it was a boy,' the first man said.

'So it's a girl,' he said. 'Does anyone have her phone number?'

'I don't have her phone number,' said the first man.

'Do you have a phone number, Rod?' he asked.

'Yes,' said Rod. 'I have a phone number.'

'Then give me the phone number,' he said. Rod gave him the phone number.

'This will arouse a lot of interest,' he said. 'Krashny's a famous name, the most famous Polish name at the Edinburgh Festival.'

'I guess you might say that,' said the first man.

'What's his first name?' he asked. 'What's his Christian name?'

'I guess it's Anton,' said the first man.

'Yes, of course,' he said. 'When exactly did he make his name at the Festival?'

'It's a few years ago now,' said the first man. 'An exhibit of his caused a lot of comment.'

'He was acclaimed,' he said.

'That's right,' said Rod. 'He was acclaimed.'

'I can't waste any more time with you people,' he said. 'I've a phone call to make.' He went off to the phone.

'That's your phone number he's calling,' said the first man.

'That's right,' said Rod. 'He asked me if I had a phone number, and I have, so I gave it to him.'

'There won't be any answer,' said the first man. 'There's nobody there.'

'No, I guess not,' said Rod. 'Wait a minute. There is this girl. She asked if she could crash down for a few nights.'

'And therefore never send to know for whom the bell tolls,' said the first man.

The bell rang several times. The girl was asleep. She awoke and found the phone.

'Rebecca here,' she said.

'Rebecca Krashny?' he asked.

The girl giggled. 'I guess that's about right,' she said.

'Are you illegitimate?' he asked.

160

'I am,' she said. She was.

'What work do you do now?' he asked.

'I'm working for the Edinburgh Festival at the moment,' she said. She was working on the temporary staff of the Festival.

'So John Drummond is going to greet Krashny officially when he flies in from Poland,' he said.

'If he has time,' she said. 'John Drummond has a very busy schedule.'

'If he can't get to the airport himself, he'll send his assistant,' he said.

'I suppose that's right,' she said.

'What will Krashny do when he gets here?' he asked.

'He'll want his dinner,' she said. She was hungry.

'Of course, he must have a dinner in his honour,' he said. 'John Drummond will be there. Your father's an artist, so *The Scotsman* will send Emilio Coia. And Richard Demarco will be present. And Mike Grieve. Are you looking forward to seeing your father?'

'Yes, of course,' she said.

'He's a great man,' he said. 'A very great man. You must be very proud.'

'I am,' she said.

'One of the foremost artists in Poland,' he said. 'It's the least we can do for the Poles, after all. They're going through a terrible time. I suppose the situation is pretty hopeless, and that's why Krashny has to fly to safety.'

'I suppose it must be,' she said.

'I must go now,' he said. 'I have a phone call to make.'

The Glasgow Evening Times *Version*

There were six columns on the front page of the Glasgow *Evening Times*, and the headline ran across five columns for its first two words, the remaining three words restricted to four columns with the story's lead running alongside them. 'TOP POLE FLEES TO SAFETY,' it roared at the hesitating purchaser. 'DRAMATIC DASH TO SCOT-LAND' nestled in one column above 'TOP'. 'EXCLUSIVE' it asserted, unnecessarily, in white capitals on black, artistically contrasting with black type on the page's white for the story. And the report began in solemnly black leaded type:

> A DISSIDENT smuggled out of Poland is on his way to Scotland to seek political asylum.

'Anton Krashny,' it proceeded, 'has been under house arrest at Kracow for three weeks, ever since industrial unrest hit Poland. A painter,' (it continued in smaller type) 'he was to have gone to Edinburgh to attend a dinner in his honour on Thursday night.'

The dinner was reported as now intended for transformation into 'a political affair with Krashny's appeal for asylum and also a plea to the Polish government to settle with the strikers and resist any Russian interference'.

Breathlessly, it revealed: 'Krashny's daughter, Rebecca, is in Edinburgh awaiting her father's arrival. When I told her today that her father was out of Poland, she said — "Thank God. I was beginning to think I would never see him again."'

With a slightly chilling indifference to its value to the authorities in Poland supposedly detaining Krashny, the report then announced the intention that he make his way to Belgium whence he would be flown 'in a light plane' to Scone airfield. Roddy Martine, editor of *Scottish Field*, was then quoted, apparently though not allegedly indicating him as discloser of the plan: 'We were hoping that we'd get Krashny out of Poland secretly — but this might now work out for the best if he is determined not to go back.' 'This' was presumably to have been interpreted as the inevitability of a report in the Glasgow *Evening Times*.

The dinner, it emerged, was scheduled for Thursday in the 369 Gallery. John Drummond, Joan Bakewell and Emilio Coia were mentioned as 'among the guests'.

'Krashny, a Marxist,' continued the story, 'lived and painted in Scotland at one time.' He was credited by the reporter with a wife in Poland but also with having 'lived with a woman' in an Islay croft. The report, continuing on page sixteen, announced that 'Rebecca was born there' but now gave her an English domicile. She was stated to have taken up Edinburgh employment in an office, temporarily, and was quoted:

'I last saw my father a few months ago.

'I honestly thought that when the troubles started in Poland and he was put under house arrest I would never see him again.

'I work and live as a poet. I know that somewhere in Poland my father has another family — a girl older than me and triplets younger than me, two girls and a boy.

'Archbishop Hume of Westminster has been in touch with me about my father, and I think has tried to help him through the Polish Roman Catholic Church.'

The remainder of the story was given the capitalised crosshead 'ACTIVE' (the only previous crosshead, similarly printed and set out, entitled 'ROUTE' as preface to the escape plan).

Krashny was entitled 'head of an arts foundation in Cracow', thus varying the spelling. The Thursday diners were 'mainly members of the foundation'. Krashny was assigned successive domiciles in Islay, Arran and Plockton (Wester Ross) 'where he continued painting', and subsequently New Mexico and Bolivia 'before returning to Poland where he was active in the Polish underground revolutionary movement'. The final paragraph disclosed that Krashny 'was befriended when he was in Scotland by Hugh MacDiarmid', helpfully identifying the latter for readers as 'the left wing Scottish poet'.

The first column of the front page was given over to advertisement — 'NEXT WEEK IN YOUR SUPER TIMES'; 'PLAY THE NAME GAME', 'WIN £500 IN A GREAT FREE CONTEST', and 'FANCY A HOLIDAY IN DRACULA COUNTRY?'. A boxed item on the front page to the story's right, headed 'YOUR TIMES', expressed regret at inability to publish 'pictures, cartoons and the crossword' because of an industrial dispute. To the right of the end of the story was a report that 'Seven toilet seats have been stolen' from a workers' hostel extension in Cumbernauld. The police requested that 'anyone with information' help them with their enquiries. 'We are investigating the thefts,' the police spokesman was quoted as asserting: 'Police are certainly not sitting down on this matter.' The report was captioned 'Who Lifted Them?'.

No further mention of Anton Krashny appears to have been made in subsequent issues of the Glasgow *Evening Times*.

1978 was The Year of the Libel. It began entirely outwith the Fringe. The Royal Lyceum Theatre had been closed for refurbishment, a complaint to which it succumbs from time to time, and, on its reopening, much was made of somewhat depressing interior decoration and even more of a new chandelier generously provided by the munificence of Carlsberg Lager. On 22 August Allen Wright began his review of the first Festival offering in the reopened theatre: 'The Lyceum's splendid new chandelier failed to light up last night but the Malaya Bronnaya Company from Moscow made up for this deficiency by giving a sparkling performance of Gogol's comedy, *The Marriage*.' On 23 August his review of the Royal Shakespeare Company's *Twelfth Night* at Daniel Stewart's and Melville College, a reflective, hilarious presentation which nevertheless strongly fore-shadowed the period of tragedy with which Shakespeare followed it, concluded its plaudits for Ian McKellen's Sir Toby Belch and the work of his colleagues with the words:

> . . . I must clear up some confusion about the Carlsberg new chandelier in the Lyceum Theatre to which I referred in yesterday's review of 'The Marriage'. The contractor who installed this ornament almost blew a fuse when he read that it had failed to light up. There was nothing wrong with it, he protested. It was just not switched on — a ceremony which for some strange reason is to be performed next Monday, instead of at the beginning of the Festival.

The contractor had threatened proceedings for defamation, and *The Scotsman* Board had ordered that an apology be printed, enjoying the same prominence as the innocent statement which had excited objurgation. Allen Wright had responded with characteristic dignity, charm and honour, but the 'I must' was revealing. He was as destitute of malice to the contractor, or to the man who turned on the chandelier at the Royal Lyceum Theatre as he is to anyone else. (His spleen was removed by surgical operation some years ago and the medical interest it excited resulted in its remaining on display in the Edinburgh Royal College of Surgeons to this day, to witness if I lie). In my capacity as his Court Fool, I sent him the following to cheer him up, and he was kind enough to say it did:

Carlsberg is my darling,
My darling, my darling,
Carlsberg is my darling,
The New Chandelier!

But if the King of the Fringe critics was thus to be forced into retraction by an individual not even connected with a Fringe company, what future might this not offer on the Fringe? The Year of the Libel was also the Day of the Jackal. It is doubtful if any of the multitude who subsequently swept to the portals of their much more financially prosperous theatrical rivals, the Courts of Law, had any anticipation of monetary returns from the pleading of their various causes, bar one or two lunatics. As Sherlock Holmes remarked, 'There are always lunatics about. It would be a dull world without them.' But what the punctual penitence of *The Scotsman* had proved was that, properly managed, additional publicity was available in answer to a judiciously managed threat of libel. The optimum circumstance would be if defamatory statements could be alleged in a *favourable* review, since this would draw further attention to an antecedent circumstance also redounding to the credit of the production.

Four cases stick in the mind. There was a company called Andy Jordan's Bristol Express Theatre Company performing at the Heriot-Watt Theatres with a revue called *The Naughtiest Girl in the School*, a title familiar to students of the work of the late Enid Blyton, but presumably carrying certain post-Blytonian connotations, self-described in the Fringe list as 'Exposé! The Directors, Performers, Musicians who created *Jump* (1976), *Bristol Cream* (1977) now reveal . . .'. And there was another company with a name of greater antiquity, Bristol Revunions, whose offerings in 1977 had included a Fringe First winner, Maxim Gorky's *A Respectable Family* and whose 1978 revue was *Pay As You Enter*, self-described in the Fringe list, 'You sprang to *Jump* (1976), poured into *Bristol Cream* (1977), now conduct yourselves to the new Bristol Revue'. This company performed at the Transport Hall, Annandale Street, off Leith Walk. *The Financial Times*, apparently in perfect innocence, described one revue as the heir of *Bristol Cream*, whereupon the other company threatened that sober journal with the law, on the ground that its own product was the true heir of *Bristol Cream* and all others were counterfeit, or possibly synthetic.

There was a journalist of international antecedents and ostensible outlets who in 1977 had applied for Festival press tickets from Iain Crawford, who had provided him with the same. Failing to discover any evidence of any of these having received any discussion from the journalist in question, in any public print or system of public broadcasting, Crawford refused his application for tickets in 1978. The journalist now commenced legal proceedings on the ground that the refusal of complimentary press tickets constituted defamation.

I, wishing to find some novel method of praise for the performance of an actress in the National Student Theatre Company's *Savage Amusement*, a new play in rather ragged production, offered the somewhat cumbersome salutation that she had proved herself either a very good actress or a very nasty person, 'and I would not care to bet which'. And the *deus in machina*, a gentleman whose student days were even langer syne than my own, informed *The Scotsman* that this statement was libellous to the young lady. *The Scotsman* Board's apology on this occasion seemed to my bemused eyes to have hit the stands almost before the later editions in which my notice appeared, which speed would the more easily enable interested persons to turn back to the original fairly favourable review of the production.

The *Festival Times*, by now edited by Steve Cooke (1977-79), administered an undoubted slating to the Cambridge Footlights revue. Cambridge held a justly great name in Festival and Fringe, having produced John Drummond, Ian McKellen, Richard Crane, and, among my own colleagues on the staff of the University occasionally writing in the *Festival Times*, Roger Savage and Frank Bechhofer. Few of these men had graced the Footlights, but others had, as was to be made clear by the subsequent display of comparable talents in the Cabinets of the Thatcher Administration. Whatever the merits of the Footlights in former times, both Cambridge and Oxford were apt to trade on their past to a degree which became counter-productive, resembling the efforts of a once-great vineyard making the best of a bad year. The Cambridge Footlights sued the *Festival Times* for the slating. I forget whether it received an apology. If it did, I doubt if it was at the direction or with the consent of the Board, on which I was still a co-opted member. In fact, the *Festival Times* in its last number that year reviewed the libel season, rather unfavourably, and noted perfectly correctly that the last person to telephone Allen

Wright had been informed coldly that the season was now officially closed, which so shattered the interlocutor that he collapsed on the instant.

As I recall, the *Festival Times* published a hypocritical expression of sympathy for persons not sued in this particular year. The instances of declared intentions of litigation I have given here are only a vulgar fraction of the whole. There has been no general outbreak since, although a few cases still surface from time to time. Allen Wright more recently took the precaution of sending a second reviewer in isolated complaints of unfairness, with the specific understanding that unless the offending notice proved unjustifiable no second review could appear, given the pressure on *Scotsman* space. The latter proviso eliminates those merely in quest of additional publicity. *The Scotsman* Board must have been persuaded by him that their promptitude in apology had been abused, and was indeed being assumed as inevitable. Second reviewers on such occasions have never to my knowledge dissented from the opinion to which the offended company had taken exception, save occasionally to remark that they would have put the objurgations more strongly. The sad part of the story is that very occasionally there may surface a rogue reviewer, though I know of none ever employed by Allen Wright; such a person, sequacious of a reputation for 'hard-hitting' or 'toughness', or some other of the Fascistoid rhetoric with which we are plagued in the long shadow of Thatcherism, deliberately rubbishes Fringe productions deserving a far better fate. Against such a traitor to critical standards there is little a company can do, for if a person should deliberately choose malignancy as a means of professional advancement, he would naturally learn as rapidly as possible the art of framing the most wounding language in such a form that the law permits of no redress. But if creatures of this kind crawl around the Fringe, they have a short life on it. The pay is far too low for their ambitions, and the hard slog destroys the endurance of anyone who cannot love the legitimate hopes of performers. I have seen some of the most venomous journalists of my acquaintance transformed into philanthropists by a good Fringe production.

Chapter Seven

Faithful to Thee, Fringe, (partly) in Thy Fashion

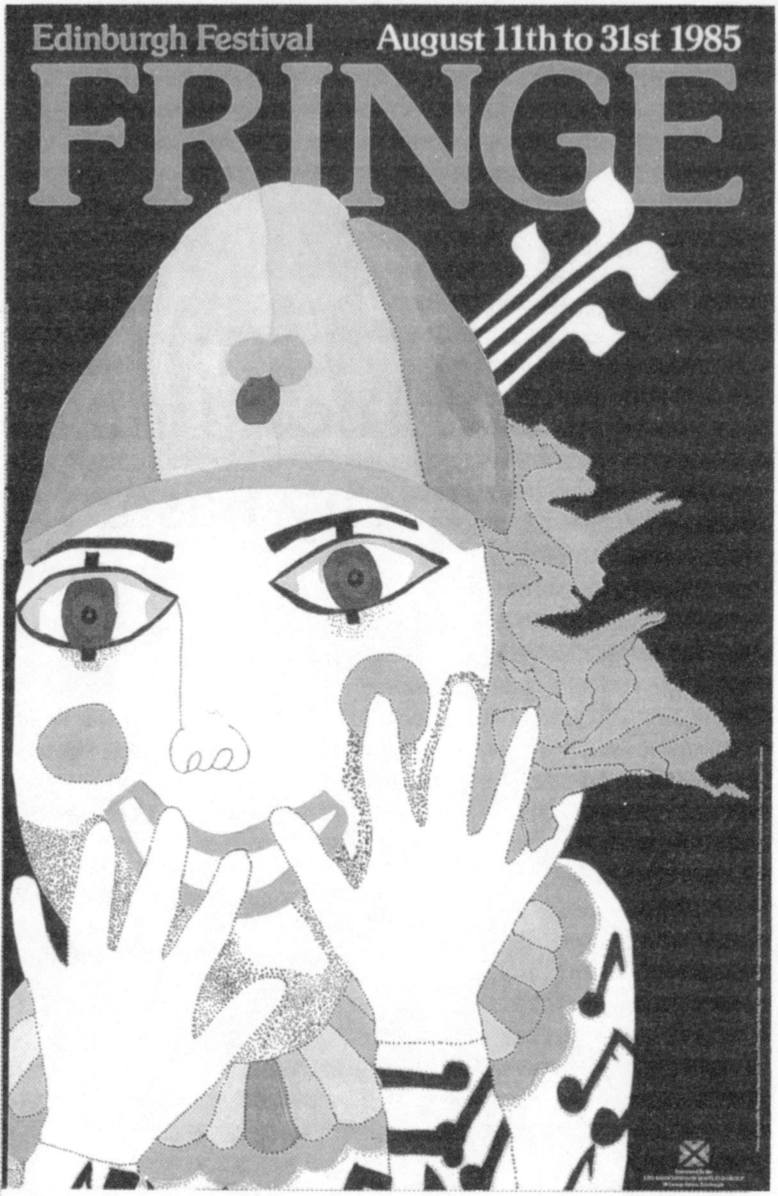
Edinburgh Festival
August 11th to 31st 1985
FRINGE

From Walter B. Scott, 'Chicago Letter', *Furioso*, Summer 1949, reprinted in Dwight Macdonald ed., *Parodies* (1960):

Where is the answer to be found?

It is clearly not to be found in the Chicago theatre. In the commodity houses of the Loop one is faced (inevitably) with pure Kitsch *— ill-made well-made plays, well-made ill-made plays, tepidly performed before drowsy lower-middle-brow audiences which wake into sudden anxious laughter at bathroom jokes, then sink back into the somnolence of the damned.*

The best theatre in Chicago was available (I use 'was' here in its sense of past tense 'to be') very distant from the Loop, in an abandoned warehouse on the Far North-west Side, where one climbed four flights of condemned wooden stairs to a makeshift hall under a decaying roof. The second-hand seats in the orchestra, gnawed incessantly by rats, were scantily occupied by bewildered bourgeois couples and drunken slummers from the Gold Coast. The rickety balcony was packed with sullen students, who showed little interest in what was going on, little sign of the passion for theatre which may once have possessed them.

Máire Ní Laoghaire took me one night to see Jean-Jean Baroque act Jeremy Irk's Les Voyeurs de Rogers Park, *in Irk's own extraordinary translation. This is (in some respects) a puzzling play and, until I have read the script, I shall not venture to pronounce a final judgment on it. 'Mordant, plangent, repellent' (in Máire Ní Laoghaire's phrase), it is at once strikingly astringent, yet rather like warm marshmallows. There are eight acts (five of them, of course, in verse) of which the first three, played in a blackout, are almost hauntingly rhetorical. But more than any other play I have seen in years (in London, Paris, New York, Rome, Moscow, Stambouli, Narvik, that is), Irk's drama comes to close grips with certain deeply imbedded constituents of the American myth — particularly various suburban* rites de passage *reminiscent — at first hearing, in any event — of those which Rudge observed in Lower Borneo. I am persuaded, however, that Irk's parallel between Salmon P. Chase and the Corn God may be at once too tenuous and too obvious.*

But I shall not attempt to summarise the play here — the fourth and seventh acts are to appear in the winter-summer Peristalsis *— because I wish to comment rather on the amazing art of Baroque. An ugly little man, with a whisky baritone which engaged one like a wood rasp (I have heard that he had been — at one time — a bouncer in the Pump*

Room), he was able to transmute himself into an entire world of characters, none of them conventional and all of them complex. In the course of the action he was by turns (one could almost swear simultaneously, and this may, indeed, have been in large measure the clef *of his achievement) an existentialist high-school junior, a 'bop' xylophonist, a sentimental police sergeant, a sort of philosophy professor, a myopic anthropologist, Raskolnikov's ghost, and the oldest sadist in Rogers Park. Baroque made impressively little use of his body: 'He seems,' Máire Ní Laoghaire told me, 'somehow to do it all with his skin.' Did Baroque betray the sense of plight? There was no time for me to ascertain an answer to this question.*

It may, very possibly, have been a greater tragedy for the Chicago stage, and for our decomposing culture in general, than we yet realise, when (two days after my visit, as it happened) the theatre suddenly caved in, and Baroque (with his entire company), three bourgeois couples, a sodden débutante and her elderly lover, innumerable rats, and the balconyful of students were plunged four flights into a flooded basement. All of them were crushed to death, or drowned. I cannot (it seems to me) escape the conviction that this incident was a further token of the city's fate — perhaps (though, of course, by no means certainly) more momentous than most.

WHAT THE POET WORDSWORTH MIGHT HAVE THOUGHT OF THE Fringe is fortunately more remote from our apprehension than what songs the sirens sang, and even more (on the Fringe) than what name Achilles took when he hid himself among women. In bleaker moments, as the critic hurries from one disaster to the next, it is not Wordsworth but his lakemate Coleridge who seems apposite: 'And a thousand thousand slimy things/Lived on; and so did I.' But the sentiment is rare. The next production cannot but be better. Wordsworth comes to mind in the effort to see the Fringe as a totality. It is its own pantheism. It is monstrous, it is magnificent. It may seem a mountain urgently pursuing the stolen boat of a critic but, probably like Wordsworth's mountain, what it wants is not retribution but attention. A few of its number may thirst for retribution, but even there any pursuit is a demand for attention.

So sing, my Fringe, that I may gain some purchase on the impossible and behold you in your entirety! You are people not buildings. Outside of the Traverse, scarcely one company of your number perpetually inhabits the space you choose in your season. And when you go, the buildings for the most part become the shadows of themselves, their eleven-month routine, however useful or admirable, haunted by the vitality with which they redound in that other month. The Bedlam will sustain something of its enFringement during University terms, maybe with results superior to those produced by its summer company and summer tenants, and maybe not. The Traverse will hold the Fringe spirit while it is open: is it not a child of the Fringe itself? The Demarco Gallery will chiefly be given over to paintings, drawings, exhibitions and Creation knows what, but wherever Demarco himself may be, there is Festival. The George Square Theatre will produce ambitious and unusual opera, and sublet itself for grand enterprising school extravaganzas, and house Freshman lectures, but its ghosts will have younger feet and their dramas the inspired interpretation of children in history, their sufferings, exploitation and alienation, spun from the wizardry of Jeremy James Taylor. The Adam House Theatre in Chambers Street will see a few elegant studio productions, and slumber in June in grateful darkness while examination candidates bake in its upper storeys. The Netherbow in the Canongate will host puppet shows or an occasional production from a new playwright or a class of drama students, few of whom are likely to employ the little upper stage which American Festival Theatre once transformed for Shimon Wincelberg's *Undertow* into a World War II combat aircraft, whence Andy McCutcheon, as a US pilot, parachuted on to the main stage, itself transformed into a desert island whose other inhabitant would prove a soldier in the Japanese army. Theatre Workshop, far to the north on Hamilton Place in Stockbridge, will house various productions, few of them likely to involve sheets of an incontinent senile patient whose impact on them was once left under the reproachful vision of successive audiences for the main duration of what seemed a fine but undirected play. And there will be other productions, intermittently theatrical. But there will also be a great silence.

Do the several lodges of Freemasons still hold their strange rituals of whose origin so few of the members dream, in the halls which in August echo to rituals much younger and much older than theirs? The secrecy of their order proscribes any information. Yet their custody of the ghosts of Fringe productions is not inapposite: Edinburgh is a town whose most remarkable layout and architecture arose under wise Masonic influence in the eighteenth century, for the greater enablement of culture to flourish. The lodges house their own ghosts also: somewhere in the shadows of Canongate Lodge Kilwinning smile the phantoms of the great painter Henry Raeburn and of the great burglar William Brodie, both of them appropriate influences for productions reaching their most *avant-garde* in the later 1980s under the Shadow Syndicate. More I may not say: the order and the Pope, at odds in so much else, join in interdicting my more profound enquiries. And what pious works now find their making in the church halls of a divided Christendom, works set on foot by virtuous persons some of whom may spare a passing thought for their August follies under somewhat but not altogether different evangelisation from fantastic nomads? The leisure centres are once more themselves, secure in the pursuit of leisurely activities unlikely to be touched by intellectual disturbance of the kind their Augusts bring to birth. Not all of these will awaken again to the monomania of directors, the narcissism of actors, the frenzy of stage managers, and the *Welt-schmerz* of prompters, and some are lost to the Fringe for admirable reasons. Ibsen's *When We Dead Awaken* realised the illusion of its mountain when I saw it in St Francis's Church Hall, on Bristo Street, diagonally across from the Bedlam and across the skate-boarders' pleasure-ground from the Fringe Club, but I do not mourn its lack of a theatrical successor, for it found one of greater reality in the mission now established there for the down-and-outs.

But where is the Lyceum Studio where once Sandy Neilson directed a hilarious fantasy on Picasso's supposed possession of the stolen *Mona Lisa*? Ask Edinburgh District Council. Where is the Hole in the Ground on which arose the Circuit tent whose profusion of offerings impinged with over-successful acoustics one on another? Ask those votaries of a dubious progress, the *soi-disant* developers. Where are the Heriot-Watt Theatres where inspired young Mancunians mingled comedy with mystery, above all in the person of a magical performer of oriental ancestry named Paul Yeung? Ask the empire-builders in the Royal Lyceum Theatre. Where is the derelict school in Drummond Street, rescued from dark stony oblivion by a cunning little clutch of Edinburgh students and non-students who attracted and in some cases produced a body of remarkable shows, winning attention by a ludicrous campaign against imaginary Fringe Society sins of bureaucracy, calling themselves the Fringe Fringe or the Edge, and secretly profiting by the kindly advice and aid of the Fringe administration they had denounced? Shut and barred. Where is the inspired management and directorship of Fringe art galleries such as the 369 Gallery and the Fruitmarket? Hounded to the verge of death by intrigues and edicts of the minions of the Scottish Arts Council. Even the George Square Theatre seemed about to be closed, for transformation into a Business School, but the University at least showed some sense of public spirit when in answer to public outcry it reconsidered the decision. Thereby it offered to the city a moral leadership away from Philistia, and it seems to have offered it in vain.

The voice of the Fringe . . . the cries of barkers for their own productions outside the Fringe office on the High Street . . . the grim voice of a performer who had given out scores of leaflets there to face a house of five that night for whom he had laughed, sung and cavorted as though to hundreds . . . the violin of a street musician playing a Handel sonata outside the Mount Royal Hotel whither I ran to get Michael Oliver from the Festival press rooms to record it for BBC Radio 4 *Kaleidoscope* . . . the cries of children in delight at the magical tricks of performers entertaining the crowd outside the Royal Scottish Academy on Princes Street . . . the schizophrenic tones of Fringe Administrator Alistair Moffat in the Fringe Club responding to the gracious demand of Princess Margaret for a large gin while endeavouring to reassure fellow-egalitarians within earshot of his undying hostility to the institution of monarchy . . . the mellifluity of Neville Garden adroitly removing a potential source of defamation proceedings from the previous live remarks of a contributor to BBC Scotland's *Festival View* by the wording of a reply ostensibly homologating the observations . . . the 'Oh God, oh God' of Allen Wright on beholding the increased size of this year's Fringe programme . . . the cut-glass gentility of drag performer Julian Clary, alias the Joan Collins Fan Club, in the utterance of a beautifully modulated and universally audible aside of quite shattering obscenity . . . the snarl of a stand-up comedian at the public indifference to his fifth witticism meeting no response notwithstanding the respect due for its antiquity . . . the rich, sinewy Scots of David Purves's pantomime *The Puddok an' the Princess* enlarging linguistic space through Theatre Alba as directed by Charles Nowosielski . . . the half-choke in the throat of a Fringe reviewer wolfing a leathery cheese roll purchased while hastening down George IV Bridge from a late-running production at one venue to another known for its impossibility of entrance after the start of performance while the schedule of subsequent commitments ensures that this must be the last meal for twelve hours . . . the sycophantic if bewildered titter from an audience in response to the single shout of laughter greeting a peculiarly incomprehensible witticism from the stage . . . the desperate tremolo of the youthful Ibsen actor endeavouring to impersonate the terminally ill Dr Rank performing against a Sheffield local councillor demonstrably over twice his age in the rôle of Torvald Helmer . . . the excruciating scream of Katharine in the Charles Marowitz *The Shrew* indicating her anal rape by Petruchio as the culmination of that variant on the Shakespeare play . . . the slow calculating vocal enticement with which Janet Dye replaced her previous anodyne syllables of Alice in Wonderland, thus disclosing her identity as a prostitute hitherto masquerading at the instance of Lewis Carroll of whose own other identity as Jack the Ripper she still remains in ignorance in the Oxygen House award-winning *Red King Rising* . . . the jeering laugh of the then manager of the Playhouse Theatre announcing his cancellation of a booking for a Fringe production at the last moment in circumstances for which the law permits no redress . . . the wholly appropriate and desperately forlorn note of isolation in the voice of the girl playing the title-rôle in Euripides's *Ion* in the splendid auditorium of a high school some twenty-five minutes outside the Edinburgh city limits . . . the successive and undistinguishable groans of a number of Fringe readers and reviewers trapped in wait for an infinitely protracted important public announcement with for solace only a single copy of *Punch* in which every single attempt at humour on the subject of the Edinburgh Festival had its origin in the reign of Queen Victoria . . . the enormous cascade of Russian in 1990 from a satirical performer from Moscow University remorselessly dedicated to the demolition of KGB terrorising followed by the elegant interpreter's version of the foregoing, to wit, 'Good evening!' . . . the exquisite harmonies of an English music group conjuring up the Vauxhall gardens during the Regency period . . . the superb use of plain chant in the classic instructions to new recruits in the Royal Flying Corps as laid down by Biggles in the Edinburgh student musical, affectionately and canon-

176

ically lampooning the most famous creation of Capt. W. E. Johns . . . the break in the voice of Philip French privately telling his contributors to the Edinburgh *Critics' Forum* that their guest production supervisor would be the Scottish drama producer Patrick Rayner stepping in to replace his friend, our former guest supervisor Martin Goldman, killed a couple of weeks before in a railcrash between Edinburgh and Glasgow . . . the note of finality in the intimation conveyed by a bouncer at the Fringe Club that it is closing forthwith.

Conclusion of Allen Wright's review of Alistair Moffat's *The Edinburgh Fringe* (*The Scotsman*, 14 August 1978):

> At its best the Fringe can be more stimulating and rewarding than anything on the more formally organised drama programme but, at its worst, the Fringe is frankly dreadful. . . . As administrator of the Fringe Society, Mr Moffat is familiar with the problems facing the performing groups, and the resourcefulness with which they overcome them. In future editions of this valuable and entertaining book he should incorporate more information about what goes on behind the scenes and examine in greater depth the motivation of the producers and actors who flock to Edinburgh every summer. Cynics used to suggest that they were all hoping to be mentioned by Harold Hobson in his weekly column but I believe that most of them are, like Alistair Moffat, enchanted by the feeling of being involved in a creative cyclone.

A couple of years ago Allen Wright's *Scotsman* team decided to give him a surprise celebration, including various gifts for him and for his wife Eleanor, and a *Scotsman* Fringe First Award plaque inscribed in his honour. Mary Gladstone, Joy Hendry and Catherine Lockerbie made the arrangements faultlessly, recruited Eleanor's conspiratorial support, arranged for her husband to be inveigled into the chosen apartment on plea of some consultation, confronted him with his apotheosis, and rounded it off with an impeccably phrased speech in expression of our love and gratitude from Peter Whitebrook. When they were leaving, the Wrights offered a lift to Bonnie Lee and myself who live in their direction. As we walked to the car I remarked that of the forty-odd reviewers in that room, I doubted if there was a single subject on which all could be got to agree, save their love of Allen Wright. He laughed, and concurred.

This is the great strength of *The Scotsman* Fringe First system, this and Allen Wright's vigilance and generalship. It is the same process which gave its particular character to the BBC Radio 3 *Critics' Forum* under Philip French. In both cases the basis lies in a recognition of the existence of worthwhile intellectual disagreement among the critics. And it also recognises silently the existence of less meritorious causes of critical conviction. In Philip French's programme (I cannot speak of its predecessor, which flourished when I lived in other lands), much of the excitement for participants and audience lay in the cut and thrust of debate, the testing of arguments and their capacity to sustain themselves against opposition. In Allen Wright's method, there was no confrontation of critics in conflict, save in accidental private meetings among themselves, but when a *Scotsman* critic feels that a Fringe entry with no more than six previous public performances in Britain before presentation in Edinburgh, is of sufficient quality in script and production to merit consideration for a Fringe First Award for its worth and originality, s/he nominates it, whereupon Allen Wright sends another critic, and occasionally also a third critic, to report on the suitability of the candidate. This may involve the nominator's defence of a nomination in some detail. But it is not a matter of weighing up the pros and cons: a proposed recipient has to pass the separate scrutinies of successive critics. The second critic may not know the identity of the nominator. Any critic on *The Scotsman* staff is entitled to nominate a production s/he has witnessed, whether s/he has reviewed it for *The Scotsman* or, say, BBC Radio Scotland, or nobody. A lukewarm review will not necessarily invalidate a subsequent nomination, though it will do it no good: it is the Arts Editor's acceptance of the nomination which dictates its investigation, and at this stage the initial reviewer may be asked to clarify his/her attitude where it is ambiguous. Ambiguity, after all, may be a critic's best friend on occasion for several reasons, but while it may give a very useful insight into a production for the punter, a clear-cut verdict on award-winning quality is needed when the Fringe First is in question.

The Fringe programme now carries an asterisk for shows declaring themselves to be of original character, acknowledging that the Edinburgh run had not been and would not be preceded by more than six previous performances. But *The Scotsman* reviewer and his/her Arts Editor cannot place all their faith in that. Companies may lie.

Hull Truck blatantly passed off as 'original' a production which had in fact toured extensively in the English provinces. It was long after that year's Festival when the perfidy came to light and the Fringe First was ignominiously withdrawn. This does not invalidate Hull Truck from a future legitimate award, and they may have had one, but it will dog the company with permanent suspicion and no person of any sense will take their uncorroborated word for a long time to come. Another instance last summer seems to have resulted from one unscrupulous figure within a company, whose weak-willed cast, when faced with tempter and temptation, succumbed to the award on the horizon. Their heroic director, however, who only heard of the award when it had been made, at once informed the authorities. In the circumstances I give no further currency to the names involved, though I saw the work, thought it a splendid example of fresh ideas on the theatre, and heartily concurred in the honour which had been given but not yet withdrawn. And I knew when the truth emerged that it had to be withdrawn. He was a very good director.

I once found myself involved in the reverse situation. Oxford Theatre Group put on *Superman on Ice*, a sensitive social drama concerning a youth, discovered self-imprisoned and dead in an American freezing room, wearing a Superman or Superboy costume. The play was managed with fierce integrity of direction, declining to milk the tear-jerking capacities of the situation and keeping the minds of the audience thoroughly engaged with the circumstances apparently innocuous in themselves yet leading remorselessly to the dreadful culmination. But the Fringe programme gave no asterisk. An enquiry from front of house as to previous production produced blanks; they knew of none. I asked for the director, a company official to whom I would normally give the widest berth. This was Deborah Parker, whose character in conversation quickly showed itself as I might have expected from her standards and austerities of direction. It appeared that the work had had a previous existence, but it had been rewritten to two-thirds of its extent, had obtained new music, and was therefore in my view eligible for a Fringe First. For excellent reasons it is now forbidden to indicate to a prospective or potential nominee that a Fringe First is under consideration; but I was of course entitled and indeed required, should it seem necessary, to get an accurate statement of the production's previous history, if any. I explained to the director that doubt had arisen in my mind as to the

179

absence of an asterisk, and that in courtesy she had to know, as her time would otherwise have seemed pointlessly exploited: any other deductions she drew, she did not openly make, which was as well since of course I could not possibly have been expected to comment. Allen Wright received my report accompanied by a nomination, discussed the question in detail with the Fringe Administrator, and agreed that the entry was eligible. The Oxford Theatre Group did indeed obtain a Fringe First after subsequent critical endorsement of my opinion.

The heterogeneity of *The Scotsman* critics provides an assurance that a nomination from one is anything but secure of further passage when transmitted for the judgment of another. What it means is that for the most part personal bases for particular affection are eliminated; also ideological biases confused by one critic with proof of cultural quality are discounted by another. In other words, a production almost invariably has to be very good indeed to gain sufficient standing in what are often very different judgments. In my experience two critics sharing many social attitudes may well view each other with the greater suspicion, as A is jealous of B's standing in the cause and B thinks that A's forms of expressing their common loyalties do more harm than good. Similarly a good BBC 3 *Critics' Forum* discussion could involve constant dissolutions of alliance as participants moved from theatre to book to film to exhibition to broadcast under review.

From Oscar Wilde, *The Picture of Dorian Gray*, Preface:

> The highest, as the lowest, form of criticism is a mode of autobiography. . . .
> Diversity of opinion about a work of art shows that the work is new, complex and vital.
> When critics disagree, the artist is in accord with himself.

The actual ceremony of *The Scotsman* Fringe First Awards is as a rule a very charming business, with thrilled recipient companies, interested individual critics alerted to be present, Allen Wright himself showing no sign of his normal beleaguered condition in Festival time, Fringe administrators radiating benevolence, and some celebrity from the official Festival or the Book Festival presenting the plaques. Magnus Linklater, the editor of *The Scotsman* since 1988, has taken to dropping in. He has proved a valuable friend to the Festival, having prevented the disappearance of the Houston Opera *Nixon in China* from its programme by masterly inauguration of a fund from the public. As a result we saw one of the most profoundly intellectual operas ever brought to the stage, as well as one of the most mordantly ironical. Occasionally Linklater's remarks at the Fringe First Awards would require the brilliant comic genius of his father, Eric Linklater, to do them justice. He may be credited with several near-ruptures of his hearers' appendices by introducing the presenter then starring at the Book Festival, a novelist best known for her raunchily sexual scenes, with the graceful apology 'but we must not keep our distinguished guest from her invaluable researches'.

The distinguished guests have normally performed their work with a fine spirit. John Drummond and Frank Dunlop were gracious and encouraging presenters. The most gallant such figure was probably Billy Connolly, in 1979, when he was an official Festival playwright. That play, *The Red Runner*, was weak, and many critics had said as much. Connolly (himself a former Fringe First winner) brought the house down with such lines as 'I am happy to present these Fringe First Awards on behalf of *The Scotchman*, a paper whose name I forget', and 'These awards derive from the high opinion formed of your work by the critics: I wish to hell they had formed it of mine'.

The only near-disaster was, in 1980, when the Fringe Administrator, Alistair Moffat (now Controller of Programmes on Scottish Television) said that an appearance on STV would be of benefit to the successful companies and that the awards should therefore be made in an STV studio. So the winners were herded under the nose of the cameras, forewarned by a floor manager who clearly hated their guts, that they were to have no friends, critics or any other supporters present. Allen Wright, looking as though he were about to be shot in all senses, delivered his official speech from a teleprompter professionally but with a staccato drum-roll all too fitting for an imminent execution. And then those of us left watching on a viewer in an adjoining chamber, suddenly abandoned our curses of Moffat, of the floor manager, and of Scottish Television. The floor manager had vetoed speeches of thanks to helpers, bank managers, *The Scotsman*, etc., and dictated that there would be no visiting Festival celebrity, merely the handing over of the plaques. But a Draconian edict of that kind was simply an invitation to Jeremy James Taylor to rise on the stepping-stones of his dead self to higher things. His Children's Music Theatre had won a Fringe First for *The Roman Invasion of Ramsbottom*. The smallest child in his company, who looked about six, was told to go up and receive the plaque. Allen Wright, suddenly confronted by this angelic if slightly apprehensive infant, forgot where he was, forgot the camera, forgot the floor manager, and turned on the child a smile of absolute serenity, encouragement and congratulation. The great grey head bowed, and the fine inscribed plaque was placed carefully in the little hands. The child trotted happily off camera, and I imagine the only dry eye was in the head of the floor manager. Then Richard Crane and Faynia Williams came up to receive their fifth Fringe First (for Crane's adaptation of Pushkin's *Evgeny Onegin* entitled *Vanity*) and gave each other a long, langorous, mutually congratulatory kiss. So what had begun in misery ended in sheer delight, except, of course, for the floor manager. The Fringe had never given a neater symbol of insistence on maintaining its own identity, and remaking the world to its own infinitely preferable specifications.

The Fringe may produce originality, and more of it may strive for originality, but it remains highly attentive to popular fashions. Promenade theatre is less frequent now, but for a time it threatened audience and critics impartially. In Kick Theatre's *The Tempest*, in King's Stables Road Church Hall, I had to leap for a window-sill and climb to safety to avoid being impaled on Antonio's sword, disturbed, as he necessarily was, by the invisible inhabitants of the island. And in the University of Pennsylvania's *Tempest*, this time at the Bedlam with fixed seating, the party of Alonso simply walked across the entire audience in their chairs, thus ensuring that the island was full of very strange noises. In the final scenes of Warwick University's *The Persecution and Assassination of Marat As Performed by the Inmates of the Asylum at Charenton under the Direction of the Marquis de Sade*, the cast pell-melled all over the Edinburgh College of Art Sculpture court, one lunatic jumping repeatedly on my review jottings, thus establishing his sanity though not mine. The first night of

Helen Come Home at the Children's Music Theatre (now the National Youth Music Theatre) in George Square Theatre featured a wholly unplanned explosion from the stage as the black children playing Trojans and the white children playing Greeks were so overjoyed by their reception at curtain-call that they leaped from the stage and darted all around the theatre hugging the very large audience, kissing them, embracing them, and then dashing off again to others and others and others. Their symbolism was perfect: I have never seen a production at whose conclusion the hearts of audience and cast were so completely at one. The fact that it was unscripted and unplanned made it all the better.

If Promenade is limited to one or two actors only in a brief and unexpected moment on stage, it can be very effective, but it also poses unexpected dangers for the production. I remember with disreputable pride such a moment in the Traverse Theatre, with its great black, carpeted steps in which the audience loomed over the players and yet sat apparently cut off save for the possibility — has it ever happened? — that a sleeping member of the public on the top row might nod over as well as off to somersault into the middle of the play with or without breaking its neck. I had gone down to see *Losing Venice* by one of *The Scotsman*'s best reviewers, John Clifford. It was well into the run, since on this I held the *Irish Times* repertorial brief and hence needed no first-night place. My son Michael, then about fifteen, kindly agreed to accompany me. This was no matter to be taken for granted. He was at this time rather forcefully in reaction to the intellectual pretensions of his grandmother, mother, father and, above all, twin sisters (senior to him by thirteen months). It meant that I had to give him as coherent an idea of what we were about to see as advance publicity and early reviews, if any, could convey, and he weighed the question carefully, though courteously. What decided him, I think, was that the play, Clifford's first, was reputedly of historical content, imagining a war between Spain and Venice in the early seventeenth century, such a conflict having actually been bruited at the time as a possibility but never having taken place. It was an outstanding piece of work, deeply sensitive to its setting in the age of Cervantes and Quevedo (Clifford later translated Calderon for an official Festival production), and dexterously using both its cultural self-limitations and self-created interstices in history to present a delicate and haunting drama of ideas, including themes of religion, diplomacy, feminism and, above all, war and peace. It was imaginatively directed by Jennie Killick, then Director of the Traverse, absolutely maximising the possibilities of the sparse props at her disposal and making them work the better for being the sparser. When the war was dramatically on, however historically off, the Spanish galleon was attacked and boarded by pirates, a couple of chairs and the Traverse carpet proving perfectly adequate ships and sea for us. One sailor took a flying leap into the Mediterranean, swum convincingly to the audience and belted half up the great steps, which certainly presented a few of the problems of a rock face, the uglier promontories being clearly supplied by the public. Behind him raced a pirate. Capture seemed certain, indeed in the script clearly was certain. But as the pirate drew himself to our level, intent on taking hold of the sailor now cowering behind us, Mickey flung an arm between them and said in a good, carrying voice which echoed at acting decibel level through the theatre, 'He's with us.' In sheer horror and shame I gazed across the three-quarter seat-banked (well, step-banked) auditorium and saw John Clifford's face, which seemed to have gone a ghastly yellow. The pirate corpsed. Mercifully the fugitive rescued all concerned with a self-sacrifice eclipsed only by that of Captain Laurence Oates on Scott's last Antarctic expedition, and turned himself in. I made a faltering apology to John in the midst of a babblement of congratulations when the play was over. He had no difficulty in discerning the underlying paternal conceit in my breast-beating, and earned canonisation honours on the spot by assuring me it had been a wonderful moment and a great testimony to my son's obvious involvement in the play. And that last was true, and the former also, but only in retrospect.

Audience Promenade could work well especially if the audience was given a little training. A fine dramatisation of the *Odyssey* at Gillespie's School involved direction for audience activity, mostly that of compositely transforming ourselves into the Homeric wine-dark sea, in varying stages of turbulency. But to have its greatest audience effect, Promenade must enlist the audience without telling them how. The most impressive example I ever engaged in, all the more memorable because of the fate of the rôle in which we were cast, was a production in 1977 of *Julius Caesar, Queen of Bythinia,* written and directed and led in performance by Paul Schoolman. I knew nothing of the company but decided that the classical world has an Irish angle (in which the *Irish Times* and my readers so far as I know entirely agree). Suetonius, rather lip-smackingly, makes something of Julius Caesar's having become the lover of the King of Bythinia, and Robert Graves's *I, Claudius* makes rather too much of the same point (and the same source), so the historical content was obvious enough. I was not absolutely startled to find a series of long pieces of paper on the table with places for the members of the audience to sign their names; something of this kind had been demanded in Manchester during a recent production of *Edward II*, I knew. So in we went, names signed as requested, my own in its correct form together with that of my gallant journal, although a few others (such as 'James Bond'), I was strongly inclined to suspect were assumed and fictitious names, much as was the Bosher Street magistrate when sentencing Bertie Wooster's friend who had declared his name to be Leon Trotsky. The play got rapidly underway, with the audience moving themselves around as best they might when representative specimens of the rival armies of Marius and Sulla brutally thrust their way through our ranks. But we had little time to congratulate ourselves on the degrees to which we had survived them unscathed. Sulla's victory led to the announcement of his famous proscriptions in which the names of those destined for execution were hung up in the Forum, and the long rolls of paper with our signatures were brought in from the front of house to be fastened to the pillars of the Crown. I therefore saw the remaining two-thirds of the play in a state of official death, and it concentrated the mind wonderfully. The Bythinian scenes, when they arrived, were effective enough, but judicious lighting and a still more judicious bedspread left the details entirely to the imaginations of James Bond, the *Irish Times* and their fellow-corpses. The major achievement of the production, apart from making Roman history come so arrestingly to life, was in its use of Caesar's genial camaraderie with the pirates who captured him, their merriment at his little joke about putting them all to death when he was ransomed, and the gruesome realisation of his promise. Graves might have learned a thing or two — or then, being Graves, perhaps he mightn't.

It is unlikely to put an audience at risk by Promenade, but the one-person show should be conceived as a play. The classic exposition of this truth in my memory took place in 1985 at the Edinburgh College of Art at an Edinburgh-Dublin Festival-within-the-Fringe as part of a grand series of exhibitions, recitals and performances brought by Michael Cuthbert as impresario. Sandy Neilson directed Finlay Welsh in Donald Campbell's *Howard's Revenge*. Campbell is a playwright and sometimes a great one, as he has shown in *The Jesuit*, his historical study of a Catholic martyr upsetting the delicate Jacobean applecart in Scotland in 1614-15, about the execution of the man recently canonised as St John Ogilvie (some doubt lingers as to whether that really was his name). Again under Neilson's direction, that got a Fringe First in 1978, as did their next enterprise, *The Widows of Clyth*, in 1979, both being staged at the Traverse. And so did *Howard's Revenge*.

It was a one-person show of the usual biographical character, insofar as the protagonist, J.B. Howard, recited the details of his life and struggles to the date (1875) at which the performance was supposedly taking place. But the whole thing turned on his efforts to learn a critical speech in the adaptation of Scott's *Rob Roy* intended to be performed at his theatre, the Edinburgh Theatre Royal, in the all too near future. (He was to become the first actor-manager of the Edinburgh Lyceum when it opened in 1883.) He was constantly distracting himself, and swinging into typical theatre reminiscence in a psychological deferment of the task of self-rehearsal which was grating on him. Moreover, Howard was represented as having a running battle with the lighting technician who, sometimes by supposed incompetence, sometimes in a fit of rage equal to the many of Howard's own, would give him the wrong lighting or plunge him and his audience into darkness. The tension of the production therefore turned on whether Howard would manage to get himself into a mood necessary to achieve his rehearsal, or whether the lighting technician, at times apparently hell-bent on wrecking Howard's efforts to the fullest of his considerable capabilities, would reduce his victim to nervous prostration. The very inadequacy of the makeshift theatre dictated by the exigences of being part of a general exhibition in an art college added its own touch of frailty to the proceedings. At the end, we gave Finlay Welsh a magnificent hand, to which he responded by a gesture towards the lighting as eloquent as any of his previous, but this time in grateful appreciation, so of course we turned in the direction of the invisible technician, gave him his hand, and were happily plunged in and out of darkness in gracious reception of our tribute. *Howard's Revenge* was great theatre, as much as anything because it *was* theatre, and the theatre man's tale was made a thing of theatre at every point of its performance.

The lesson here, of course, is that the one-person script and direction should be conceived by theatre people if at all possible. The very slackness with which the art-form has been so often presented is all the more reason to recognise the need to restore its theatrical status. And one of the major questions to be kept before the minds of producer, presenter and scriptwriter, is, what part is the audience to play? It may or may not be taken by the figure on stage to be present; but if it is not to be directly involved, it must be held in mind, to be seduced, tricked, cosseted, defied, bewildered, and ultimately to be wrapped up. If there is an interval, it must be preceded by a high note; and if the end is not correspondingly high, it must at least be conclusive if only in new statement of unanswered questions. The one-person audience, then, must be treated as consisting of intelligent human beings, not, in the repulsive phrase of the profit-obsessed, as so many 'bums on seats'. (And bums they are considered in every sense of the term, it often seems.)

Campbell gave a wonderful example of his audience control in a production of his own a couple of years later, at the Netherbow. Entitled *An Audience for McGonagall*, it apparently depicted the slightly crazy and self-obsessed late-nineteenth-century Scot, William McGonagall, immortal for his hideous concoctions of whose poetic fibre he was absolutely convinced, approaching the Royal Estate at Balmoral in insistence on reading his effusions to Queen Victoria. Ultimately he breaks down the resistance of the servant, and declaims by royal command; presumably he knows the servant is John Brown, the Queen's favoured highland ghillie of rough but intimate manners. Meanwhile the audience was troubled. Campbell's direction seemed as baselessly optimistic as McGonagall's self-estimate. The woman did not look like Victoria, even if she was making an effort to sound like her; the man similarly did not look like John Brown, even if he, also, was making some efforts to achieve Brown's conversational and official styles. McGonagall, admittedly, sounded like what one took him to have been, and the make-up and physique resembled what is known of his appearance. And then when the self-styled bard has withdrawn, all is discovered. McGonagall has made a fool of himself once more, characteristically, if in a new form: the man and woman are actually a couple of minor servants amusing themselves by a pretence of being Victoria and Brown. So the very critical censures summoned up in the minds of the audience now become the greatest laugh of all, and the play ends in the discovery that we have trapped ourselves.

From a letter of Oscar Wilde to Lord Alfred Douglas, from Berneval, ? 2 June 1897:

> André Gide's book fails to fascinate me. The egoistic note is, of course, and always has been to me, the primal and ultimate note of modern art, but *to be an Egoist one must have an Ego*. It is not everyone who says 'I, I' who can enter the Kingdom of Art.

The Rex Harrison *débacle* may, indeed, have had its origin in some attempt at theatrical convention with a vague notion of Shaw signing off as dramatic critic, remembering what awful things he had seen and dreadful things he had said, as well as more salutary recollections. But a token gesture with no real fulfilment is if anything worse than none at all, quite apart from Harrison's own unremittingly tedious contribution to the disaster. The antecedent principle in that case, where it was much more obviously artificial and creaky than what was done in *Howard's Revenge*, does get some decent service on the Fringe. In 1988, for instance, Northern Production Company staged the one-woman *An Audience with Dorothy Parker*, whose title was a rather neat answer to the conundrum of the rôle of the audience. That was us, we were there, and we were 'with' Dorothy Parker who, on her side, was alone in her bedroom waiting for her latest flame to ring. The structure lay within the monologue, obviously autobiographical, which Parker wrote as a short story on this theme, but the script compiler shrewdly and realistically assumed that the wait for the telephone bell could last an hour, and that its additional filling beyond the contents of the short story might be several more monologues. The lady knew how to do the work. Reminiscence was also fair enough, as was some verse (which Parker might reasonably remember to bolster her self-respect for her achievement as a writer, and to denounce herself for her ludicrous pursuit of a young man obviously immeasurably below her own intellect). The result was a fine presentation of

Parker's work, with a sufficiency of plot to maintain tension at the back of our appreciation for her performance of individual items, and with a happy ending which nevertheless had its own irony, indicating that all in the future would be far from well, and Dorothy Parker would die, having previously buried herself in frustration and alcohol. The biography had been satisfactorily faithful to its subject's texts, and had given enough insights to make it far more credible and far more abiding in its impact, than a life-and-times wrap-up could have been.

In one form the one-person show can do great things by the reassertion of the oldest theatrical identity known to humanity: the story-teller. Homer did it, Herodotus did it, the great epic bards of Celtic civilisation did it, and God knows how many countless entertainers from the dawn of humankind did it as well. Thus in the Festival Julian Glover could do it for *Beowulf*, admirably demonstrating the truth J.R.R. Tolkien's famous essay taught to hitherto arid scholars, that *Beowulf* is a work of literature, and a very exciting and engaging one too. And what more obvious challenge could be posed to the one-person show than Tolkien himself? Rob Inglis in 1980 in the magic interior of St Columba's-by-the-Castle, and, ten years later in the less promising but under his spell highly effective hall of Marco's Leisure Centre, revealed how much of the intricacy and symbol, and even linguist's pleasure-ground, in Tolkien's epic, could be subordinated to the simple thrust of the narrative in the hands of a bard. His cunningly altered voice seemed to diminish and enlarge his height for the effects he needed: snake-like and hugging the ground for Gollum, child-size and child-innocent for the hobbits, ironic and tall for Gandulf, towering in the bass register for the largest monsters. It was primarily with the awareness that story-telling demanded consistent hold on the progress of the noble but vulnerable Frodo, and the faithful, realistic Sam — a Don Quixote and Sancho Panza facing real enemies and actual enchantments — that Inglis cut out the third of the six books. One regretted the loss of the greatest vocal challenge of all, the sweet voice of the corrupted and false Saruman now keyed to base intents where formerly he had been among the forces of light, but the logic held good, and *The Lord of Rings* in the voice of one man had become an entity of the theatre.

189

Rob Inglis brought to full-bodied life so many different favourites — he is one of the wonders of the Fringe. There was his *Dr Jekyll and Mr Hyde*, for instance, in which he held the Lyceum Studio in two incredibly contrasting performances, again making his voice carry so much of the force of character-building. Inglis's Jekyll is an Edinburgh academic doctor, as Simpson of the chloroform auto-experimentation had been; but, with just diagnosis of how ambition normally metamorphoses Edinburgh people in search of success, his Hyde is English. Where innumerable Hollywood adaptations messed around with dark plots against heroines to get over the text's undoubted coyness on the depravities of Hyde, Inglis achieved infinitely greater effect by drawing from his throat a peculiarly horrible male chauvinist slavering anticipation of 'fun'. And, still enchanting the watchers, he evoked the hideous boredom of obsession with predatory sex: had Hannah Arendt been among those present she could have hailed it as 'the banality of evil'. He also showed how theatre deepened the story's impact, when Hyde conscripted his audience to 'sing-along' routines to further his self-aggrandisement, and made us his gutless accomplices.

As story-teller, Inglis made his voice act out his characters, as a good story-teller will; as interpreter of fictional characters, he acted them out in full. So did another giant of the Fringe, Peter Florence, who began as a pre-university juvenile in 1983 in the Warriors' Chapel of Old St Paul's Episcopal Church. There he resurrected the war poet and war victim Wilfred Owen in a compilation he called *The Pity of War*. 'His voice is rich and varied,' wrote Bonnie Lee in *The Scotsman*, 'eager, musical, passionate, clarion, soft.' I have never known her so insistent that I see a performance. His extreme youth, raven-dark hair, lightness and energy, as he leaped and marched along the Communion rail's white marble, his supernatural stillness in the articulation of certain poems, and his strong English tonal variations built on the rich music of the Welsh larynx, all combined to make it a haunted chapel. His performance inevitably resulted in my annual weep, and in a lasting friendship with Peter Florence and his parents, whose place was absolutely integral to the success of the production. Rhoda Lewis is an actress of remarkable versatility and rich voice while Norman Florence drove himself to the limit — on my visit to Old St Paul's he was handling the box-office with a broken arm — with the closest direction and the most thoroughgoing stage management imaginable. Father and son later built up the Hay-on-Wye Festival of the Arts on the Welsh border, in several increasingly impressive seasons.

They took later shows to Edinburgh. I think Peter produced Christopher Logue's *War Music* at the Bedlam solely outside Fringetime, but it has every Festival relevance. In 1977 the Prospect Theatre Company brought to Diamand's Festival *War Music*, a version of the *Iliad* from the fight at the ships to Achilles's return to battle: it played in the Assembly Hall with varying performances by Toby Robertson's large cast, who ranged from the fine, clipped, military narration by Timothy West to Rupert Frazer's apparent conviction that Achilles suffered from St Vitus's Dance. Ten years later, Peter Florence performed alone. He was a narrator of subtle and sensitive transitions and he realised to the full the dramatic implications of every single character, from ordinary soldiers on the briefest of appearances to Hera's wholly delicious seductive shimmering in her diplomacy to immobilise Zeus. His Achilles was splendidly built from the initial sulks through the rather paternal concern about Patroclus, the abandoned grief at his death, the implacable determination on revenge, to the grim resignation for his own ultimate destruction. And all was permeated by the theme of his Wilfred Owen work, the pity of war, the endless succession of sacrifices, the flaring up of character to be cut short in death, the reversion of ambition into savagery, and the intrusion of personal emotion destined to sway events more decisively than any strategy. Every one of his cast of characters deserved separate ovations. His props consisted chiefly of a staff, and a light jacket discarded when the fighting became intense. His performance was the ideal one-person show, directly descended from Homer.

Bonnie and I would talk about the day's shows when we met at home, usually after midnight, and might supply one another with some errant reference needed for the ultimate verdicts we were preparing for early morning delivery to *The Scotsman*. The lunchtime after one such exchange I found myself in the YWCA looking at a Cambridge Mummers' *Prometheus Bound*, in translation from Aeschylus. It failed to set me on fire, but it was not bad. My departure was stopped

191

in its tracks by the President of the Mummers, no less. He asked me my opinion. True to the practice of my great chief, I produced my customary formula, namely meaningless response rather than curt refusal.

'Interesting,' I said, as nasally as possible. His gaze continued importunate, so I thought for a moment, swallowed, and pronounced: 'Interesting.'

'That's very interesting,' he said, infringing my copyright courteously. 'Yesterday we had a different show at this time, and the lady from *The Scotsman* said it was interesting.'

That sounded like one of the more indelicate Donald McGill postcards. Well, *The Scotsman* had many ladies, and the self-exculpatory participle was, as Mr President had just shown, nobody's monopoly.

'And when will your review appear?' On this I could speak with some generous freedom.

'God alone knows,' I said piously. 'At the moment there are seventy-five reviews in the pipeline awaiting appearance.'

'So it could be some days,' he said, 'and some days before the lady's review is printed also.'

'What was that show?' I asked, uninterested but feeling the need of some courtesy before I got out.

He told me.

'That was no lady,' I said, 'that was my wife.'

I can still see the horror in his face. There he was, impeccable origins, no doubt, public school and whatnot, Cambridge and the Presidency of its Mummers, and all to supply the basis for the ex-humation of this idiot's delight! I felt so sorry for him I hurriedly took him out for a rapid drink. He seemed a decent enough bloke, and someone should have warned him the earth was still polluted by creatures like me.

Bonnie's show had been about Verlaine and Rimbaud. She disliked it intensely, and there had been some hunting up relevant literature which I recalled next day when meeting Mark Bunyan, a gay liberationist Fringeperson of splendid dramatic material, performance and philosophy. Obviously I was forbidden to discuss Bonnie's judgment, but I said that she had been thinking of an appropriate quotation on the great men, and I thought had considered but probably not used Dorothy Parker's 'I don't like Verlaine either.

192

He was always chasing Rimbauds' to which Mark replied, without an instant's hesitation though with an expression a seraph would have given its wings for, 'I thought Rimbaud was a little boy who lived down Verlaine'.

For a time one of the fashions which widely infected and occasionally improved the Fringe was an opening-scene plot-symbolising tableau. I first saw one when I took Chris Hite, who at about twelve years of age was the youngest Theater Wagoneer of 1974, in pursuit of our common enthusiasm of horror plays, and we drew Steve Berkoff's version of Poe's *The Fall of the House of Usher* at the Traverse. Berkoff was then a closed mouth to me, and I remember how kind Chris was at having been dragged to what we both agreed afterwards was an appalling disappointment for serious Povians. The thing began with a scream reminiscent of a *prima donna* finding her Butterflying understudy on stage irretrievably embarked on *'un bel di'*, and its main impact on the two of us was to supply the grimmest of forebodings, prophesying butchery of the great text we had arrived to celebrate. (I saw the same mess many years later at *The Scotsman*'s behest, but on this occasion much of the ruin was averted by the fine comic results of the cast performing in the richest of Lancashire accents. It was the pretentiousness of Berkoff which took a mauling from them, whereas the Lancastrians supplied a good local identity, given witches of Pendle and all that, to the dark grandeur of Poe.) Other uses of the same opening technique did nothing to alleviate my dislike of it, and my conviction that it fundamentally disordered the audience in its attempts to follow the story. But my objections were swept away in 1985 in a roaring torrent of veneration when The Shadow Syndicate employed this device to commence their Canongate Lodge production of *Scream Blue Murder*, adapted by Peter Grainger-Taylor and Adrian Johnstone from Zola's *Thérèse Raquin*. I had expectations of the singularly unusual from these two former Edinburgh students, whose 1983 Bedlam production of *The Phantom of the Opera* had added innumerable intricacies to the slightly creaking old spine-chiller, culminating in the discovery that this phantom was an unborn child. But the three opening minutes in the variation on Zola shattered the sensibilities more constructively than all the ingenuity of the sizzlingly intelligent *Phantom* had done. The long, low stage was illuminated only by dim blue lighting on an obviously French, obviously bourgeois, and obviously stultifyingly dull family circle seated around a table in formal aspect and exquisite civility. Dinner was commencing itself. One spoke, one replied, one made conversation. Then the table divided, and there swum up beneath it a yellow drowned face followed by its attendant corpse.

The rest of the play ensued with considerable fidelity, so closely that actors and scriptwriters eloquently conveyed the tedium on which Zola insists, while the ingenuity and passion of the production immunised the audience against its infection. And the overture — mordant, plangent, repellent (in Máire Ní Laoghaire's phrase) — hung over our minds throughout the proceedings, most notably in the persistence of enquiries as to the absence of Thérèse Raquin's husband.

The Shadow Syndicate later acquired Jon Pope, a lean, dark, sardonic product of at least some drama studies at Edinburgh (afterwards a director in Glasgow Cits productions, raising eyebrows supposedly frozen into immunity from the Cits' habitual challenges to the conventions). He may have allowed himself to be faintly intimidated by Henry James, when staging *The Turn of the Screw* in the Crown Theatre, for all of his inspired use of visual images on screen to create the supernatural dimension: his uncharacteristic textual fidelity seemed to imprison him a little, although if it deepened his fine claustrofying effect, its merit is not to be questioned. But I had hoped (against Pope) the governess would stifle the child whose salvation she achieves at the cost of his life, of which her hysterical condition indicated a strong possibility. (My favourite theory of the story in any case is that the uncle deliberately arranged for the demise of his nephew by the hiring of a governess like that, while eliminating himself from the body of the narrative.)

Jon Pope seemed to me more firmly in his element for Shadow when he reworked Wilde's *Salomé* into a radical chic party psychoanalysis of a drunken beggar, who is transmuted into John the Baptist. As the modern figures evolved into Wilde's characters, the esoteric opening became a road to the exoteric, and the modern ambiguities made his idea of their ancient counterpart apprehensible in a new form. The ending, using the resources of the long, low Canongate space, became a Johannine-contrived sandstorm burying the court of Herod as absolutely as though Shelley, fresh from his obliteration of Ozymandias king of kings, had improbably joined forces with the Baptist: and it posed the nice moral that involuntary victims of psychological experiment may bury their more condescending investigators and cultural profiteers. When Berkoff directed *Salomé* for the Dublin Gate Theatre production as the Festival officially saw it in 1989, modernity became the enemy and not the friend of the work. Philip French, convening the Edinburgh Festival *Critics' Forum*, said that in opening the programme, he momentarily misread the scene direction as 'a dinner at Harrod's' (for 'Herod's') and then when the curtain rose he saw he had been right. Movement from the cast in perambulatory moments was kept at a mincing tread, apparently through invisible water — had there been a less fortunate directorial allusion to the Judaean terrain causing the Court to simulate life under the Dead Sea? But lighting was magnificent, the Baptist when necessary being illuminated in his prison cistern, sometimes after the manner of the bowed shoulders in Dali's *Christ of St John of the Cross*, a painting much prized by its fellow-citizens of Glasgow. (I mean it: when I first visited Glasgow in 1957 a railway porter asked when I was leaving for Dublin, and on hearing it was that night, said in a tone of reproof which would have met the specifications of John Knox, 'You'll no' leave this town wi'out seein' Christ', patiently explaining his reference was to Dali as my ignorance gibbered in his face. I then went and sat before Christ for half an hour.) Unfortunately Berkoff chose to improve on Wilde's use of Ezekiel for his Iokanaan, or John, by interpolating hunks of the Sermon on the Mount; but Joe Savino, already an Edinburgh favourite from his work as Johnny in the stupendous Gate production of O'Casey's *Juno and the Paycock* brought by Frank Dunlop for the 1987 Festival, thundered his reproaches from the fullest recesses of the Irish traditions of druidism, anchorites, and the rural Roman Catholic parish clergy. Olwen Fouere in the title-rôle had undoubtedly a face and form a man might die for, had his martyrdom not been committed to higher causes, and Berkoff won few additional friends when he rubbished his performers and departed to his London production for which he summoned up what he declared to be fresh talent, including himself. Some critics, apprehensive of a thunderbolt were they to blaspheme against the name of Berkoff, explained they disliked the production because *Salomé* is a bad play. It is in fact a great play, but (apart from the passages originally from Ezekiel) it is an untranslateable one, as from his own experience in translating it Jon Pope heartily agreed. Perhaps some future Festival Director will bring it as a French-language performance, realised by a director with a modicum of respect for the play and his cast.

Chapter Eight

No Safe Place

A Memory of Oak Grove Theatre days in 1973:

Our five-year-old daughter Leila:

Let's play 'Play'. I'm the Director. I stand in a safe place and tell everyone what to do.

RICHARD DEMARCO IS THE FRONTIERSMAN *PAR EXCELLENCE* OF Edinburgh culture in or out of Festival. Time and again he has hurtled forward into the lonely forefront of new ideas, new forms, new space, whether in exhibitions, in theatre, in symposia, conferences, events, happenings, breaking wilderness, leaping beyond all established boundaries, evangelising endlessly as he goes, making the *avant-garde* look staid and cosy as it blinks at the new horizons into which he has vanished. It was inevitable that he would be the conqueror to extend the frontiers of Edinburgh in Festival far beyond the city and even the land, as in 1988 he led his pilgrims to Inchcolm Island in the Firth of Forth, his organisation as always miraculously following in his wake through the devoted resourcefulness of Jane McAllister. *Towards Macbeth — a Prologue* was presented by the Demarco Gallery with the Italian Institute and the Regione Siciliana/Assessorito Turismo e Beni Culturali, directed by Carlo Quartucci and performed by his wife Carla Tato with Scottish actors John Bett and Juliet Cadzow and support from the Quartucci-Tato company 'La Zattere di Babele'.

I was covering it for BBC Scotland, to report for Neville Garden and his radio listeners at the dawn patrol next day, and was directed to arrive at the gallery, where, with the rest of the customers, I was requested to clothe myself (additionally) in a blanket, which I declined as a member of the impartial press, whose impartiality depended on distancing itself from any herding into the audience apart from the conventional acceptance of a place within its ranks. What I suspected was that the audience was going to form a spectacle also: I have no objection to forming part of a spectacle, even the main part, but I wanted the freedom to see what contribution the blanketed audience would furnish to the proceedings. The nice young men gave up on me, and we stood around

Blackfriars Street until we were admitted into the great upstairs theatre, in use for its first Festival. Three young ladies, possibly waiting to grow up to be witches, performed with violin (badly), dance (with ravishing eroticism) and song (tolerably). Images flashed on the walls revealing *Macbeth* productions. Then we were herded into buses and roared down the Mound to Princes Street with Richard Demarco managing to ride in three buses at the same time, or very nearly, while Verdi's *Macbeth* thundered its might on the customers. I disapprove of the labour-cutting single-staff buses regrettably introduced in recent years, especially in their failure to protect drivers threatened with thugs late at night, but if the Verdi *Macbeth* was introduced, it would probably intimidate any malefactors into terrified silence. The traffic, for some reason, sheered delicately from us and the proverbial impossibility of making headway through Edinburgh on wheels during the Festival melted away. A remarkable man, Verdi. We reached the pier, ultimately, and found ourselves in a well-filled craft, reaching the island without incident. (Nobody was quite sure that the initial Thane of Cawdor might not attempt to retrieve his fortunes with the assistance of his Viking chums in their natural element, since we were, after all, only promised 'towards' *Macbeth*, and the Norwegian overture reported by the Bloody Sergeant to commence Act I, Scene 2, might well epiphanise as a stepping-stone with an option as a sinking-stone.)

Since I first came to know Edinburgh through Stevenson's novel *Catriona*, islands in the Forth mean the Bass Rock to me, but I was happy to accept Inchcolm as a substitute; and Stevenson lies even deeper in my mental foundations with *Treasure Island*. Two years later Frank Dunlop was to encounter much criticism for his *Treasure Island* in the Assembly Hall, but his use of a ten-year-old boy actor was magic for me and, regardless of other proceedings, I happily hurled my soul into the diminutive person of Iain Hathorne and in his person confronted Jimmy Logan as a splendid Billy Bones, raced around the perimeter built half-way up the side of the auditorium, fearfully faced pirates in combat, got back to the *Hispaniola* by coracle (actually carried through the darkened auditorium by the invisible extras) and performed the wholly insuperable rites of (*Hispaniola*) passage with Israel Hands. Iain Hathorne as the kid was great (Dunlop is at his finest as a director of young actors), and the kid was me. In 1988 I had no idea on Inchcolm that I was playing my own

Towards Treasure Island, but when Jim gets to the island in Silver's boat, he jumps for the shore and makes his own way as quickly as he can. The attendants directed the blanketeers right, towards the ruined monastery, and BBC Scotland raced off to the left, around a curving path, up to the height where a kilted piper was exciting bitter remonstrances from the seagulls at this blatant monopoly infringement. I took what cover I might from the piper (and the seagulls) — it was not yet time for Ben Gunn — and wormed my way over to the headland. I had the whole Inchcolm theatre before me, with a perfect view of the Firth beyond.

Standing before the ruins was Johnny Bett, late of 7:84's *The Cheviot, The Stag and The Black, Black Oil*, and many another gallant theatre statement in the causes of Scottish national self-awareness and the sister/brotherhood of humankind, declaiming individual lines from *Macbeth*, isolated and apparently little connected on any principle; Bett was taking no chances with the acoustics, and his sharp, keen voice rose high and perfectly audible on the wind. The effect was that of fragments of the play tearing through the air, spinning themselves into some sort of nebular state. He had made no concessions in dress: he confronted what was evidently a large congregation of monks in an ancient raincoat, which might perfectly well have done duty in a social drama of London on the problems of an exhibitionist. The blanket-clad monks looked quiescent: after all, their relations with Macbeth had been notoriously pacific. Were they headed by Walter Bower, the fifteenth-century Abbot of Inchcolm and author of the fiercely nationalist *Scotichronicon*? The piper gave the full generosity of his lungs to his work; more and more of *Macbeth* fluttered from the air; I lay on my belly in ecstasy, with the best view in the entire place. The Forth gently murmured its blue and white salutation to the endless clear blue skies awaiting annexation by Richard Demarco. God, it was Heaven!

Eventually the monks, hugging their habits around them, showed signs of being directed back into their fastness, and I hurried down to join them for Vespers. Now we were inside the stone remains, and by hiding in clefts in the walls as the monks (under firm guidance) made their processions here and there, it was possible to test the boom of the lines in their stone echoes, and imagine the remoter replies from the surf. Upper clefts captured different effects, and the nebula continued its indiscriminate growth. And then we were thrust down to the bowels of the earth, into a long, low chamber, where Carla Tato in white, bloodstained, with a blonde head, and Juliet Cadzow, in funereal dark matching her raven hair, dominated from a long table, Tato perpetually smashing a stone on the table-top crying great raucous gusts of passion in Italian while Cadzow, speaking from the depths of her vocal register, made a heart of darkness of Lady Macbeth's several most significant speeches. We were confronted by evil, and madness, and deadly resolution; ambition, and diplomacy, and deceit, and the implacable resolution to violate even the aged sanctity of protection for a guest. It was as though the nebula suddenly and dreadfully concentrated itself in the thought of murder.

Richard Demarco had spent an artistic lifetime in intricate manoeuvres between Cosmos and Chaos, and treated these two impostors just the same, so there was only a deep fitness in his having so signally forced them to his purpose on Inchcolm. The finale in iron tension tightened the invisible spider-threads of all that had preceded it, and symbolised a play and a production spinning itself into being around the terrifying centre. The full production was to follow in 1989. Alas, in the last days of July 1989 came the devastating news that Quartucci and Tato were medically unfit to make the return journey, and the official Festival promptly pulled out. Bookings were returned. I like to think of Richard Demarco at that moment, with all of his great preparations, all of the triumph of the prologue, all the hopes of his intended audience in ashes before him, and he, standing among the ruins, with implacable purpose in his dark eyes. He would stage a *Macbeth* at Inchcolm! But how in God's name was he to do it? How on earth was a cast to be recruited, with the Festival looming practically within spitting distance? I myself had no choice but to betray him. With grief in my heart, I advised Philip French of the situation — *Critics' Forum* simply would not have the time to get to Inchcolm and back or to devote any more than the moments given each Fringe production for what was now simply another Fringe show — if it was even to become that. *Macbeth*'s loss of Festival status took terrible toll of review possibilities elsewhere, even when it became clear that Johnny Bett had worked like a demon to get a cast together. The Festival gets space which, in fairness to the necessary equality for each member company of the enormous Fringe, just does not go to individual Fringe productions. *The Scotsman*'s coverage must now fall from good, well-flagged Festival space, to the two hundred words for the massed Fringereviews. Some individualist might make an exception in a London journal, but for those of us with unavoidable wide-ranging commitments, the time could not be found. Yet everything that was reported of the new Inchcolm *Macbeth* was heartening, if one's heart had not been eaten out by inability to attend it. In one respect, the good news was dismaying. We had wondered how sufficiently experienced Scottish actors could possibly be found on such notice to produce a *Macbeth* of sufficient stature to fight off the inevitable comparisons with what had been promised by the advance publicity and, still more, by the Prologue, and I, for one, had been sure that they could not. But Johnny Bett found them, and several of them were the heads of their profession. I rejoiced for Demarco and Bett, but I found it a grim thought that so many actors should be at liberty so close to the Festival. Have we built up the theatrical wonder of the world to leave the cream of the Scottish theatre unemployed while basking in our Festival? But Demarco at least had conquered again, won back his audience, and provided a *Macbeth* long proclaimed for its innovative daring and its unquestionable strengths. An excellent cast was headed by Roy Hanlon, veteran of many outstanding productions including Sandy Neilson's launching *The Jesuit* by Donald Campbell, and Chris Parr's *Nero and the Golden House* by Richard Crane when, as now, Hanlon had appeared with Juliet Cadzow. The Gaelic poet Aonghas MacNeacail played the soothsayer. But there isn't a soothsayer? Well, Shakespeare probably didn't speak Gaelic, but Macbeth certainly did. As I said, it was an innovative production. There are many Fringe productions I regret to my depths having missed, but none more than Johnny Bett's *Macbeth* on Inchcolm. The floating passages of *Macbeth* in 1988 had been all too applicable, and magnificent though its Lady Macbeths had been, Richard Demarco had shown everyone how to play one and a half of her lines: 'But screw your courage to the sticking-place,/And we'll not fail.'

There stands outside Greyfriars Kirkyard, at the junction of Forrest Road, Candlemaker Row, and George IV Bridge, and facing the Bedlam, a dry fountain with a small statue of a little dog, the famous Greyfriars Bobby, who allegedly guarded his deceased master's grave in the cemetery. In the fullness of time the dog died, was denied burial in the churchyard (which sounds as though the custodians were reverting to the place's former Popery in the matter of sacred ground), and would be much commemorated in subsequent song, story, Disney film, and Fringeplay; and Angela Georgina, the Baroness Burdett-Coutts, a great Victorian philanthropist who played a noble part in the education of the poor, erected the fountain. Recent researches have unfortunately elicited the circumstance that the deceased master was not buried in Greyfriars Kirkyard either, but in Preston Street cemetery, so what was the dog doing? Well, the place did have a plentiful supply of bones, admittedly vintage, but he may have developed refined tastes.

The Baroness Burdett-Coutts had little future association with Edinburgh, of which she was nonetheless made a Freeman, and in 1906 she died, and was buried in Westminster Abbey, where presumably her bones lie untroubled. It is improbable that her title descends, after the Scottish fashion, to her posterity, the senior of whom in sufficiently Caledonian circumstances would presumably become the Baroness irrespective of sex, but among more potent irritations, William Burdett-Coutts, Fringe lessee of the Assembly Rooms, is alluded to by the frivolous as 'the Baroness', which he tholes, as he tholes most things, with a slightly weary good humour. When the Assembly Rooms was in Festival hands, in the last decade, it had a mausolear effect, and Fringedirectors were said to throw an eye over its Festival Club as a potential location for a staging of Dorothy L. Sayers's *The Unpleasantness at the Bellona Club* in which the corpse is discovered to have been in undetected inanimity for some days. But since the Festival relinquished it (apart from subsequent subleasings from the Baroness for a few productions), it has become a buzzing, pulsing location, something of a cross between a mini-Festival and the more over-populated passages of Gibbon's *Decline and Fall of the Roman Empire*. It is heartily cursed by Fringe companies in other locations because of the notorious refusal of the impartial London press to stir beyond its borders for most of its stay, but that is hardly a matter for self-reproach on the part of the Artistic Director of the Rooms.

William Burdett-Coutts is, naturally, anxious to make a profit, as is every other impresario on the Fringe, and his successes in awards, box-office and press notices have not failed to draw dark suggestions from rivals that his sole interest lies in taking the cash and letting the credit go, nor heeding the rumble of their distant drums. He is not content merely to sit back and wait for the bookings he would undoubtedly receive. His rooms from time to time show drivel, as which other venue in Festival or Fringe does not, and if the Cambridge Footlights or the National Theatre of Brent are perpetrating soul-destroying hogwash on his premises, he can legitimately point to better work from them in a previous year (as problematic in its dating as the Greyfriars bones, in the case of the Footlights). He needs to keep a closer eye on the technical services he provides, or get the services of an authoritative vigilante from elsewhere. But he looks long and far for exciting and challenging companies to supply the cultural high points among his offerings, and his net has extended from Japan to South Africa to Ireland. In 1986 he induced the great breakthrough of Ireland on the Edinburgh Fringe, prompting 1987's first official Festival invitation to Ireland since 1974. The Druid Theatre of Galway had produced a few imitative Fringe flickers, but no worthy successors. Burdett-Coutts now went for the Abbey and the Gate, and in no leave-it-to-yourself-sir spirit. He booked the Abbey production of Tom McIntyre's adaptation of Patrick Kavanagh's *The Great Hunger*, which objective Dublin cultural opinion (if any) regarded as the finest expression of *avant-garde* theatre to have shown its head in a long time. He also secured the Gate one-man *I'll Go On* by Barry McGovern, based on the early novels of Samuel Beckett.

Patrick Kavanagh (1905-67) was a Monaghan poet who published during the years of World War II *The Great Hunger*, a remarkable long poem in Cyril Connolly's unquestionably highbrow magazine, *Horizon*, describing the sexual and aesthetic isolation of his remote, parochial, native county. He subsequently lived in Dublin, a bitter, uncompromising, outwardly squalid and repulsive figure, resentful of cultivation, profoundly alienated, anti-social and at war with authority to the extent of conducting all his correspondence through an accommodation address. McIntyre, though a sardonically genial person in private, had an uncompromising integrity equal to Kavanagh himself; and he had no intention of prettifying his material. More, he and his director pursued the staging of Kavanagh in high symbolic form. They certainly looked for, and caught, the strange, bleak, poetic spirit, and the love of landscape expressed in unyielding naturalism. They also expressed the frustration in a series of visions which, again like their original author, made no concessions to blander or cruder responses. The company performed magnificent gyrations, worked in almost unimaginable turns of speed or statuesque blocking, made the internal war of Kavanagh against his Monaghan a thing of comparable genius in visualising the conscious and subconscious mind. Máire Ní Laoghaire would very justly have termed it 'mordant, plangent, repellent'. And about half the audience left at the interval never to return, many more having preceded them. The reason was simple: Cecil Woodham-Smith's best-seller *The Great Hunger* had led them to take it as a play about the Great Famine, origin of the great Irish immigration to the English-speaking world. Kavanagh had chosen his title (a popular allusion to the Famine before Woodham-Smith) with deliberate near-blasphemy and need to convey enormity of horror.

A row of seats in the large auditorium separated me from William Burdett-Coutts, but from the speed with which they had been vacated, I had not the slightest difficulty in reaching him. He was standing, looking at the stage, a man entranced. The recent great migration could have left nobody in doubt that most of its iron-faced participants had not the slightest intention of returning. If one-hundredth of the reputation rivals had built up around Burdett-Coutts had a basis in reality, he should be tearing his medium-length black hair. As I approached, he was murmuring, certainly more to himself than to me, 'Wonderful! wonderful! marvellous!' I agreed that it was. He glanced at me — he is naturally courteous, although seldom effusive — and smiled, a little shyly, like a small boy discovering an adult has noticed, without apparent hostility, a much-loved but very private make-believe. I have not been very much impressed by subsequent chatter about his Philistinism.

For the rest of the week, his confidence in the performers was nevertheless justified in box-office terms. The Abbey had leaped into the next century in one of the most fascinating Fringe productions memory could know. The great silences of the first night gave way to rapture on successive nights. The Assembly Rooms in Fringetime is particularly circumstanced for news of good and bad to fly far and wide. But Burdett-Coutts had no reason to expect anything of the kind when he half-whispered his lonely homage to a show apparently with scarcely another friend in the hall.

For the following week Beckett was Beckett, but here again

Burdett-Coutts had taken his risks, although this time perhaps with more awareness of his pitfalls. Frank Dunlop had had a Beckett mini-festival in his first year as Festival Director, 1984. The great David Warrilow (of the crystal-clear murmur) had appeared in authoritative versions of *Ohio Impromptu, A Piece of Monologue, That Time, Catastrophe* and *What Where* directed by Alan Schneider and produced by the Harold Clurman Theater of New York (Schneider had also directed John Calder's compilation *From Its Beginning to Its End*), and, in some ways most daunting precursor of all, Max Wall had appeared in a dramatisation of *Malone Dies*, one of the three novels whence Barry McGovern had based his show. Would Edinburgh support more Beckett, and not necessarily fashionable Beckett either? To this day I have on my wall a photograph of McGovern lying supine in his Malone persona, diminutive against a great empty background: it comes from a Gate press pack I recovered from a Hanover Street garbage receptacle into which I saw a passer-by thrust it half an hour before *I'll Go On* went on. The circumstances of retrieval were Beckettian enough to make it a prize possession, apart from the inspired rendition it commemorates: yet it was no good box-office omen. But the box office had no cause for alarm. McGovern held his audience enthralled, above all in the magnificent survival of the human spirit he asserted in the context of a humanity in dissolution to the point of invisibility. His first (non-)appearance was a behind-the-scene voice Hamletting its refusal-agreement-neutrality-uncertainty-psychosis about going on and the mingling of the novels' meaning of it with the stage use of it perfectly translated the pre-stage writing into the medium which made Beckett immortal.

Where Festival proclaims itself 'indoors and out-of-doors' it is happiest. The great Circuit venue — spanning the Church Hall at King's Stables Road, the tents and open-air bars of the Hole-in-the-Ground at Castle Terrace, the Lyceum Studio and the Heriot-Watt Theatres — induced endless mutual entertainment of conversation outside reacting to the stimulus of challenging, infuriating and heart-warming productions within, but it passed away in the early 1980s. Sometimes a company dares the climate with open-air productions, as John Retallack's Actors' Touring Company did in a Newington garden in the late 1970s with an uproarious *Tempest* and a deeply sensitive *Don Quixote*, both of them seeming to draw from the air the illusory or imagined enchantments so necessary for the remotest dimension of both works. Today the great venue combining inside and outside is the Pleasance, off the eponymous thoroughfare arising to the right of the Cowgate east end, and presided over by a large, genial, plump impresario named Christopher Richardson. He sounds like a former English public school master. As a matter of fact he *is* a former English public school master. He is also a fanatical, if gentlemanly, theatre buff, and his collaborations include assisting Jeremy James Taylor with the designing of his Russian Revolution seventieth anniversary play *October's Children*, awesome in the swiftness of its dissolution of the pageant affirming Maxim Gorky's ideal society into the harsh chaos which proved the Revolution's immediate impact.

The central courtyard of the Pleasance, entered through two pseudo-medieval gateways each of which causes the nervous to strain their necks for a presumed portcullis, provides a variety of conversation-tables, while indoors several bars (including one for stand-up comedians, some officially in performance) refresh audiences in quest of the two theatres. Richardson himself is responsible for the creation of the second, Pleasance Two, reached by an outdoor stair, and it was there I saw in 1987 the only Sherlock Holmes play to have left me with sentiments of unalloyed gratitude. Most of these naturally accrue to the two performers, especially Tim Norton, the Holmes, also author-director; but its absolutely satisfying clincher was the *coup de théatre* justifying its title *The Final Revelation of Sherlock Holmes*, and the inspiration for the means by which that was staged came from Richardson.

Snobbery insists on trying to make Holmes and Watson conventional figures of fun, just as in Conan Doyle's lifetime it sought to belittle his great literary achievements by mildly jeering consistent allusions to 'Sherlock', whatever his immediate subject. *The Final Revelation of Sherlock Holmes* succeeded because of its reverence to the creator, although, in good Fringestyle, it was homage concealing much of its nature until the moment of revelation. The plot assumed a series of fantastic adventures, all of which seemed more and more implausible within the conventions of Conan Doyle's characters, and yet pace, ingenuity, title, and a continued tension hinted with increasing strength that more was at stake than the usual *pastiche*. The hand of the playwright was too firm to heighten fears of what Dorothy Parker would call a reversion to tripe. The plot had its anatomical contradictions, but they seemed to possess self-diagnosis. And then both men die. And the voice of a BBC announcer on the radio states that Sir Arthur Conan Doyle died this morning at half-past eight, at his home at Crowborough in Sussex. We have been watching the death-gyrations of two brain-children whose Creator is no more. In its way it was an outstanding comment on the apocryphal Holmeses and Watsons perpetrated after Conan Doyle's death: animated corpses, all. Since much of Tim Norton's work was in literally deadly satire of the apocrypha, it did not stray far from conventional stage methods in portraying Holmes and Watson, save that both were good, strong performances. Their venue was excellent for them. Pleasance Two had become a fine, steeply-banked, commodious auditorium with a wide, fairly deep stage.

There was a curious sequel, noteworthy as one of the many often unperceived ways in which the Fringe benefits the culture of its not always appreciative city. Walking from Pleasance Two into the courtyard from an early performance (probably its first, for I was *The Scotsman*), I noticed a diffident but slightly official-sounding gentleman making inquiries about communication with the actors. I think I must have explained that the stage door gave onto the courtyard north-east corner; anyhow, I was drawn into the conversation. He turned out to be Councillor Tait, a Tory, and it was an honour to meet him. He was animated by no self-serving or vote-snouting instinct, simply by civic spirit. He was not a particular Conan Doyle fan or Sherlockian enthusiast, but he thought Edinburgh should have a memorial to our rather neglected son — 221b Baker Street, which had never existed, and whose number had never been assigned to any building, was nevertheless the object of honour; but what of Conan Doyle Edinburgh residences in his first twenty-one years? The birthplace was razed: where else would be appropriate? I explained that I had found his other domiciliary sites, and we settled on 23 George Square, in which the family had lived during most of young Arthur's years as medical student in our university. Tim Norton entered constructively into the discussion, intended for him in the first place, my presence in the Pleasance being fortuitous (but not fully so, since in strict logic the encounter is yet another of the many beneficial results of the strategic hand of Allen Wright). To our great regret Tim could not be present when the plaque was finally erected with the consent of the Dominicans who now owned the property (in whose basement Theater Wagon had performed so long ago). Significantly the next-door house is 23b, whose only entry is by interior steps. (Unlike Holmes I have never counted them.) Dame Jean Conan Doyle had approved the design, and afterwards visited the plaque, with which she was delighted. Edinburgh must hope for more city fathers with the spirit of Councillor Tait, and more Fringe playwrights with the ingenuity of Tim Norton. As for duplicating the meeting-ground which consolidated the idea, there is only one Pleasance; there is only one Christopher Richardson.

Theatrical entrepreneurs are not normally lovable people, but I knew one once whom I ultimately found a tragic figure. He had a great production on his hands. He knew it. He had it all sorted out. He knew where the big money was. The notices were right, the locale was right, the box-office was a marvel, and if there wasn't a Fringe First (and there may have been — I forget), there was everything else but. The London dailies had spoken enthusiastically of it, and that meant much to him, as his sights were on the West End. He alluded to the cast in somewhat patronising terms, although he spoke in just raptures of the excellence of the lead actor. The playwright was a good fellow who had done a good piece of work. Despite all the hard-bitten manner and the rhetoric of gain, there was conviction about the social message of the work, when you dug a bit. Anyhow, I mildly liked him, and had thought well of one performance of his as an actor which I had seen a Fringe or two earlier. I looked in one evening to his company's bar area to find the poor devil almost in tears, which up to that point he would probably have denied possessing. The money men had come as expected, had liked the work, had booked it for the West End, and had taken it out from under him without a penny of compensation, or the shadow of a place for his work as impresario. By his own ethical standards, he had not the faintest basis for sympathy. I was very sorry for him. He had nailed down everything in sight apart from his own situation. When you thought about it, he had given his heart to the production, and his head as well.

American Festival Theatre impresario Harold Easton has straightened out several nasty little difficulties into which he had the right of entry but in which he had no company stake or involvement, and the health of the Fringe is the greater because of his thoughtful diplomacy. He has acquired a highly impressive knowledge of Fringe-spaces, although he has been largely satisfied with those he has used himself, notably the Royal Scots Club whose crusted traditionalism melts under his wand into a relaxed American haven, respecting its visitors as well as its premises, but transformed so effectively that its ambience becomes a warm transatlantic vibration operating in a firm and comfortable discipline. Easton's good nature in the facilitating of possible Fringe productions, whether he stands to benefit or not, is incomparable. He has worked himself to the bone to give information to the neophyte, to explain the strengths and weaknesses in a situation where the greatest names may be fighting for slivers of publicity, and to help guard against the kind of disappointment avoidable by judicious warning. In brief, he loves the Fringe, and the Fringe has every reason to love him.

In 1986 he won a *Scotsman* Fringe First for the British première of Arthur Miller's *Playing for Time*, an adaptation of the memoir of a member of a Jewish women's orchestra in a Nazi death-camp, Fania Fenelon. His belief in the Fringe has enabled him to ease out options of certain American rights tied up for London, but neglected for the rest of the island by Americans incapable of seeing beyond the metropolis. He is very American, jimcrack-alert, with friendly little explosions of incessant information and meditation, capable of giving intricate organisation a poetry lacking a less staccato voice or a less vibrant nature; he also has a touch of an American looking for home, not birthplace, not homeland-of-ancestors, not nostalgiaville, just home and, as a rule, knee-deep in Fringepressures, Fringe-anxieties, Fringehopes, Fringeheartbreaks and Fringehappiness, he seems to find it. He lays down the law with assurance, a bright eye, and an instantaneous pause if questioned: he actually does want to be shown where he might be wrong. This takes unusual forms: 'That was a nice review, but you didn't have space to say what mistakes we are making, so tell us, what do you think is wrong with the show, what should we think about again, look here I'd like you to have a word with our director, Rob Mulholland, he'll want to hear what you have to say and he's too nice a guy to bother people. How about lunch?' Nothing about lunch: I don't take lunch from people whose productions I review. Quick nod. 'I respect your position. But you wouldn't say no to a cup of coffee.' Fair enough. Actually, I should have stood that cup of coffee to Mulholland who talks in dreams that conjure themselves before your eyes, now with this variation, now with that, your ideas worked in and out with the precision of an artistic scientist. I realise that H. Easton and, if put to it, R. Mulholland, know perfectly well that it probably does their futures no harm to sound as if they respect positive criticism from persons who may in the future review them. But, introvert and extrovert, they are fascinated by ideas from critics or anyone else.

The fare American Festival Theatre brings is normally North American, with steady reliables from successful but not overexposed stock items of the past — Gurney's *Scenes from American Life*, Inge's *Bus Stop*, Ferber and Kaufman's *Stage Door*, Durang's *Baby with the Bathwater*. Each season carries a star item, given the main thrust of everything, publicity, public relations, talking campaigns, and frequently a separate theatre location — Netherbow very often, or maybe Assembly Rooms. In 1990 it was *The Boys Next Door*, a glittering comedy mingled with realism and pathos about a rehabilitated group of retarded adults, performed and presented with respect, honour, a great absence of patronising and only the faintest whiff of *kitsch*. Their obsessions were often cousins to the more socially acceptable obsessions presumably well represented in the audience. In 1989 it was Michael Cristofer's *The Lady and the Clarinet* in which a lady recalls what Lady Bracknell might justly have termed a life crowded with incident to a clarinet-player, silent in speech but highly responsive in clarinet, the confection again beautifully composed of satisfactory emotional fodder on many levels. In 1988 it was *Undertow*, confronting two marooned soldier enemies discovering one another's deeper and more admirable natures, with very few punches pulled and yet with a great vindication of human decency triumphing over war pressures.

Of the great achievement of 1987, the dramatisation of John Steinbeck's *The Grapes of Wrath*, it would be otiose to speak, for its adapter, *The Scotsman* critic Peter Whitebrook, wrote and revised a most instructive diary of the experience which he published as *Staging Steinbeck*, in the process of capturing the atmosphere of Edinburgh at Fringetime most memorably. Virtually his last word picks up a major problem for such a production — what it can add to successful screen treatment. He quotes Philip French on *Critics' Forum*, saying the American Festival Theatre production 'bears comparison with, and is in fact tougher than, John Ford's classic film'. And Philip French's encylopaedic knowledge of films of the past, and phenomenally sound judgment as a reviewer of cinema and indeed everything else, make this the ideal critical note on which to close Peter's tale of labour and love. What *Staging Steinbeck*, being from the inside, may not convey is the sense given the Netherbow audience of its own entry into a strange, lost rural America of the Depression years, the sense of discovery all the greater because of Peter Whitebrook's transmission of his own innocence on things American, of the magic he himself found in trying to project himself into the unknown terrain in time and space he sought to make manageable within the confines of Fringetheatre. He is an assured and confident critic, but it is not an assured and confident diary, and much the better for the vulnerability it displays. A produc-tion of that kind, with vigorous professionalism in its management but with sensitive, human, cautious and initially self-doubting exploration at its heart, possessed the strength which was vital to its success, but also the youth of spirit realised so well above all by the oldest and most experienced actors — Faith Geer and Albert Bennett, Ma and Pa Joad.

If the company director is also the company playwright, it may prove inspirational, and perhaps cathartic. Jeremy James Taylor is an intensely lovable person but, if some of his writing is a guide, the person questioning the justice of this general affection is frequently himself. A director has to be hard, and in directing small children hardness may seem harshness to the recipient, and perhaps to the dealer. Amid all the plaudits for *Helen Come Home*, he was haunted by the child whom he'd had to send home the day before the production opened. As a director he sees the necessity for hardness and acts upon it when he has to; as a human being he has never, so far as I can see, fully accepted it. So a theme in some of his plays is the exploitation of children by adults, sometimes in a fairly obvious Dickensian context, sometimes in contexts nearer home. Much of his work is based on one of the most important, and one of the most ignored, aspects of history: the history of children, especially the children cut off from security or from love. His evidence comes from fragmentary stories in old newspapers on occasion, and very often must give little more than the initial inspiration for a specific plot, given how little has been recorded of the origins and ultimate fate of the children in question. Sometimes he will leave a particular story focused on a heartwinning child without any conclusion: in *October's Children* the most interesting child of all simply goes out of the story, his fate deliberately left unknown to symbolise the countless victims of the Russian Revolution. He calls his play *Captain Stirrick* Dickensian, but its sources are pre-Dickensian, the report of the organisation of pickpocket infant gangs by an older youth himself being ruthlessly exploited by a fence: it is the Artful Dodger story, with the original Dodger having his boasts and dreams, his successes and destruction, where the apparent fantasy becomes ugly reality but, unlike Dickens's appropriate ending for the arch-exploiter Fagin, the ultimate profiteer goes free, as in the newspaper story from the beginning of the nineteenth century where the original fence went free. In *Solomon Pavy* he took the question of exploitation right into his own anxieties and preoccupations, and studied the use of child actors by unscrupulous Elizabethans, basing his work on the known examples of Evans, and of Nathaniel Giles, the master of the children of the Chapel Royal, and of the child actor Solomon or Salathiel Pavy or Pavey who was famed for his astonishing rendition of old men's parts, commemorated by Ben Jonson in a beautiful elegy when he died of fever. It seems an impertinence for a parasitic onlooker such as a critic even to offer praise for so much integrity, or to attempt understanding of so much sorrow. What is undeniable is that Jeremy James Taylor's often tortured perception transcends the centuries, and by agonising over his own situation he has produced great artistic insight. History begins at home.

It is perilous to try to read origins of artistry from the work itself. One of the most remarkable beginnings of a play I have ever witnessed was that in a company calling itself D.O.A. Theatre Company performing *Poor Paddy Works on a Chain Gang*, whose author was Robert Cohen. The venue was unpromising, being the Royal Mile Primary

School, very far down the Canongate, although great things have been done with its functional classroom, notably by Faynia Williams when she staged the award-winning *Soldier, Soldier*. In 1989 the venue was being managed by Bill Dunlop, an almost incredibly ascetic devotee of theatre, whose concern for his sub-lessees was so outstanding that he pushed their productions instead of his own play on the seventeenth-century dramatist and novelist Aphra Behn. He spoke great things of *Poor Paddy*, whose name was rather against it, as the names of good Fringe plays often are. In particular, he advised intending customers to be sure to guard against their own late arrival, and with reason, for the auditorium and stage opened in darkness whence it became possible to discover two men in bed together evidently at the conclusion of a deeply affectionate night. As they dressed and conversed it became evident that one was in the Provisional IRA and the other in the British SAS, and that each had been on a mission to spy on the other and elicit vital information, culminating in the discovery that the house was surrounded by forces intent on the destruction of the Provo while measures had been taken by the Provos to wipe out a group of British soldiers on information distilled from the disclosures of the SAS man. And yet at the back of their ingenuity for their mutual destruction, and their envenomed rhetoric against one another as the spiral of appalling disclosures mounted, some residue of genuine love remained. The play seemed slightly more sympathetic to the Provo than to the SAS man, but both of them were shown as having destroyed themselves as well as one another. It would have been natural inference to deduce that the author was either a passionately involved Ulster sectarian, or a passionately involved gay liberationist, or both. In fact Robert Cohen was none of these things, and his original inspiration for the play had not been of Ulster origin at all, the most likely fount being the Israeli-Palestinian pattern of confrontation. Yet the accumulation of learning which had gone into the Ulster location was so impressive, and so well deployed, as to leave little doubt as to the author's Ulster antecedents, and the sense of gay patterns of love, betrayal and residual affection would surely have merited as much of a compliment as any theatrical work would be likely to get from Jean Genet. Robert Cohen is a fine playwright: that is what matters. As for the supposed Provo loyalties, he simply felt it his duty to be harsher in criticism of his own side. His actors were English.

D. G. Steffes is an American whose son in 1990 was at Sussex University. Steffes wrote a couple of one-act plays which his son directed at the Fringe. Sussex had made several appearances on the Fringe, but not continuously enough for the inherited wisdom of its own past generations to have much effect, and they were singularly unlucky in their venue. The Pharmaceutical Society at 36 York Place looks central on the map, but it often proves to be a dead point, missing the northbound traffic down nearby Leith Walk and Broughton Street. Here *The Scotsman*, virtually on its own, found itself in contemplation of great work. The greatness was not that of Steffes and son, although the plays were good, and were directed with punctilious filial devotion, worth watching in its own right. The Steffes plays both turned on the same theme, the imprisonment of the actor in the design of the author (and possibly — it was not a clear distinction — of the director). One, *Fantoccini*, was a nice new twist on the old Petrouchka story: the puppets are discovered in the box, with their handsome, charismatic lead increasingly determined to revolt, break out and seek real life. He has varying successes in convincing his colleagues, and then his search for freedom is aborted by the showman's removal of their personalities and determination on his rebel's metamorphosis into an old, ugly, leering, hump-backed Punchinello. It was open to the audience to take the argument as a reworking of *Paradise Lost*, if it liked. The other, *The Tree's the Thing*, among several other symbolic points reasserted the argument of the inability of the actor to say or do anything on his own in the ideal conditions of theatre.

The irony was that these two plays on the powerless actor featured some of the most powerful acting I had seen in sixteen Fringegoing summers. Jamie Richardson, as the lead on both occasions, gave both performances everything the Steffes family could have asked. Yet his work symbolised the unimaginable gulf between good and sublime acting. In his hands the puppet's search for life and freedom became epic, and the discourse in the second play a profound philosophy. The director obviously knew he had the services of a fine actor, the youngest in his cast, as I learned (for the amiable front of house and interval refreshment staff were only too ready to chat to their almost solitary client). But did Steffes and son realise that the quality of the lead performance negated the major thesis of each play? Perhaps they did, and had succeeded in offering the charm of a thesis refuted by the excellence of the vehicle which so ably expressed the flaw in the argument its work brought to such triumphant life. The success of the author's work ultimately depended on the destruction of his case. If acting is a prison, Jamie Richardson made it also a liberation.

Theatre West End operates at the designated compass point of Princes Street Gardens, featuring a shallow but very long stage faced by several rows of banked seating. I had luxuriated in Charlie Snow's drunken Heracles seeming to stride across its length with force enough to suggest one of his previous labours had received payment by a gift of seven-league boots. I had bitten morose nails over bad Shaw there, and I had counted the minutes until some self-styled stand-up comedian had served his allowance of purgatory to the customers. I was now confronted by rows of grimly effective World War I sandbags.

My grandfather had risen to lance-corporal in the trenches (my Irish grandfather, this is; my English grandfather had opposed the war). In hospital recently I had the good fortune to meet a nonagenarian in my ward, with memories as vivid as yesterday; he remembered the day that he was wounded as the happiest in his life, releasing him as it did from the endless wet and lice and rats and death around him. In the bitter revulsion of the after-war years, the disenchanted rallied to the anti-war narrative of a German, Erich Maria Remarque's *Im Westen nichts neues* (1929). Mother had taken me to see a revived screening of its film, *All Quiet on the Western Front* starring Lew Ayres, whose commitment to the work's message he had the courage to express in conscientious objection to the next war, with disastrous effects on his career. She had stressed very much that it was as relevant to what her father had experienced in the British army as it was to the German. And it was that point on which the admirable work of Stephen Johnstone turned.

How could one man and a few sandbags hope to do something more for me than the memory of the courage and honesty of the movie, with its harsh landscapes, haunted lighting, and the final shot of a hand reaching out to freeze in death, to say nothing of its deployment of a fine cast portraying the ugliness of war reality and the self-serving myths on the home front? Johnstone had not spoken a sentence before

217

he showed me how much simplicity, scarce resources and a single actor *using a Liverpool accent* could do. Ayres in the 1930 film must have had an American accent, but that was simply the inevitable all-purpose strain on the suspension of disbelief genially lavished by Hollywood to any society it chose to portray. Stephen Johnstone wrought revolution in his communication of the work by simultaneously telling two stories, that of his narrative as a German soldier and that of his intonation as a British soldier. Received standard pronunciation would simply have repeated the Lew Ayres formula. Scouse meant that we were gaining purchase on two sides of the battle-front and two home fronts; it was as though the entire German experience as distilled through Johnstone's acting version of Remarque's novel was being translated simultaneously (to employ that construction with absolute accuracy for once) into the observations of an unknown Merseyside recruit. German allusions, personal and placenames, military style and whatnot, simply registered on the brain for what they were with no disturbance to the other almost identical story conveyed with identical pathos and dignity asserting itself in sound.

Gulliver's Travels was presented in the Southside Centre in Nicolson Street by a two-man team called the Lords of Misrule, one performer playing Gulliver, and the other, the manager and scriptwriter, Alan Leigh, playing everything else. Here the stage was an absolute essential and the endless apparent improvisation was actually faultlessly and intricately worked out. Brilliant voice-throwing achieved the contrast between the piping sounds Gulliver heard from Lilliputians and the Stentorian roars they intended to deliver, with similar management of Brobdingnag in reverse. At times the illusion was so well realised that in retrospect there is an impression of Gulliver actually having stood on the King of Brobdingnag's hand to receive the famous denunciations of war and politics. Make-up and symbolic disguise were pushed to their fullest extent when the horrible, filthy Yahoo gambolled off to be replaced by a wonderfully masked and aristocratically pawing Master Horse, apparently whinnying his way into speech when he was actually whinnying out of it. The whole work was conceived in a deep sense of respect for

Swift. Following the direction of modern research inaugurated by the medical findings of Sir William Wilde, Swift is not mad, but on his first appearance, Gulliver is. The play therefore turned on what had driven him mad. Swift complicated the issue by making Gulliver so greatly varying a protagonist in the successive books: in Lilliput a sympathetic victim, in Brobdingnag a nasty chauvinist, in Laputa a sardonic observer, and in the Houyhnhnms' country a tragic victim of psychological alienation. But by forecasting his ultimate fate, the dramatic tension was carried through with purpose, and Gulliver became something of a pilgrim destined to mental destruction rather than spiritual regeneration. His initial difficulties with the politics of the Lilliputians, and the monstrous size of domestic pets and pests among the Brobdingnagians, therefore ensured that he was seen to encounter and withstand the various perils of his pilgrimage, while Swift's many hard parables and morals were held up with the force he intended as memorable cameos.

Present *Gulliver* on film, supported by every device of modern technology, and the messages are blunted; present *Gulliver* in reading aloud, and the wonders seem hollow; read it, and you get them both; see it staged by the Lords of Misrule, and you get them both, but with an immediacy all the greater from the ingenious use of basic materials at human disposal. Theatre using basic props, if supported by performances far beyond most capacities, retains the simplicity of the parable. Ostentation and profligacy in staging would directly contradict what Swift was passionately declaiming: a richly serviced production in high-priced theatres is as convincing in preaching against human greed and competitiveness as Marie Antoinette was convincing as a shepherdess. And the essentially human achievement in simulation of big and little men, scientific lunacy, degenerate humans and Superhorses, is what Swift must require as the basis for theatre transmission of his work. He read it to his servants to ensure its intelligibility, and perhaps to check up on his accurate use of the Irish-language sources; he would want an audience with no greater material basis whence to make demands.

Freddie Anderson's *Oiney Hoy*, a sort of *Candide* about modern Ireland, later published as a novel, was performed in 1987 by the

Easterhouse Summer Festival in the Mandela Gateway Exchange at Abbeymount, beyond the Palace at Holyrood. The actors were from the young people perpetually marooned in the wastes of Glasgow's possibly most deprived district. Acting was not great or notably accomplished, although there were some appealing and vigorous performances. The director, a local government leisure officer, had exhausted herself in the effort, but was clearly immensely gratified by the pleasure of the audiences, and even more by the continued enjoyment being evinced by the cast. As far as she was concerned, this was a holiday for her charges from their present wretched environment and there was no way she intended to spoil it by pestering them with pseudo-professional standards. She wanted them to be as good as they could become without losing their happiness. Everyone seemed happy. Nobody wanted any awards. The former convict Jimmy Boyle had played a great part in making it all possible by leasing the theatre. The Fringe happens for many motives, and the good may be far above the great.

James O'Brien, a Birmingham crusader for the release of the Birmingham Six, brought his agit-prop play demanding their release to the Demarco Gallery in 1987. The play itself confused the converted with the unconvinced, and made its own contribution to alienation techniques by white-painted faces, explosion-sounds, explosion-stinks, and so forth while chanting doggerel on the injustices of the sentence, need for an enquiry, questionable decisions of Authority, etc., to its audience. On the other hand the passionate sincerity of James O'Brien himself had very forceful impact. The problem about the cause of the Six was that much of it was being manipulated in the interest of support for the Provisional IRA, the undoubted murderers of the pub-drinkers in Birmingham. People were not prepared to question such blatantly false statements as the judicial insistence that no British policeman would strike a prisoner, fudge evidence or allow natural feelings of fury at murders of civilians to sweat confessions. It was vaguely felt that sympathy for the Six played into IRA hands. O'Brien's heartfelt indignation and simple personal decency made a great impact on visitors to the venue, and his readiness to pitch in to help other shows in difficulties, and the management when otherwise overwhelmed, drew people of little interest in his cause to his play. The support he aroused kept his show (and its sequel on the Stalker affair) on the road, and he unquestionably played an important and self-sacrificing part in releasing the innocent prisoners and exposing a great stain on British justice, to its considerable benefit.

In 1978 my first *Scotsman* assignment was unable to go on, and I fled in the rain to look at a nearby venue offering, in the Crown at Hill Place, for possible coverage in the *Irish Times*. Its title, *The Burning of Carthage*, suggested an interesting and tragic episode in Roman history. It proved to be an improvised idea from Cambridge Amateur Dramatic Company of post-nuclear-holocaust survival whose tedium, uncertainty of purpose and general chaos may have been felt to symbolise the character of a devastated world, but was in my view unendurable. I telephoned Allen Wright, discovered that I could have the case, and seethed a nuclear strike of my own into review form. It ended, 'OK, we get the message, Cambridge: any damn thing is good enough for the Fringe'. I learned that at the end of the run the cast party had as its prime success 'Owen Dudley Edwards presenting the Festival Fringe Worsts: no. 1, *The Burning of Carthage*'. Immediately after Festival 1989 I had to attend a conference in Liverpool and then leave it early on Sunday morning for a London lecture: this necessitated a long bus trip to Manchester airport on which I was joined by a member of the *Carthage* cast who thanked me for my review, stated that it enabled him to rethink his ideas on the theatre, and told me that after an interval he had become a professional. But even these gallantries were eclipsed by a Cambridge A.D.C. person named Peter Rumney, who wrote to me at *The Scotsman* just after my onsaulght was printed, stating that he had no part in *The Burning of Carthage* and that it was my right to say what I believed, his view on the production being neither relevant nor in need of expression. However, the last sentence of my review could be taken as implying that I thought all Cambridge A.D.C. productions came into the any-damn-thing category. He therefore was inviting me to review his Cambridge A.D.C. production, a new play by Mark Wheatley, *Jael*. Would it be possible for me to get *The Scotsman* commission to review it? As director, he wanted to know if I would consider it any damn thing. Allen Wright agreed with me that the sheer guts of this appeal merited respect, and back to the Crown I went. The biblical subject of the play had been a childhood nightmare of mine, featuring the lady who hammered the tent-peg into the head of Sisera, the enemy of her people, although I later became more interested in the strong feminist preoccupation of the whole passage in *Judges* with its unexpected beginning in asserting the female leadership of Deborah. The play looked as if it had been unduly influenced by the Hollywood biblical preoccupation with extraneous human interest, was ably directed, finished in fine style, and in overall ambition and dedication merited considerable respect. I said as much, ending on a plea to my readers, 'Go to *Jael*'. Many years later I was very pleased to see Peter Rumney performing impressively under the auspices of the Glasgow Citizens' Theatre.

In 1979 *The Scotsman* assigned me to cover a University of Rhode Island adaptation of John Dos Passos's *USA* at the Roxburgh Rooms. The complimentary two seats are essential to reviewers in order to ensure that a second opinion is present, with a second pair of eyes and ears to pick up what one might miss: the thing is to choose a companion of reliable judgment, good observation and, if possible, special knowledge (as with bringing children to children's shows). My graduate student Colin Affleck had obtained a First with us partly in the light of his splendid thesis on the value of *USA* to the historian. But on arrival I found that, as occasionally happens in the press of business at *The Scotsman* in Fringetime, it had double-booked, and my amiable colleague David Campbell, otherwise an education producer for BBC Scotland, was already ensconced. We agreed to discuss our redundancy in the interval, and retired round the corner to Peter Cunningham's excellent pub, Stewart's Bar in Drummond Street. I pointed out that Colin knew more about the original work than either of us, and David good-naturedly consented that we sign a joint abdication in his favour. Colin duly put in the first of his characteristically judicious and constructively but not excessively well-informed judgments, showing what had been lost in the drastically cut version, complimenting the production on its realisation of Dos Passos's news headlines interspersed in the text, and assessing the strengths and weaknesses of the dramatisation of what had been left in the main story. Allen Wright printed the piece with pleasure, regretted that he could not use Colin further since his roster was complete for this season, but was happy to add him to the strength of foot-soldiers for Fringe 1980, and, as it has turned out, ever since.

Welsh Theatre has been coming to the Fringe with increasing strength in the later 1980s. First, there was a mysterious company called Red Dragon, who were from the Welsh College of Music and Drama, forbidden by some officious bureaucrat to employ the name of their institution for fear of discrediting it. Red Dragon put on some perfectly decent Howard Brenton, showing more originality in the production than was evident in the play, *Christie in Love*, and some effective Charles Marowitz. Eventually bureaucracy gave way, or suffered a loss which was in fact a gain, and the students performed under the College's name. In 1990 it included a remarkable new play by Andrew Neil, a Scot on the staff, with a wonderfully intricate (Scottish) plot to justify a title whose explanation brought the house down, *My Mother Answered the Phone to Stanislavski* (which proved a nickname of a crucial character in the complex life of the central figure). It made a slight effort to milk TV by starring John Stahl, famous for his rôle in the Scottish TV soap opera *Take The High Road*. This was gratifying to home punters and people in search of good plays, but in general the work of the College has been insufficiently Welsh.

In 1989, the group *Made in Wales* performed *The Scam* at the Traverse, in which Ian Puleston-Davies and Nick Dowsett gave hard, strong performances as two Welsh migrant workers perfecting a scheme to rip off the system in which they are enmeshed, only to see their friendship endangered by the profit motive and their own self-liberation imprisoned in the far more intractable confines of the free market economy. Welsh-language theatre made its first Fringe appearance in 1986 when Cwmni Cyri Tri produced an intricate and highly visual fantasy; pantomimed neo-mythology was also rendered in Welsh by Y Cwmni, who performed well at the Harry Younger Hall alongside the Welsh College, in 1989. The work of the most remarkable recent playwright to come from Wales formed the other part of its bill, Edward Thomas's *House of America*, where the American dreams and self-identifications of a dangerously isolated Welsh family prove the catalyst in the destruction of their lives. It was a riveting piece of contemporary Welsh self-analysis, and the Fringe appearance has done much to arouse Welsh public interest.

The growing exploration of Scots in the years since MacDiarmid's death began by touching its roots. Frank Dunlop invited Tom Fleming to revive the old anti-clerical pre-Reformation *Ane Satyre of the Thrie Estaites* in the Assembly Hall where Tyrone Guthrie had staged it in the early Festivals, and then to produce Sydney Goodsir Smith's great play on the hero of the first stage of the Scottish War of Independence against Edward I, *The Wallace*. Leadership on this cultural level produced its natural response on the Fringe, and is a good example of how the Festival may prompt constructive reflection elsewhere. In the best sense, the past called to the future.

The most ambitious application of Scots to the Fringe to date has been Bill Dunlop's version of Aeschylus's *Agamemnon*, which he intends to be followed by productions of *The Libation Bearers* and *The Eumenides*. By opening on the Monday of week 0, *Agamemnon* actually inaugurated Fringe 1990, and hence Festival 1990 also, in its wider sense. It performed in Riddle's Court in the High Street, much hallowed by many years of the Workers' Educational Association. The hard-bitten question of all work in Scots must be, whether it adds anything to the sum of cultural excellence. The National Theatre *Oresteia* in Tony Harrison's translation had for once satisfied both the lovers of theatre and the Beautiful, Beautiful People, and what more was needed, short of a revival in the ancient Greek vernacular?

Scots is a more democratic language than English, as no doubt King James I of England felt in conning the King James Bible and recalling — and it was probably a memory that haunted him — his days as King James VI of Scotland when he was theologically instructed in his identity as 'God's silly vassal'. It is also earthier. It may take some pride in also being a more barbarous language, given the dog's dinner Civilisation has been making of itself. It strongly reflects primitive agrarian usage. Its more modern practitioners have been persons renowned for direct speech. It possesses a sharper precision.

There was much in this production which carried its message for any stage or time: Bill Dunlop had every intention of giving Clytemnestra a good feminist run for her husband's real estate. Cassandra alone speaks in English. She was performed, extremely well, by Lyndsay Maples who is English. This really took matters farther. Cassandra in the Aeschylus *Agamemnon* is alien to her audience in the play and out of it, not because she is a Trojan, but because she is divinely inspired and hence apparently mad. But the Cassandra of Bill Dunlop's version and his company's production was not mad at all. Her insistence on having been raped by the Sun-God seemed a very English kind of claim, especially if delivered to a Scots-speaking audience. She was most effectively directed, not towards hysteria, but to an icy calm, in context far more unsettling an indication of her mental state to the excited Scots chorus. She was a deeply sympathetic figure, but with an isolation of origins much deeper than her captive status and theological entanglement. She suggested a cultural void between her and her hearers, over which they could make but faint efforts to leap. Cassandra's allusion, at the climax of the murder-vision, to Agamemnon as a bull and Clytemnestra as a cow, came very naturally to her urban eyes viewing the hierarchs of a primitive agrarian society. And she was firmly urban, making her Troy come alive as a cosmopolitan centre in contrast to this remote backwater. Ostensibly the palace of Agamemnon is in an urban setting — what else would the Athenians expect? — but on Cassandra's tongue, description rather than disdain placed it in ancient Hicksville.

The Scots themselves made blunt but dignified appearances, Clytemnestra an enraged victim whose ferocious decision for liberation induces her metamorphosis into very ugly self-control. Agamemnon directed, which dual function was a mistake; his directing was masterly, but his performance was that of a village worthy who has crushed an obnoxious amendment at the town council, thereby wallowing in Hicksville. The more general pattern was one of a society frightened by its own daring in having gone so far against a more civilised adversary, and the advent of Cassandra thus realised its worst forebodings as well as fulfilling hers. The Scots *Agamemnon* in itself gave the proof of the remarkable, if not altogether predictable, potentialities of Scots in the theatre of the future.

In 1989 Richard Crane performed in his *Rolling the Stone* under Faynia Williams's direction at the great space established by Richard Demarco in Blackfriars Street. It was a wholly characteristic piece of Crane rethinking of classical legend, this time on Sisyphus, taking in Camus and various other appropriate or inappropriate commentators and creative artists on the way, mixing Sisyphus's sardonic comments on them with mysticism, theology, anti-heroic send-up of legend and life, wicked and hard-hitting puns and, above all, the optimism of Man battling against previous experience and all the probabilities in his efforts to get the accursed stone over the top. It was realised by a complex network of ropes driven against the uppermost part of the wall (somewhat to the consternation of the administrators of the Theatre of the Future) up which Sisyphus struggled and down, tumbling in every conceivable fall known to Man and Hades. It duly won Crane's ninth Fringe First Award, but it may have symbolised also his memories of Fringemanship. Here he was, battling once more for his audience and his triumph, experience in his case on his side, but past successes being no insurance for the present venture, as he and Faynia and all former winners of awards know. Yesterday's success will make today's comparative failure all the more dismal. Perhaps it may matter little to the brass necks of revue casts, but serious theatre is haunted by it. But what a series of triumphs Richard's and Faynia's were: 1988 was *Red Magic*, his meditation in the Assembly Rooms on Eisenstein, the set a moviola dolly doing duty in various capacities including a train: Faynia had thought of an old camera crane, but found it less effective, and probably less accessible. Their sons, Leo and Sam Crane, had taken the part of the infant Eisenstein on alternative nights, and showed every inheritance of crowd-conquering capacity. Richard said that what fascinated him about Eisenstein 'was the way he always said he never really grew up'. Eisenstein as Fringe-person, in fact. Like *The Happy Prince*, the Fringe is for all ages, and all ages are one. And before that there was their *Pushkin*, beginning with its marvellously white tableau of the dead playwright in the snow after his fatal duel, the actors standing in dreadful silence while the audience became seated. And then . . . but they are a book in themselves.

Something very like Cranery in the early stages reigned in Baden-Powell House, Fisher's Close, off the Lawnmarket, at the Edinburgh Youth Theatre in the early 1980s under the producer-journalist David Clayton and his colleagues Iain Johnstone, Gavin Pagan and Gerard Lohan who wrote and composed its best work. Amid several great events, I remember particularly *Clutter*, a crowd-energising play about a theatre family decimated by service in World War II; *Frankie*, where Chris Annets played a heartrending child-creation of Frankenstein caught up in a Cinderella situation at Castle Frankenstein and subsequently in a magnificently multifarious freak-show, all mingling comedy of performance and tragedy of identity; and *Maurice the Minotaur*.

Production was straightforward: it was Richard's, not Faynia's genius, which the material recalled. *Maurice* was based on the story of Theseus and the Minotaur, but reworked in Richard's iconoclastic and inventive spirit. Theseus was a silly upper-class twit, boastful and cowardly, pushed into the Labyrinth where he cautiously sidled around watching out for the Minotaur. The Minotaur found him, in a very neat set of hidden half-encounters and pretend-discoveries which greatly delighted the youthful audience, mostly slightly younger than the teenage actors. The Minotaur made his capture, to reveal himself as a former intended victim of the original Minotaur whom he had managed to kill, and now maintained prisoner by the evil female Gorgon who had forced him to take the Minotaur's place. Eventually she was killed and the children rescued, all by the wits and courage of the Minotaur, who, being a very modest boy, then made Theseus the hero. They had great fun inventing the original myth so that it would become history, and asserted a very fine point in criticism of standard history in so doing. I wonder if actors or audience ever took history seriously again, and occasionally as I listen to the infallible-sounding pronouncements of historians I have to kill an unseemly snicker at the thought of little Maurice, and his achievements in conspiracy, diplomacy, and mendacity (apart from the detail of his heroism which he was so anxious to conceal). The notion of the Minotaur saving the expedition and its hero then credited with having killed him was as neat an irony as anyone could ask.

Kathy Howden made a magnificently horrible Gorgon, wallowing in genteel malevolence: she subsequently proved herself a radiation of talent on stage, reaching pathos, bitchiness and schizophrenia all at once in *Frankie* as Geminee/Gemineye, a Siamese twinset combined completely into one body. She went on to the Royal Scottish Academy of Music and Drama where I had much delight in presenting her with a Royal Lyceum Theatre Club award, and was later to perform in the Lyceum Company under the resourceful directorship of Ian Wooldridge. Alas, Edinburgh Youth Theatre ultimately stopped using its own material, and sought box-office success scripts from London. If the Scots will only have confidence in themselves, they have excellent work to show: dependence on tried and proven crowd-winners from the metropolis inevitably provincialises the spirit as well as the players and audience. What London does so well for itself is unlikely to serve needs accustomed to Edinburgh originality. We need another slogan: Keep the Cringe off the Fringe.

Michael Westcott, the vice-chairman of the Fringe, retired in 1990 and was presented with a Festival Fringe First plaque. He is also retired from an assistant secretaryship within the University, where for years he was the invaluable master of ceremonies on all major occasions, and a pillar of integrity as well as a remarkable diplomat in nurturing cultural creativity. He is one of the most perfectly organised people, and one of the masters of effective procedure, whom anyone can know, and there is a magnificent symbolism in so punctilious an agent of order having worked for so long and with such dedication for an institution priding itself on the anarchy of its spirit. He has visited probably far more Fringe shows than I have ever known, and in addition is interested in many charitable ventures, public and private, some with stage ramifications, some not. At the end of 1990's Festival he drove me to St Andrews to see a performance in the Byre by a young actor, Ali de Souza, in whose career he was interested. We sat in his car and looked at the sea while we ate a meal provided by Michael, which though lost to sight is to memory dear. De Souza was splendid: lightness and strength entered the stage with him, perfection in what he touched, illumination of the most commonplace lines, a needful reminder that budding Scottish genius in the theatre is not only to be found on Fringestage. It was so like Michael to wind up my Festival with a vision of its potential future. I may revel in the paradox of his integral place in the Fringe, helping it to weather so many storms

228

and presiding over its needs in the absence of prestigious — and, for a time, dead — chairpersons. But I can never wonder at how much the Fringe loves him.

Chapter Nine

Last Words

FESTIVAL
FRINGE 1981

From *Saki* (Hector Hugh Munro), 'Reginald at the Theatre':

'That is the worst of a tragedy,' he observed, 'one can't always hear oneself talk. . . .'

MICHAEL McEVOY, AN ACTOR OF DELICATE, GENTLE, YET SOUL-enlivening force, performed a one-person show on Vincent Van Gogh for the most recent Fringes, making much use of Van Gogh's letters to his brother, his relations with Gauguin, and so forth. Scripted by Patrick Haley, *Portrait of Vincent* began with the recorded sound of an art auction at the present day in which a Van Gogh is knocked down for a sum unprecedented by any painting. It ended with Van Gogh's decision to commit suicide on the grounds that only thus could his genius win its audience. For once the one-person show made a devastating achievement in overturning the conventions by deliberate use of the I-died formula, although the death took place offstage. McEvoy's deeply personal interpretation made sure of its hold on its audience's heart; whoever had bought the auction record-breaker, Van Gogh was ours and we were his, acts of identification rather than possession. The genius of his artistic creation might lie beyond our apprehension, but the character behind it stood before us, quietly, explicitly, sometimes with terrifying turbulence. And what that character said in the end was the legendary price to be paid by heroes — to succeed, you must die.

Death does not, of course, have to be tragic, though its comic possibilities are too rarely in evidence to justify the present-day enthusiasm for alluding to any demise under discussion as a 'tragic death'. Noël Coward's *Blithe Spirit* makes hilarious capital out of two deaths, those of the first and second wives of the writer Charles Condomine (sometimes three, ending with Charles's own death, in stage productions as well as in Coward's film version). It was an old favourite of mine, romantically through Kay Kendall's performance, paternally in that my daughter Leila, having realised with restraint the rôle's comic potential, projected a judicious chill of fear on her school production's audience in her last moments on stage as the Medium Madame Arcati. So my voyage to the Bedlam one bright Fringe morning in 1990 was undertaken with no greater expectations than a touch of gooseflesh pleasantly enhancing what I consider Coward's finest comedy. I survived it without goose-pimples, for this Madame Arcati was oddly donnish and unconvincing, but in general the company, S.F.A. Ventures, of whom I knew nothing, proved eminently capable. Yet what I saw brought home to me a death of overwhelming tragedy in the life of an author of comic genius far superior to Coward.

Charles, the Coward clone, was obviously too young to play an established author settled well into his second marriage. But who could complain about that when Charles did his work with such zest and charm, infectious high spirits and wit formed of sheer exuberance? Coward's indulgently cynical self-realisation here became so captivating and so entrancing that it hit a harder reality: the idea of a husband whose wife's ghost loved him well enough to murder him in her yearning to possess him once more. I looked back to the programme in the interval — Hugh Cazalet. Something about that name seemed connected with the effervescence of this performance. But where had I encountered it before? The mind whizzed back, threshed around, flapped about, and then darted down. There was nothing effeminate about this Charles, nor indeed had there been about the part's creators on stage (Cecil Parker) and screen (Rex Harrison). Cazalet's performance was not obtrusively sexual, but it quite definitely captured a husband's marital, indeed bimarital, appeal as radiated towards each of his wives. Yet what I had now remembered brought female images rising into conscious memory.

Jill the Reckless, not the adult heroine of P. G. Wodehouse's novel of that name, but her girlhood recalled by her feckless uncle in the name he had then given her, a name also given for the book's American title *The Little Warrior*. Eve, in Wodehouse's *Leave It To Psmith*, recalling how her father sent her to charm away a dun at the door. Gladys, the little slum child befriended by Wodehouse's Lord Emsworth, who gives him courage at a moment of crisis by slipping her hand into his. The schoolboyish, joke-perpetrating, anti-authority Wodehouse girls in their early twenties: Bobbie Wickham, Stiffy Byng, Nobby Hopwood, Corky Pirbright. The greatest of all his heroines, Sue Brown, of *Heavy Weather* and its precursor *Summer Lightning*, Wodehouse's *Twelfth Night*, the Viola who becomes the firm ally and surrogate daughter of the novel's Sir Toby Belch, the Hon. Galahad Threepwood (also starring the Efficient Baxter as Malvolio, the Schopenhauer-reading Millicent as Olivia, Beach the butler unusually singing to do duty as Feste). 'To my daughter Leonora, Queen of her Species.' 'To my daughter Leonora without whose never-failing Sympathy and Encouragement this book would have been finished in half the time.' Wodehouse's step-daughter Leonora, whom he probably loved more than any being on earth. His letters to her had not then been published, but what prompted my train of thought was her marriage to a man called Cazalet.

I remembered Mother's telling me how Leonora had died when Wodehouse was a prisoner in Germany, and how, when he was told, he said, 'But I thought she was immortal.' His last full character conceived with her in mind is Sally Painter, the heroine of *Uncle Dynamite*, which he was writing when he heard of Leonora's death. Sally is offstage for the last tenth of the book.

My review went off to *The Scotsman*, favourable, with some little criticism about a minor error in costume, noting Cazalet's youth and stressing how his performance more than compensated for it. As I waited for the paper to appear, I took a look in the National Library at *Who's Who*, and at Burke or Debrett. Leonora had one son, afterwards Mr Justice Cazalet. He had two. When what I had said was in print, so that there might be no embarrassment in the confrontation of cast-member with as yet unpublished critic, I returned to the Bedlam and sent in my name to the leading actor. It was a fine, clear morning. We talked in front of the theatre, looking down George IV Bridge and Candlemaker Row.

'I have one question to put to you, Mr Cazalet,' I said. 'Was your grandmother called Leonora?'

He stammered slightly, as well he might. 'Why, yes, that is, she died long before I was born.'

'I know,' I said.

'But it was Leonora! How on earth did you know that?'

'It was your acting,' I said.

Death sponsored a famous partnership with which both I and the Fringe have been jointly and severally involved. I suppose I could make a good case for William Burke, who murdered sixteen people to sell their bodies to the anatomists in 1828 and whose rejoicing at the not-proven verdict on his beloved Helen MacDougal clearly out-weighed any regrets about his own fatal verdict of guilty, to argue that he was a man of soul and, perhaps, in my book *Burke and Hare* (1980) I have. I could discover nothing to the credit of William Hare, his partner in murder, who with his wife turned King's Evidence against Burke and MacDougal; so you might think of him as a man of body: though 'body' in the context is really the preserve of their victims. For a century and a half Scottish stages had given various shows on Burke and Hare, all more or less presenting them as fiends incarnate. My book had one origin in a Lyceum revival, starring Tom Fleming in James Bridie's *The Anatomist*, whose slightly precious treatment of the moral guilt or innocence of Dr Robert Knox in receiving the bodies was in marked contrast to the distinguished playwright's obvious indifference to any question of seeking human dimensions in Burke and Hare. They were to be funny but homicidal Irishmen, all of which qualities apparently took them out of legitimate enquiry.

I was in fact irritated into writing my book, though it took some years to solidify my intention. After it was published, the co-operative spirit of the publishers of Edinburgh, who organised the early 'Book Festivals', despatched Kim Wolfe-Murray (now a Buddhist monk) to lure me into fine shenanigans with a beguilement as charming as that of his mother Stephanie, of Canongate Publishing. So, from several midnights in Festival 1981, I led hordes of the public through sites associated with Burke and Hare, while various characters in the story mysteriously flashed into view performing certain actions illuminating my narrative. The Wolfe-Murrays found me a splendid derelict house in which the duo were beheld arriving to murder the crippled idiot of the West Port, 'Daft Jamie' Wilson. It was exhausting but thrilling fun for me, and I hope for the audiences, and the young actors showed a fine spirit. The midnight tour has had many, more commercial, imitators since.

I had hopes of someone writing a new Burke and Hare play based on my own revisionist study. And in the fullness of time they did. One Fringeday I was sent by Allen Wright to cover a new Burke and Hare play, found it a documentary, and suddenly began hearing an eerie ring of familiarity. I had, in fact, been sent to review what was proving to be myself, or large hunks of myself. In a sense my situation was like that of one of the victims of Burke and Hare, making a contribution to knowledge while having given no permission for that purpose. The author, when invited to explain, stated that he realised he had used so much of my work that a refusal of permission would have torpedoed the production. Certainly no resurrectionist could have viewed the revivification of one of his victims, such as Stevenson imagines in *The Body-Snatcher*, with a horror equal to his, when he looked at the house on being told *The Scotsman* was present, and realised the form taken in its epiphany. I invited him to lunch: the thing was really too funny, and besides it was a good production. My review necessarily explained that as I had written much of what I was reviewing, my favourable judgment had to be considered in the light of this. I made it clear that I had no intention of suing the subject of my review (which made a nice change, when you think about it), and this, of course, had to be examined by *The Scotsman*'s legal advisers to ensure that the review did not in itself constitute potential evidence in any future action I might take, and decided it would not since it showed I would not take it. This is not as daft as it seems: there are authentic cases of actionable material being placed in newspapers by persons who subsequently arrange for legal proceedings involving the newspaper — Fringe 1979 brought the *Festival Times* under one such threat, neatly torpedoed by its Board chairman, at that time the future BBC Scotland producer (whose remit would include *Festival View*) Bruce Young. I thoroughly enjoyed my lunch with my repentant poacher and so did he; and he drafted, and I redrafted, a suitable statement to appear in any further programme of the work, as it did, in an even better revival, and I shall watch his career with considerable interest.

Ultimately, a playwright unconnected with his predecessor, Chris Ballance, wrote *Water of Life*, about Burke and Hare, making acknowledged use of my book, and I had pleasure in nominating it for a Fringe First in 1989, which it got. It was a well-produced, well-acted, coherent, riveting drama, making excellent sense within its own confines. Like my friend the poacher, the author had agreed with me in seeing the potential tragic quality of William Burke, lured by circumstances into murder whence he could not break free, for the first murders were committed not primarily from gain but from fear of the Hare house being closed for sheltering fever-ridden dying persons.

237

But the most original twist I saw on the Burke-Hare theme was by Chris Begg, a schoolmaster in Hazelhead Academy, Aberdeen, who had not read my book or had dismissed it if he had. It was good reworking of the Bad Quarto. Burke was a horrendous villain. Hare, actually a much uglier figure than Burke physically and I think mentally, was peripheral, but, in a nice bit of gruesome symbolism, he ended the play by hanging Burke. The genius of the thing was the use of a pre-teen schoolboy actor, playing the part of Daft Jamie. Steven Milne, the diminutive Daft Jamie, darted around the stage, brilliantly making it clear to the audience that he alone had realised the truth of the murders, but unable to convince anyone in the cast until his message got through to Burke. Jamie stammers out a Burke and Hare rhyme, Burke replies savagely with 'Wee Willie Winkie', corners the elusive waif, and exit, bearing the intended body. There are many dramas of children foiling a criminal, even a murderer; but the idea of the child detective being killed after his solution of the mystery but before its disclosure to Authority, was absolutely spine-freezing. It was comparable in its way to Hitchcock's *Psycho*, with its killing of the investigating private detective — but Hazelhead Academy had gone Hitchcock one better by making the murdered detective a child.

Theatre may offer ritual as substitute for death, much as Konrad Lorenz describes cranes acting out aggression as substitute for engaging in it, and Conor Cruise O'Brien describes United Nations diplomats in Assembly performance on the same system. Yet theatre may inflame its audience to seek death, for themselves or for some oppressor, as Cruise O'Brien would feel Yeats did, in his play *Cathleen Ni Houlihan*, and as Yeats came to believe he had done. The theatre of politics alters its ritual when an extreme votary brings into real action the principle that the King must Die. Today one playwright has become Pope, another has become premier of Czechoslovakia; today also political assassination grows, much more noticeably choosing its victims among charismatic leaders. The boring political performer may deserve assassination more than anyone, but he seldom receives it. Thus when Gordon DeMarco, a fine creator of US thriller fiction, transferred his fictional locale and personal presence here to write and subsequently stage *Murder at the Fringe*, his victim

238

was a charismatic performer-playwright, loosely based on the great folklorist-anarchist Dario Fo. The real Fo is much less like the Gordon DeMarco corpse as revealed in *post-mortem* souvenirs than Gordon DeMarco may have intended; but Fo embodies personal radiation of electricity, with powers of communication overleaping commonplace norms. When I interviewed him, I found I understood him better if our interpreter, Stuart Hood, did not intervene, and I have no Italian. DeMarco is correct in that Fringemurder would seem dramatically to require someone as earth-shaking as Dario Fo.

But the most obvious place for murder in the theatre (apart from director maddening actor beyond endurance or *vice versa*) is among rival creators. In his press conference, called for 7.30 a.m., to launch the 1991 Festival programme, Frank Dunlop, Puck as always but this time Puck momentarily trying on the head of John Knox, indignantly championed 'the very neglected and traduced composer Salieri'; Salieri deserves the celebration commissioned by Dunlop for his last Festival, and one wishes it celebrity, but for the next few years the vulgar will continue to think of Salieri as Mozart's murderer thanks to the plays of Pushkin and Peter Shaffer. It is actually Pushkin on whom the story reflects: the idea of murder of a rival was in *his* head, as he showed by getting killed in a duel, as well as by fashioning Mozart's murder in his play. (I wonder how Peter Shaffer will die?) So Fringe-theatre knew what it was about when Stage of Fools in 1987 produced a play, *Tomtom*, by Nick Vivian and Tom Morris, at Heriot-Watt Theatres in which two ventriloquists operate the same dummy in apparently schizophrenic conversation only to have one quit the act for a better contract for which the other in love-hatred-rivalry murders him.

The grand master of the *avant-garde* (or, as the Scottish Enlightenment would have said, the *avant-gardez-loo*), Joe Orton, was of course himself a spectacular victim of such a murder on 9 August 1967 (assuming it really was Kenneth Halliwell who killed him, and that the whole thing was not an Ortonesque revenge or theocratic confection cooked up by the police). This inspired some weary drivel from Strode Jackson some dozen Fringes later, in exploitation of its box-office possibilities, but in 1990 an Edinburgh undergraduate playwright, Roddy McDevitt, made quite spectacular theological horrorscope of the murder-cum-suicide. *Halliwell's Hell* sucked inspirational blood from Halliwell documentary material, fuelling an infernal machine of inevitability whose agents in the play include Orton's creation Sergeant Truscott and God's creation T. S. Eliot; and the inevitability proves itself part of the greater apparatus of infernal retribution with Halliwell condemned to repeat endlessly his own supersession by his protégé Orton to recapture whom in death he damns himself.

Dogs was a musical, originally devised as a satire on rock-group cults, pop-star idolatry, showbiz inflationary tactics. All of this David Llewellyn manipulated as author and director. His conception of its origins lay in a hilariously revolting cult of canine metamorphosis among Liverpool teenagers. When the pack is removed in the paddy-wagon by the police, there is a marvellous number worked out by percussion simulation of their rhythmical banging on the sides and roof of their invisible van-prison. The populist exchanges with the local superintendent, their efforts to explain the dog cult to him, and his understandably hygienic anxiety to get rid of them as fast as possible when he finally understands the full repulsive implications of their dog-rôleing, showed writer-director and cast in full co-ordinated celebration of comedy in the customarily envenomed confrontation of Authority vs. Ethnicity, whether in reality or in theatre.

But something happened to *Dogs*. In part, it was the inspired performance of the student musical co-ordinator of the production, Andy Frizell, cast as 'Wolfie' Nutley, the waif-like bourgeois boy who became the pack-leader. There was his moving, unschmaltzy relationship with his most devoted disciple, his little sister. The two of them swung the story more and more powerfully into a strange, entrancing if dotty saga, in which Satire began to make room for Sentiment, but Sentiment in armour lent by Satire. Very different ghosts from that of Elvis Presley haunted directors and actors: Spike Milligan's *Puckoon*, a previous Llewellyn Fringe success; Jack London's *Call of the Wild* and *White Fang*, with heroic quality more irresistible than David Llewellyn may have realised at first. The children adrift in the showbiz world caught innumerable shadows from the root-*motifs* of the babes in the wood or Hansel and Gretel — or the Children's Crusade. And then, in a flicker of *Manon Lescaut*, Wolfie and Shitsu are marooned in an American desert where Wolfie dies. His posthumous cult as a Messiah returned to the satirical, but there was no satire in the desert lament of his sister over his corpse, and if the Messianism was credible it was so by enslaving the audience to the integrity of the martyr, lunatic as it was. The very end blazed its mockery at every exploiter of dead Messiahs from St Paul to Jesse Jackson. (On the other hand, it was quite uninfluenced by the musical *Cats*, having preceded it.)

It ran briefly at the Walpole Hall's adjoining tent, and returned for another Fringe to the Heriot-Watt. It had great numbers, zest and fire and laughter and a cast who obviously enjoyed almost every minute, comedy origins giving all the greater bite to the death in the desert and the lone lament. And those last remain for me as one of the finest expressions of Fringe tragedy, although their original purpose was an illusion within an illusion. As John Retallack had shown so ably in his version of *Don Quixote*, Cervantes concluded in tragedy what he had begun as uproarious satire.

Eibhlín Dubh Ní Chonaill, *Caoineadh Airt Uí Laoghaire (Lament for Art O'Leary)*, first verse (my translation):

> *My fortress of love for you!*
> *The day I beheld you*
> *At the head of the market*
> *My eye gave heed to you*
> *My heart gave light to you*
> *I eloped from my father with you*
> *Far from my home with you.*

It happened in 1773. She was then twenty-five. She was from one of the few surviving Catholic landholding families, the O'Connells of Derrynane, in Kerry: two years after it her nephew, Daniel O'Connell, the future architect of Irish popular nationalism, was born. Art Ó Laoghaire was an officer in Austrian service, one of the many who had emigrated illegally because of the prohibition against acceptance of Irish Catholics into British service. He returned a Colonel, won Dark Eileen O'Connell's heart, took her to a home near Macroom, in Cork, and then became involved in a feud with a Protestant neighbour who asserted his legal right to buy Art O'Leary's mare for £5, the highest value on a Catholic's horse. His attempt to assert military conventions by challenging his adversary to a duel simply had him outlawed. He fought off a siege of his house, but was ambushed and shot by soldiers, the bloody steed summoning Eileen to his corpse. *Lament for Arthur Cleary*, a play by Dermot Bolger, appeared at the Traverse under David Byrne's direction in the 1990 Fringe. I suppose that when it played in Ireland its harsh, dense setting in the mushrooming contemporary Dublin, twice the size of today's Edinburgh and of the Dublin I knew, would have been the obvious basis for association by most of the audience. But for me, it was Eileen O'Connell's poem which gave me my first hold on the play. What Bolger had created, and what Byrne and his actors realised in the almost incredibly small acting space of the Traverse minor auditorium, was a vivid and terrifying lesson in Irish contemporary history: the world of rack-rents, squatting, promiscuous violence, rackets, dance-halls, nomads, spiritual emptiness save for a probably transient and highly sexual love, a society I knew only through the grim and rather fearful reflections of septuagenarian parents. Dublin has become a very frightening city, especially if you are old. Bolger's use of the poem inviting a likening, but not an identifying, of the lower-caste misery into which mid-eighteenth-century Irish Catholics had been forced with what their own people had now made for them. Symbolically it is important that O'Leary resembles but is not the same name as Cleary, although the more intimate Christian name is identical. Both men are older than the girls who love them, and perhaps Art O'Leary was as conscious of it as Arthur Cleary, and as ready to overcall his youthful prowess. Both remember a kind of freedom in the European career which intervened before return to Ireland, and both are ready to challenge the restrictions on that freedom in Ireland to the alarm and foreboding of the women who have taken them. The title of each work asserts the inevitability of its Arthur's fate. They are heroic figures who know they fight the licensed jackals of the State, whether a greedy Protestant or an extortionate rent man; their sole weapon, the preservation of Arthurian chivalry, protects only for limited time and is then the instrument of their destruction.

David Byrne's direction ostensibly gave all to the contemporary story, firmly restricting the original poem to a voice and a programme note. But the very fidelity, the hard realism of its instruction, provided the means for the play's reception into a historical dimension. The majority of Irish people in the Republic are today under thirty, perhaps under twenty-five, and may well be losing their historical consciousness in the wake of their language and their religion. But to those who retain it, the dimension is there. And to those who do not, the play has the message that those who forget their history are condemned to repeat it. Yet it has its other message, that expressed in Wells's *The Time Machine*, whose horrific future society bore witness 'that even when mind and strength had gone, gratitude and a mutual tenderness still lived on in the heart of man'. Wells had his fictional vision of the future to bring that comfort; Bolger had his poetic document from the past.

The Mass is central to Roman Catholic religious expression, and the Mass is theatre. It is symbolic and not realistic theatre, but Roman Catholics such as myself believe that the Mass actually embodies the self-sacrifice of Jesus Christ, coterminous both with His own symbolical expression of it at the Last Supper and His actual martyrdom on the Cross the following day, something possible because of Christ as God being outside time as we know it. Edinburgh undergraduate playwright Colin Teevan does not share my religious views, but he is of Catholic origin, and his *Till Human Voices Wake Us* on the Fringe in 1989 at the Bedlam put the Mass at the heart of what it wanted to say. A man lies dead: the priest celebrates Mass for the salvation of his soul. Simultaneously there appears at various points the reality of what the man's life has been, its different meanings in the minds of his various family members and what his life was like in his own mind when alive. There was some powerful acting, notably by Tom Phillips as the savagely and smoulderingly resentful son. But it was no mere equation of bereavement with the hypocrisy of appearance. Teevan's was a cold, ironic pity, but pity nonetheless, for the false starts, and seemingly trivial but irretrievable blunders. It was profoundly concerned with acting, in the lives of all of the parties, by implication in the appropriate sentiments required for the priest to express to God, Who knew perfectly well what they were worth according to the doctrines of the faith in which His acceptance of the departed spirit was being expressed. Oscar Wilde was pompous (perhaps because of internal unease on the implications of Walt

Whitman, implications with which he had yet to come to terms himself) when he said, in compliment, that if Poetry had passed Whitman by, Philosophy would take note of him. So far philosophy, at least in the hands of its official practitioners, does not seem to have done, but we can hope. For Colin Teevan it might be tempting to say that if Playmaking has passed him by, Theology would take note of him, and God knows it should. But he is a remarkable playwright, whether or not he takes further note of theology. He was to express it outside Fringetime with his play on the murder of Federico García Lorca, in which the last hours of that playwright — gay, republican, murdered early in the Spanish Civil War — are passed in forms of creating and acting out drama within drama of his imminent death. Life is theatre, and we are all performing within it, both consciously and subconsciously, sometimes imagining we play our own scripts while unaware of how much we play exclusive of our scripting. Teevan is an unusual case of a playwright thinking about such things.

The Falangist leader José Antonio Primo de Rivera, on being sentenced to death by a Republic Court early in the Spanish Civil War, answering a proposal to include his sister in the sentence:

> Me, certainly! In your position, I would do the same for you. But not her! Human lives are not to be disposed of causelessly, like setting off fireworks at the end of a party.

One quarter of a million people watched the Glenlivet Fireworks Concert in 1990, on the official estimates. The best immediate seats for seeing and hearing are at the Ross Bandstand in Princes Street Gardens, from which various bands cheer the passers-by on some Festival mornings. Ticket orders, and press complimentaries, and the Beautiful, Beautiful People, and various dignitaries fill the Ross. Garden standing tickets are obtained by booking at the Festival Office only. Some parties find havens in adjoining premises with tolerable views, much as they used to do for prominent hangings at the Tolbooth and Libberton's Wynd at the west end of High Street a century and a half since. (My friend Burke, of Burke and Hare, was turned off to a crowd of 5,000, being hanged in space now covered by the National Library of Scotland, where no doubt he inspired my researches.)

The press used to view it from the Festival Press balcony at the Mount Royal Hotel, Princes Street; premises also famous as the location of the would-be protective murder on which Bernard MacLaverty based his novel *Lamb* (later filmed). But in his first year, 1984, Frank Dunlop reserved it for special guests: Elizabeth Taylor (not making a Festival appearance) kept the Courts where formerly the press Jamshyds gloried and drank deep. That year, my daughter Sara and I saw the concert from the floor below, where Tom Sutcliffe, head of Arts in *The Independent* and once an inspirational producer for my stint on the BBC 3 *Words* programme, had a bedroom: Tom's aethereal charm was far more rewarding than Elizabeth Taylor could possibly have been. She sent a message to the press thanking it for respecting her privacy, which, however intended, was like a bailiff thanking evicted tenants for their co-operation. And for once her notions of press interest in her movements were excessive; at Festival time, non-performing visitors rate a couple of lines at best. *The Scotsman* ran a photograph of her with Frank Dunlop, and rumour promptly declared it was Samuel Beckett in drag, come to see the splendid mini-Festival-within-Festival Dunlop had so resourcefully staged in his honour. In any case the Festival Press Bureau left the Mount Royal and decamped to the Sheraton, off Lothian Road, whence the Fireworks Concert and most other Edinburgh phenomena were invisible to break the anonymous luxury; and later found a bleak structure on Jeffrey Street out of all sight (promptly baptised Colditz); and most recently settled down in the Scandic Crown Hotel which was likeable, well lit and cheery in a functional, pleasant Scandinavianism, but also inaccessible to a sight of the fireworks.

In 1990 I watched the spectacle with a group of friends on Princes Street. One of my companions was a little apprehensive that her French guest might be offended by the choice of Tchaikovsky's *1812* (or Chaikovsky, as Conrad Wilson in lonely literacy would call him as usual in tomorrow's *Scotsman*, on which orthography he had been formerly much twitted in the letters column by correspondents who retaliated by spelling him 'Konrad'). I was less concerned, especially since the French lady showed no sign of distaste, nor was I much concerned that a piece of music commemorating successful resistance against an invading power seeking domination might be given application to comparable problems within this island. The previous year the concert had culminated in Elgar's *Pomp and Circumstance, No. 1,* whose inapplicability to Scottish tradition had been loudly asseverated far and wide; in 1990, however, *1812,* followed by George McIlwhane's *Alba,* reassured Scots that the Festival had at least acknowledged its musicological imperialistic sins. Of course the 1989 band may have celebrated the land of hope and glory in a spirit of high irony, given the governmental withering of that glory in the garden of the arts with scant hope of any improvement; or it may have been prompted by some malevolent understrapper in the government personnel determined to lose no opportunity of infuriating the 3:1 Scottish majority against it. It was possible to see all Princes Street craning its ear at the encore to make sure that no further abomination of desolation sounded from the holy place, and the whisper 'Alba' wafted its way down the lines, necessarily, since the work is unhappily less well known than what it happily replaced.

The great centrepiece is of course Handel's Music for the Royal Fireworks, and the Scottish Chamber Orchestra under Ivor Bolton gave a grand account of it, while the pyrotechnician exceeded all possibilities. It is the only fireworks performance I enjoy, since the proceedings on November the Fifth are an incongruous subject for rejoicing to a Catholic whose coreligionists were tricked and tortured into scapegoats for a government frame-up. Apart from annual ritual sadistics against the memory of the wretched Guy Fawkes, the Fifth of November is productive of God knows what maiming and disfigurement by promiscuous pyrotechnics in the private sector. But the only unpleasing association of the Festival fireworks is the Hanover Georges in whose honour the music was first composed by unfortunate Handel, pursued by the tetchiness of their patronage all the way to London. The Edinburgh proceedings of 1990 were not entirely happy. The Castle hill grass went on fire, and the Ross Bandstand audience were sufficiently drenched in smoke to elicit expletives and expectorations from the Beautiful, Beautiful People, and the music was exceedingly loud in the Ross area, more particularly when joined by four twenty-four-pound field guns from the Castle for the *1812.* Unidentified burnt-out flying objects descended on the Princes Street crowd, apparently with little serious effect, and visitors found their cars clamped by a private English security firm whose refusal to give release without instant payment conflicted with previous police warnings against carrying money or cheque-books. As Adam Smith pointed out long ago, private enterprise usually results in conspiracy against the public interest, and it is idle to point out to such licensed vigilantes that they injure Edinburgh Festival tourism.

I am a total patsy for the pyrotechnical effects themselves. Princes Street Gardens are magic at the worst of times, sometimes at their most magical in the worst of weathers, and here Science and Nature abandon their mutual jealousies so that the mysterious shadows, great outcrops of rock and enchantment of the Castle resolve themselves into fresh mysteries of blazing, changing colour while the air is momentarily a haunted green or blue, or some great cluster aloft transforms itself into gravity-defying temples in red and gold. Our city, the child of a volcano, seems to celebrate its origin. It conjures up with it a great fellowship in the enormous crowd. The spectators are largely passive while the darkling spirits of earth and air make ghastly revel at the moon's eclipse; murmurs arise during firework intervals in hopes of yet further wonders, and time and again are stilled as some grand achievement suddenly holds the entire sky in just awareness that it was indeed worth waiting for. At last the finale is indicated, and reluctantly but happily dispersal begins. In 1990 I bade farewell to my friends, all travelling northward, and made my way south in the incredible mass of humanity holding the Mound and then into George IV Bridge through which the people alone could make progress while the few bold cars were forced into snail's pace or immobility. A nearby man shouted, 'The people have won back the city, even in Edinburgh!' Someone else jocularly placed a parking cone on top of a car frozen in the endless human ranks. Onward we marched, rejoicing in the moment when the city was ours. For once the voices of exaltation on the air were not the cries of arrogant invaders from the Thames Valley annexing the space indifferent to the existence of mere natives, but the silent Scottish people now out in carnival and repossessing their own. Humanity in its sheer vastness had become one magnificent expression of freedom. The Festival had found the people, and the people had found the Festival.

If there is one single person who sums up for me the Fringe at its most rapturously entrancing, it is Mark Bunyan, composer, pianist, lyricist, writer, gay liberationist, embattled pilgrim who will reveal capacities of undreamed-of invective if anyone compares him to the protagonist of his namesake John, a sore trial to his implacably atheistic conscience. He is an impossible person to write about, his entertainments ranging into so many different forms and moods that it is an impertinence to summarise them. In his successive one-person shows he has what he calls his soap-opera, the trials of a very Somerset amateur actor, caught up in village problems of sexism, repression, gay and lesbian self-realisation, snobbery, environmentalism, and generally the unexpected, turning on a wonderfully lunatic version of staging some *genre* of musical comedy the intricacy of whose parody leaves listeners ill with laughter.

One year it was Gilbert and Sullivan, and another it was *The Student Vagabond*, and a third some act of inhomage to what 'he' (the unnamed Somerset Thespian) terms 'Andrew Lloyd'. In the process 'he' has assumed a very real identity, seeming oddly smaller, and certainly more frightened than his creator and performer: and his crises usually involve an act of great personal courage on his own part or on that of someone else, and Mark has admirably realised the terrors to be overcome in 'his' need to stand up and count his opponent out. It is always a shock when the 'soap' ends and 'his' little gnome-like face and staunch bewilderment in 'his' confusing and sometimes oppres-sive world vanishes, and the professional leaps to his feet, bows with glorious *élan* to his public, rattles off a list of other shows appearing at his venue, however unconnected with himself and his concerns, throws out an all-embracing hand and exit.

But the 'soap' follows a cascade of other songs and delicious patter, covering everything from the boredom of a French provincial *bourgeoise* linked to a monument of male selfishness until liberated by sudden and glorious widowhood, to an ironic discussion of misadventures for the package vacationer in Spain, to a virtual Eugene O'Neill performance on what everyone was thinking about in the wedding group, and *Agatha* which conjured up the infancy of Agatha Christie as she supposedly conjured up future murder mysteries to remain untold as yet, and . . . and . . . and . . .

In *Yesterday's Blonde*, his novel, James Dean has not crashed to his death, and Marilyn Monroe is unsuccessful in committing suicide, and they discover one another in what he complains so seldom is celebrated, friendship as distinct from love.

. . . and he is also an elegist. His last Fringe appearance, in 1988, included a terrifying storm-like composition describing the advance of AIDS, and listing acquaintances and friends who had died of it, and preaching the necessity for courage in frank avowal of terror. Among the names was Neil Cunningham, abrasive and mordant performer who so impressed Fringe audiences around the late 1970s with his rendition of Heathcote Williams's 295-year-old man interviewed in *The Immortalist*, the production's name now a hideous mockery.

Mark Bunyan is one of the best and wisest men I have ever known, as well as one of the funniest. If I had to think of one word to describe him, it would be 'honour'.

AIDS is closer now. One day in spring 1990 I was filming in Wales, and rang Bonnie, who told me she had just learned of the death of someone we had loved and admired: Vaughan Williams, of the gay group calling themselves the Insinuendos. It was as if a great hand swept through a blue sky, crunching within its grasp a being lighter than air, whose songs and jokes and nonsense and conviction had borne us all into the air with him, laughing and throwing out his lean arms, his eager quizzical face talking of identity and integrity and meaning freedom. He was, he told us in his introduction bits, born in Swindon of Methodist stock; his father worshipped the music of Ralph Vaughan Williams, whence the name he gave his son. As the sky which darkened for me that morning was Welsh, so I imagine the paternal name-cult of Vaughan Williams may have been of filio-pietistic origin and the dry, demure tones, and flexible ironic bass, derived from Welsh inheritance. Vaughan was thin, almost transparent, it might have seemed, and Welsh supernatural beings have their last epiphany in that shimmering transparency. Naturally I never said that to him, and having said it now, I can see him looking down at me through long, amused eyelashes, too polite to say he expected this sort of Irish metaphysics, too honest to play up to it. Enough: all I know is that he was born in Swindon, and however frozen in popular consciousness as a commuter junction, I will remember it as birthplace of an air spirit.

Statement of Gered Windle sent to Edinburgh University Students'
Association President for 1989-1990 Jimmy Quinn and to Owen
Dudley Edwards, 5 June 1990:

> We met in 1985, that is Peter Tamm, Vaughan Williams, and myself,
> Gered P. Windle. We said to each other, why don't we do some singing
> etc. and see what happens. We thought we'd reinterpret the 'love-song'
> (Man I Love etc.) but people found us very funny — as well as musical!
> First performance was in a tiny restaurant 'Bon Ton Roulet' in South
> London, Brixton — we did three numbers with a wobbly tape!! And
> really it took off from there — lots of evenings and days spent together
> drinking cheap red wine — Vaughan's favourite was that Sainsbury's
> French stuff in plastic screw top (£1.50 a litre then!).
>
> Very creative early days — we just loved being together and
> produced a lot out of which came the first Edinburgh Festival 1986 after
> performances in London. We got lots of bookings from that — toured
> the country's small theatres and arts centres — London too. Best
> Festival we did was the following year 1987 at Gilded Balloon — very
> successful. Great fun. Did 1988 at Pleasance. Also by this time did a
> tour of Germany and were making an AIDS education video for
> Lambeth Council and had a couple of TV auditions — I think they were
> a bit frightened to take us on — I mean three up-front gay men *not* in
> dresses, celebrating their lives — it was too much! for TV producers.
> However, we did a spot on '01 for London' in 1988 autumn. By the way,
> we ran ourselves completely, never got a penny funding from anybody
> (do I sound bitter?!!).
>
> Peter Tamm left the group in autumn 1988 and since then two others
> stood in — Max Sinclair and Brian Ross. There were various pianists,
> the last one being Caroline Humphries. The last two shows at
> Edinburgh were directed by Allan Ferris.
>
> We did our last run at Lewisham Studio Theatre in February 1989.
>
> Vaughan became more ill about this time and died in February 1990
> — a great loss.

It may seem odd, in retrospect, that Gered speaks of their work as too
risqué for television, but this was before Mrs Mary Whitehouse had
cost the BBC huge damages for transmitting her libellous fantasies
about the alleged sexual lives of mothers of playwrights whose work
she disliked. TV was increasingly panic-stricken in the Thatcher years
and the Prime Minister was making much of family values and

domesticated mothers. Certain gay comedians were 'coming out' as a gag, others were making use of drag with increasing popularity, and a few, such as Mark Bunyan, were themselves combining inventive entertainment with ideological demands for gay solidarity and an end to showbiz denials of sexual identity. Mark's atheism would repudiate the analogy, but his attacks on the well-established movie-star closet-hangers whose cowardice left their gay brethren much more vulnerable were and are asserting precisely the case made to persuade the secure Queen Esther to endanger her well-provided circumstances by self-identification with her fellow-Jews under persecution, and the self-serving lies of the closet gays in limelight are in the tradition of Peter's denials of Jesus under indictment. The Insinuendos agreed with Mark, and indeed performed some of his songs especially in their vein, with his permission — 'Is *he* one?', for instance. But they differed from him in their stress on their own religious upbringing — Peter Tamm was Lithuanian-American ex-Catholic, and Gered Liverpool Irish ex-Catholic, identifications announced when Vaughan was recalling his (originally Welsh?) former Methodism. They sent up stereotypes on homosexuality by implying in several songs that they advocated sexual partnership for three — 'Tea for Three', 'Three of Us' — and pointed out in the latter that God is a Trinity. This was certainly likely to frighten off the media: God was treated as a personal fief shared between Mrs Thatcher and Mrs Whitehouse at this time.

The simplest principle at work in the Insinuendos' repertoire was the substitution of threes for twos and men for women in standard love lyrics, with wonderfully comic results. It doesn't detract from the gallant Drew Griffiths's work for gay drama and gay history to say Mark Bunyan and the Insinuendos conquered territory by laughter which formal confrontation left unscathed. Balding, pony-tailed Gered Windle devastated audiences with:

> *I feel pretty*
> *Oh so pretty*
> *I feel pretty, and witty, and gay*
> *And I pity*
> *Anyone who isn't me*
> *Today.*

I feel charming
Oh so charming
It's alarming
How Charming
I feel
And so pretty
That I hardly can believe
I'm real.

See that pretty boy in the mirror there:
Who can that attractive boy be?
Such a pretty face
Such a pretty dress
Such a pretty pot
Such a pretty butt
Oh such a lot
Such a pretty me!

All this was accompanied by posturing and fussing with fake handmirrors and handquiverings and a doll's dress to suggest a *toilette* not precisely likely to send the Beardsley Salomé or Belinda into litigation for breach of copyright. It was not a drag performance — it was vital for it that it wasn't — but it used the appeal of the old vaudeville comedy drag acts.

The Insinuendos threw lyric lines between one another in various numbers and Vaughan was rather appropriately established as the ideologue, Peter the romantic, and Gered the satirist who would explode over-serious atmopshere by Irish-Scouse ribaldry. This might be followed by indignant protests from the others, and they perfected anti-sexist ethics by mock-rebuke. Sometimes they exchanged rôle identities — Vaughan had a lyrical fantasy about an island — and sometimes they introduced a grimmer note. 'Love for Sale', for instance, again taking over a standard heterosexual lyric, this time by Cole Porter, became a very dark, menacing impression of gay prostitution. One lyric, 'My Man', they rendered in three languages, Peter in emotive American, Gered in send-up German, and Vaughan in beautiful and mesmerising French. Sometimes their patter could seriously concern itself with advice against sexual fears of inadequacy in the act of love, making the most explicit statements on the Fringe without the slightest touch of smut. They talked worldly wisdom, and yet they reflected some quite primeval innocence, even when producing lines with the grimmest of *double entendre* as in 'Love for Sale': 'Who's prepared to pay the price/For a trip to Paradise?' Though that, in the starkest tragedy, now adds a third meaning in recollection.

In 1987, the Insinuendos at the comedy centre on the Cowgate, the Gilded Balloon, were much more AIDS-conscious, and characteristically discussed the subject with courage and information as part of their overall programme: set on educating by comedy, they pelted the audience with contraceptives evangelising safe sex. For the *Irish Times* — they being an angle I was anxious to make Irish — I had met them the previous year to get photographs and possible tour plans. And now in 1987 we rediscovered each other at the Gilded Balloon opening party when Bonnie and Vaughan met and talked at length. Vaughan was now working as an AIDS counsellor in his time outside performances. I, too, had learned more about AIDS and while charmed as always by his ideology and wit, I was left worrying about an almost unnoticeable hard, dry, little cough only faintly interrupting what he was saying.

Peter Tamm was no longer with them when they returned in 1988, and the act suffered badly from his absence. The new talent was not equal to his predecessor, and some spark had gone from the other two, Vaughan at times lacklustre yet with great moments of recovery. I could not lie to them — integrity had always been their watchword — so I did not call on them after the show; but after the interval when they had resumed in Pleasance Two, Vaughan made a late entrance, not from the stage exit but from the audience upper door, seemed absolutely to fly down, more ethereal than ever, suddenly saw me, smiled at his most enchanting 'Hullo!' and then down to the stage.

He worked to spread education about AIDS as long as he could continue, teaching innocents about its dangers, guiding victims into learning to live with it in the light of his own experience when he knew. It was in this way that he met Jimmy Quinn, who brought the Students' Association at Edinburgh into co-operation with Vaughan on the question, and it was from Jimmy's public announcement that Bonnie learned what she had to tell me when I telephoned.

The skies were blue, clear, and tinged with white. The summer was coming, and with it Festival. The swallow, which had carried so much to so many in need of its healing arrival, was dead.

253

Roger Savage had staged several productions at the Fringe including the 1970 *The Pantaloonatic*, Ian Charleson and David Rintoul being in the cast. Hilton McRae also worked as a student with Roger, playing Peter Quince in Purcell's *The Fairy Queen* at the same period. From Roger Savage, 'Remembering Ian Charleson (1949-1990)', Edinburgh University *Bulletin*, Spring 1990:

'He disappeared in the dead of winter.' It was in fact on Twelfth Night, 6 January 1990, that Ian Charleson died. He was forty. Little more than two months before, he had been playing Hamlet at the National Theatre in London. It was a Hamlet which the actor Ian McKellen had called the finest Shakespearean performance of the year and which (as the obituary in *The Independent* said) some held to be 'the definitive Hamlet for the new generation'. . . . I was able to tap the memories of Peter and Marylin Johnstone . . . and of actors David Rintoul and Hilton McRae.

Hilton first: 'We all met at Edinburgh University, 1968: golden days. We wore loons, long scarves, kohl on the eyes, fur coats inside-out, brightly-painted clogs. We tackled Shakespeare, Marlowe, Weiss, Tardieu; we sang *all* the time; we played bridge till four in the morning; we loved each other. And we were just provincial Scots boys, knowing very little but awesome in our humour.' The Johnstones remembered that 'it was as Malvolio in *Twelfth Night* that Ian sprang onto the Edinburgh University stage, with such vigour that we jaded third-year Thespians fell back in awe.' David Rintoul was in that Dramsoc production. 'Ian was an architecture student, a local boy fresh from the Royal High School, a young man of enormous dash and charm. He joined EUDS, was immediately cast as Malvolio, and brought it off splendidly. I was cast as Sir Toby Belch and didn't. (Bring it off, I mean. I did belch a lot.) He became a dear friend. . . .

'There was a great explosion of energy in the EUDS at that time, and Ian was very much part of it. I suppose he must have been involved in over twenty plays in his three years, as actor, director and designer; and he always looked back on his University days with great affection.'

As a youngish English lecturer I was lucky enough myself to direct Ian in a couple of those twenty shows. He doubled deftly for me as a scurrilous harlequin and a limp lover in a mimed madrigal comedy, and was a scary Caligari-type Doctor in Buchner's *Woyzek*. Inventive, eye-catching and tractable on stage, off it he was mordant but unpretentious, though given to rattling off tumultuous improvisations on any piano which lay in his path. I think I gave him a bit of coaching for his LAMDA audition; I certainly had a hunch that, if he got in, he wouldn't emerge just as a spear-holder. And he didn't. The metropolitan career which followed — Frank Dunlop launched it — included substantial film parts (Derek Jarman's *Jubilee*, Attenborough's *Gandhi* and, of course, *Chariots of Fire*), some fine Shakespeares (among them a Bertram in *All's Well That Ends Well* on TV and an Ariel in an RSC *Tempest*), plus an American troika for the National: *Guys and Dolls*, a Sam Shepard and a Tennessee Williams. Richard Eyre, who directed his last appearance on the South Bank, wrote that he had till then seen Ian as "a fine, light, unfailingly truthful romantic actor, but with Brick in *Cat on a Hot Tin Roof* and with his Hamlet he discovered a new gravity, a real weight and depth".

Ian took his growing success with grace, aplomb and a good deal of clear-eyed irony. Hilton McRae recalled their later friendship: 'Really we never changed. We always laughed, mostly at ourselves, struggling over Schubert piano duets or wryly baiting actors in "be-seen" restaurants. We had a blissful year at Stratford living in converted stables as a two-man coterie. He is an irreplaceable truth of my life.' By early 1989, though, Ian's own life was shadowed. He had become HIV positive and his health was deteriorating — his sinuses being especially troublesome — as AIDS began to claim him. Marylin and Peter Johnstone: 'Through the years we kept in touch and thought of him as part of the fabric of our lives. When he told us last summer that he had AIDS, it was though an iron door had slammed shut. But he was absolutely brave and unsentimental, saying everything through his great, unforgettable Hamlet. . . .'

Oscar Wilde, conclusion of 'The Happy Prince':

'Bring me the two most precious things in the city,' said God to one of His Angels; and the Angel brought Him the leaden heart and the dead bird.

'You have rightly chosen,' said God, 'for in my garden of Paradise this little bird shall sing for evermore, and in my city of gold the Happy Prince shall praise me.'

Edinburgh Fringe Venues & Street Plan